LEARNING TO TALK BEAR

SO BEARS CAN LISTEN

God's music is wind soughing through treetops, dove wings whispering at waterholes, the mournful cry of a lost-in-the-fog honker. It's a harmony that became addictive, and carries even into my dotage. Elk music took me to the dance. Bears—particularly grizzly bears—keep me dancing.

Grizzlies, you see, are the Marine Band of the animal world. They swagger with the calm indifference of an animal who knows he has nothing left to prove. So why does this John Philip Sousa of wildlife resonance—an animal who may really believe us superior, but in no way is reconciled that we are masters—receive such a bum rap from the planet's most fearsome other creature—us?

Good question; not all grizzly bears are Jeffrey Dahmers or Jack the Rippers in fur coats. Perhaps that's the "why" for this book.

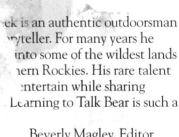

...ek is an authentic outdoorsman ...ryteller. For many years he ...into some of the wildest lands ...ern Rockies. His rare talent ...entertain while sharing ...Learning to Talk Bear is such a

Beverly Magley, Editor
Montana Magazine

"Provides a treasure trove of information for any wishing to understand the nature and science of the grizzly bear. . ."

The Midwest Book Review

"This is as fine an outdoor book as I can remember ever reading. I became so wrapped up in the fate of *Ursus horribilis* that I hated to put the book down."

Jack Oliver/Allison Park, PA

"A major literary contribution in an effort to save the magnificent grizzly."

Marin Independent Journal
San Rafael, CA

"A fine book. Reading it was almost like sitting around a campfire and listening to Roland."

Don Johnson/Menomonie, WI

"[Roland Cheek] is a born storyteller."

The Register Herald
Eaton, OH

"I've just come to the last sentence. I didn't peek ahead. I read it word for word, and I learned more about bears than I ever thought I'd want to know."

Jewell Wolk
Cut Bank, MT

"A masterful job entwining personal observation, often combined with humor or suspense with biological research into the lives of grizzly bears."

The Couer d'Alene Press
Couer d'Alene, ID

"Really enjoyed the book. Hope we never have to put some of the advice to a test."

Tim McMahon/Santa Ynez, CA

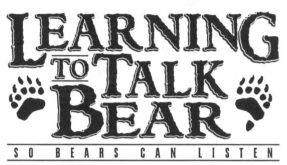

SO BEARS CAN LISTEN

Roland Cheek

a Skyline Publishing Book

First printing May 1997
Second printing June 1997
Third printing September 1997
Fourth printing May 2000
Fifth printing January 2004

Cover design by Laura Donovan, Dogsonics, Kalispell, Montana
Text design and formatting by Michael Dougherty
Typesetting by Type & Graphics, Bozeman, Montana

Publisher's Cataloging in Publication
(Prepared by Quality Books Inc.)

Cheek, Roland.
  Learning to talk bear : so bears can listen / Roland Cheek. —
1st ed.
    p. cm.
    Includes bibliograph
    Preassigned LC
    ISBN 0-918981-02-6

  1. Grizzly bear. 2. Human-animal relationships. I. Title.

QL737.C37C44 1997   599.74'446
                               QBI96-40821

Published by   Skyline Publishing
                    P.O. Box 1118
                    Columbia Falls, Montana 59912

Printed in Canada

Table of Contents

"*To understand is hard.
Once one understands,
action is easy*"

-Sun Yat-Sen

Dedication

To those selfless field biologists who study bears. Wildlife biologists are, without exception, men and women most attracted by a labor of love, usually underpaid, and with fewer opportunities for advancement than college graduates in any other field. May they live forever.

Jane—my copy editor, chief critic, appointments secretary, purchasing agent, household maid, chef, girl Friday, and lifetime companion. Nobody ever had a better partner.

Incidently, she's standing atop Lena Mountain in the Bob Marshall Wilderness. Lena Lake lies in the background. It's grizzly country.

Acknowledgement

Each time I pick up this book and see my picture, or read my name on its spine, I blush. Learning To Talk Bear, you see, is a composite of information gathered from many sources and I'm merely the vehicle for its dissemination. I would not be that vehicle without my old Oregon hunting buddy, Mark Worsley, painting such a vivid picture of Montana that I had to see it. (Mark also thought I had enough talent and experience to make a passable wilderness guide. And he's the one who first suggested I write about my adventures.)

Montana Fish, Wildlife & Parks biologist Shawn Riley put me on the track of his agency's South Fork Grizzly Study. And what can I say about Rick Mace—except that his assistance and cooperation has been superb. Other MDFWP biologists who contributed much are Terry Werner and John Waller. Mike Madel and Tim Manley are MDFWP Grizzly Bear Management Specialists kind enough to share vital insight about "problem" bears. Supervisors Dan Vincent of Region I and Mike Aderhold of Region IV were most helpful. Other MDFWP professionals offering assistance and encouragement were Endangered Species Coordinator Arnold Dood and Wildlife Bureau Chief Glenn Erickson.

Additional professional biologists providing information were Steve Gniadek of Glacier National Park, Kate Kendall of the U.S. Biological Survey, Dan Carney of the Blackfeet Nation,

Dale Becker of the Confederated Salish & Kootenai Tribes, Jim Claar of the U.S. Forest Service, and Chris Servheen and Nancy Kehoe of the U.S. Fish & Wildlife Service.

I'm indebted for the special insight provided during a lengthy interview with bear researcher emeritus, Dr. Charles Jonkel.

Mountain Lion hunter Tom Parker shared extraordinary information. Fred Matt and Tony Incashola, prominent members of the Confederated Salish & Kootenai Tribes, gave freely of their specialized knowledge. Bob Frauson's historical perspective relative to grizzly bear management in Glacier National Park was extensive and invaluable. Pat O'Herren, Art and Jack Whitney, Jim Lafever, and Doug Chadwick all provided insightful views about the great bears.

Environmental activists Keith Hammer of the Swan View Coalition and Mike Bader of the Alliance for the Wild Rockies opened up their conservation research for my perusal.

At the risk of his being too busy to edit my next book, I'll cut you in on a little secret: Bob Elman is an old-style editor, of the Maxwell Perkins mold.

And finally, it's fair for me to wonder if this book would have been without the encouragement of Ruth and Royce Satterlee? Or *could* have been without that of John Montagne?

Prologue

In all the world, few creatures are better equipped to go where they want, when they want, for whatever reason they choose. The Doberman knew he was outgunned before the bear even emerged from garage shadow into yard light. The mutt barked once, then squirreled back into his dog house to lie still as a church mouse—except for the chain rattling a tattoo against his water dish.

Fat as a Hampshire hog at harvest, tall as a yearling Hereford at fair, the monster grizzly with moonstruck hair over his hump and along the flanks paused to lift snout to the wind, then ambled ponderously along a hedgerow to the garbage cans, nosing briefly, quietly, then pushed through the carigana and crossed the drive-way, three-and-a-half-inch claws clicking on the hard packed road surface like tap dancers jockeying for off-stage position.

Daylight sneaks up on foothills snuggling against the west-erly side of mountain country. It caught the grizzly digging skunk cabbage from a tiny marsh almost within sight, and certainly within sound, of the relieved Doberman noisily greeting his breakfast.

It took the great bear only minutes to find a spot for his day bed, a promontory of dry land thrusting into the marsh from the north—a kame terrace left during the retreat of the last ice age. The terrace (or bench) was capped with a thick stand of lodge-pole pines and ringed on three sides by head-high paper birch and a hawthorn thicket. The bruin took only a couple of minutes to scoop a shallow pit to fit his bulk, then settled in like a corset-free fat lady oozing into an overstuffed chair.

While settling his beachball-sized head onto his forepaws the grizzly heard the station wagon traversing the lane.

It was after church and a leisurely dinner when the man reminded his children of their Mother's Day tradition: picking mom a bouquet of fairy slippers while she enjoyed an afternoon nap.

"We can take Prince, can't we?" the nine-year-old asked, already unsnapping the Doberman's chain as the dog leaped and yipped about the boy in ecstasy.

The bear heard the kids romping long before they neared. "Look, Daddy, is this one?"

"No, Melissa, that's a birdbill. See how the flower looks like a robin's bill. See? What we're looking for is a tiny pink orchid that could be a little slipper for your Barbie doll."

"I can't find any."

"They only grow in forest shade, near where it's moist." The man paused. "Like in the woods around this marsh."

"Dad!" the boy called from behind. "Prince won't come." The lad grasped the dog's collar, but the Doberman shook free and scampered a short distance toward home before turning and squatting on his haunches. "What's wrong with him, Dad?"

"I don't know, son. Prince, come! Prince!"

The dog only whined. So the boy ran toward him. Again the dog fled. "Let him go, Jaimie," the father called. "We don't need Prince to help us pick your mother's bouquet, anyway."

The bruin followed sounds of their passage as the humans circled the marsh. But when they turned toward him on the terrace, there was a low rumble deep in his throat.

"Look, Daddy, here's one!"

"It sure is, honey. But look around. See? There's another growing near that uprooted tree."

The tiny girl in the white flower print-dress bent over at the waist to pick the tree-root orchid. Had she been less absorbed with Barbie slippers and more alert to her surroundings, the child could have peered between hawthorn shoots into the red-rimmed eyes of a monster grizzly bear lying just fifteen feet away. "Daddy, come see what I got."

The bear tensed at the man's approach, ears flattening against the skull and silvertipped guard hair standing aloft on his hump.

"Isn't that pretty, dear?" The man paused to loosen his tie and roll up the sleeves on his Sunday-go-to-meeting shirt. He called, "Jaimie!"

"Here! I'm down by the water, dad!"

"Stay out of the pond, hear!"

The absurdly tiny ears pricked at the boy's shout from his left, then flattened again as the man took the tiny girl's hand and the two ducked beneath the limbs of a leaning birch, angling away from unseen danger. "There's one, Melissa. See?"

As the girl ran to their latest find, the man stretched and gazed idly about, eyes sweeping over the tangle where terror lay, passing on without pause.

Father and daughter strolled on and the bear's ears again pricked, while the guard hair slowly lowered along his hump. Then the boy was running! The boy burst through the nearest hawthorn thicket, skirting the windthrown tree roots only four steps from the bear's nose, snagging his jacket on a thorn. The lad paused to examine the tear, then dashed on to join his father and sister and somewhere find a stupid dog who, for some wild reason, didn't want to help pick Mom a bunch of fairy slippers for her special day. . . .

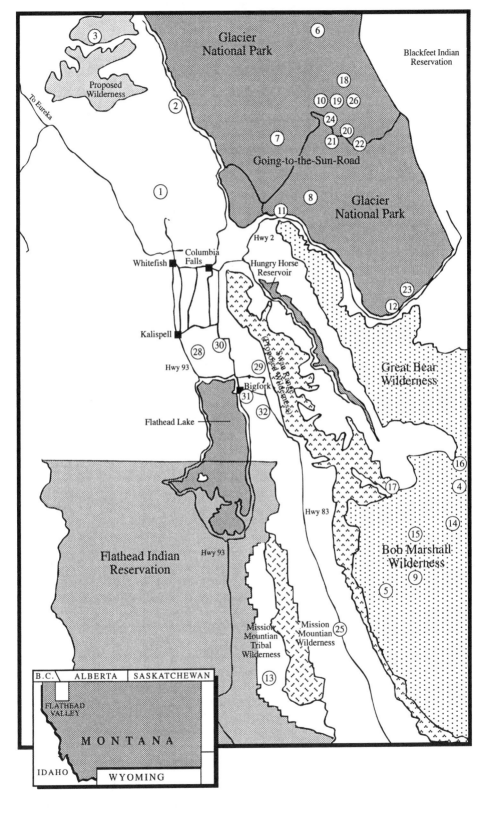

Big hump dish-face Grizzly bear.

Tom Ulrich Photo

Chapter 1

Learning Curve

The Brittany spaniel burst over the hill. That the mutt was in unaccustomed flight didn't register until the angered grizzly bear exploded into sight, hind feet spinning past ears in hot pursuit.

Hunter had, for eight years and thousands of wilderness trail miles, traveled as my companion. Over those miles and during those years, I'd seen him put the run on several bears met in surprise encounters. And I know the wide-ranging dog had confronted others beyond my ken without so much as a speck of unpleasantness. But this bruin was different; this one appeared to have no clear grasp of either canine or ursine custom. Prudence dictated the dog's options.

The spaniel was, of course, more fleet than his pursuer. But each time he gained ground, the dog, disbelieving a bear like this existed, slowed to hurl another intended-to-be-intimidating bark over his shoulder.

To the grizzly, the dog's pauses served as teasers and the barks insults. I might have thought the scene hilarious had not the runaway caboose and its trailing locomotive been headed for my station. The dog gained a few steps and again lost ground by slowing to curse his ursine pursuer, then wheeling and racing toward his master. If the stupid mutt expected me to get us out of this brouhaha, he would've been comforted to know my thoughts were coursing along the same lines.

It all began with the high-pitched, excited bark. I'd heard it dozens of times, and with our spaniel it always meant "Bear!" Then Hunter settled into his clamor-bark, intended to intimidate everything from titmouse to tyrannosaur.

I paused to lean against a whitebark pine, slipping off the daypack and rummaging for my water bottle. The clamor was still going on—out of sight, beyond where the trail disappeared over the hilltop, perhaps three hundred yards away. I stared at the bottle, shook it, then swallowed the last of its water, wondering how much farther to the slumbering ski lift.

The clamor settled into a deeper pitch. Had the fool dog stirred up and treed a brood of blue grouse? I cocked my head. No, his barking was spaced out, more routine, and seemed to be coming nearer. I dropped the empty water bottle into the daypack and took out the last of my lunch, a candy bar. Now all that remained was a camera, a block of "fat wood" for fire starter, and the empty water bottle. I stripped the wrapper.

He barked again; still out of sight, but definitely closer.

I hiked here in mid-July to see if this particular portion of the Whitefish Range might lend itself to "hut-to-hut" crosscountry ski touring. By developing a winter recreational venture, my wife and I hoped to expand our seasonal wilderness outfitting business into one viable year-round. The lay of the land would have taxed a San Francisco streetcar, but the hill was rounded and the forest scattered—easy enough to negotiate on touring skis. This might be it.

Hunter barked again. I munched on the Snickers bar and eyed the hill's crest. . . .

Though memory continues to play back the affair in slow motion, it all happened rapid-time. From the moment bear and Brittany burst over the hill until they'd covered the distance to where I stood between twin pines took but fifteen seconds. I remember glancing up. Both pines were as big around as steel barrels and just as smooth for twenty feet to their lowest limbs—no chance to climb. Nor was there a suitable tree to scramble into within sprinting range.

The bear's big, dish-faced head swung low to the ground, ears flattened, teeth clacking so loudly they could be heard at fifty paces. No growling or roaring here. No posturing. Just single-minded purpose—to catch and pulverize. I needed no mathematics to calculate there was little chance for a knobby-kneed, flatfooted, overweight outfitter to outdistance the runaway freight. What I needed was a rapid transit to a distant siding.

It's odd details were so clear: the bear was unusually dark, like polished cordovan shoes, shading almost to tan on the hump and just behind the front legs.

It seems now, from a decade-and-a-half distance, as though it happened on a giant panoramic screen and I was merely a detached observer. But when the dog raced to within thirty feet I felt a cold wind on the back of my neck and heard a distant voice whispering, *Boy, you better do something!* So I pointed to the left and shouted with all the authority I could muster, "Hunter—go!"

Darned if the dog didn't do it.

The bear, however, was not nearly so well trained, altering its original course to hone in on a new target. And I hadn't even barked!

With an angry grizzly bearing down at express-train speed from thirty feet, I remember thinking, *I wonder how this is going to come out.* The bear was small for a grizzly, perhaps a hundred and eighty pounds. I probably would have outweighed it. But, shod as I was in a pair of leather hiking boots and clad in tennis shorts and a T-shirt—none of which seemed formidable enough to deter a bruin bent on brigandage—there was no way I'd come out ahead in a kicking match. Neither was I armed, not even with so much as a pocket knife. And my opponent's clacking teeth (now deafening) and long claws (still churning) might as well have been sweat-seeking missiles honing in on the drippingest thing on that ridge.

When the bear abandoned pursuit of the spaniel to bore in on the dog's master, I began waving my arms and shouting at the top of my lungs. Except for the I-wonder-how-this-is-going-to-come-out question, the only thought occurring to me was when the bruin closed to eight feet, I would swing my camera-laden daypack at its face and step behind the left pine tree. Beyond that, there was no plan, no escape. Not even untidy, shorts-wetting fear.

Still madly shouting, I raised the daypack. At twelve feet, the bear slowed. At ten, it stopped, turned, and began pacing away.

Meanwhile, the Brittany had circled and, unnoticed, he came up from my rear. With the insufferable bear at last in retreat, Hunter saw a chance to rescue his master. With hackles raised, he darted between my legs to hurl a torrent of canine epithets. The bear spun and rushed back, ears flush to skull, head swinging, teeth clattering. My camera-laden daypack flattened . . . the dog.

The grizzly again turned, this time at twelve feet, and stalked off up the trail as a mute spaniel and his quivering master watched.

I collapsed against the pine, hand gripping my canine buddy's fur, taking great gulps of air, gradually calming. Amid the adrenaline high, wheels spun: "Holy cow! I stood my ground! I stood up to a grizzly charge and wasn't even scared!" A more important realization, however, was the fact that my brain functioned throughout, as if one part had been detached from the other: analysis opposed to emotion. Minutes passed. The dog lifted his head from my lap, leaped to his feet, and began a low growl. Little more than a hundred yards away, the cordovan bear with the tan hump stalked back and forth atop a fallen tree. It seemed almost as if the animal was pulling sentry duty.

Then beyond, I saw what Hunter heard—a cub no more than porcupine-size backed its hesitant way down a tall spruce. Indeed, the mother *was* patrolling between her cub and the threat we posed.

I learned a lot about bears that July day. And lessons learned are still to be plumbed to the utmost. Simply writing about it a dozen years later, recalling the sequence that occurred and reinterpreting those recollections, brings fresh perspectives. Having never been charged by a bear until then, my experience was limited. Until then, my encounters with bears had largely occurred while armed with a high-powered rifle. I wondered if a certain arrogance goes with dominating power? Would the sow have died had my fingers stroked my old standby, the familiar 30-06? Perhaps. But perhaps not, for by the time of that summer incident near the idle ski resort, a personal metamorphosis relative to bears had begun—was, in fact, already in an advanced stage.

At the approach of danger, the sow had sent her cub up the dead spruce tree, then retreated over the hill to avoid our approach. But when the free-ranging dog, incessantly in search of grouse, came upon her, she at first held her ground, then with Hunter's aggressive behavior, launched a charge. In retrospect I'm convinced the sow would have been content to let the dog speed out of her life; she did, in fact, several times slow her charge to allow it. But when the obstinate canine also slowed, half-turning to make himself a noisy threat, the sow shifted back to full attack mode.

Its probable the sow knew of my presence all along, but the transfer of her charge from dog to human occurred only after I constituted the greatest threat to her cub by pointing and shouting to dominate the dog and, to her mind, threatening her. There was no change in expression with the change in targets; only the beady eyes, flattened ears, low-swinging head, ominously clacking teeth, and raised hackles along her hump.

Was the analytical side of her brain also plugged in? Did she, too, wonder how this was going to come out? She had almost certainly never tussled with a human, so perhaps all she saw was a sort of super bear towering over her, roaring at the top of his lungs and waving his front legs in the most frightful manner. Could she have known about my inferior musculature and useless fat? That my teeth are false instead of sharp? That my begrimed nails had been trimmed just hours before and were at best unsuited for slashing and clawing in the first place?

Somewhere between thirty and ten feet, did prudence become the better part of valor? She surely knew she would serve her cub no purpose by fighting even a winning battle if she risked becoming disabled in the process. But to flee precipitously might invite counterattack. So she chose to turn and pace away—a veiled threat.

To fight or to flee must still have been in the sow's mind when the dog pushed between my legs to begin his clamor once again. In an instant, fight overcame flight and she spun into another charge. What went on in her head during that second charge I cannot guess. But the fact that she broke off at twelve feet instead of ten might indicate waning anger or burgeoning doubt. Or it may have been influenced by prompt removal of the dog-threat by that scary super bear.

Whatever the reason, I was impressed by her measured retreat. It was already clear to me that grizzly bears are endowed with what might seem prideful arrogance to us humans. But I had not thus far experienced that disdain at close quarters.

Grizzlies, I knew by this stage in a life of outdoor adventure, function under an operating paradigm or system different from that of black bears. Even a shy grizzly, low in their social hierarchy, can turn frightful if pushed or cornered. And the tools of a grizzly are awesome compared to either mine or those of the average black bear. But I also knew most grizzlies to be retiring creatures, largely nocturnal, given to avoiding humans under most circumstances.

But not all grizzlies.

There are, I already recognized, aggressive animals who are neither shy nor retiring, who tend to view as their own the territory surrounding them as they move. I knew by mid-July, 1982, that such territory can vary in size from the site of a discovered elk carcass in an avalanche fan to a hillside covered with huckleberries. Depending on the time of year and on circumstances varying from spring mating to fall food gathering (or when they feel their offspring threatened), such bears can become violent in an instant. Very few bears of any kind, I was certain, had turned to humans as a viable protein source.

What I did not then know—and what the cordovan sow had just conclusively proved—is that gradations exist from one extreme of bear behavior to the other. This book is about my sometimes fumbling efforts to learn about bears, particularly *Ursus arctos horribilis*—the grizzly bear. That my interest in the species pre-dated a surge of national awareness of America's premier undaunted-by-civilization indicator of God-given wildness was my good fortune. ■

Chapter 2

Boys, Bears, and a Grizzly Rug

My experience with bears dates to my years in knee pants. That's not to say I actually saw any bears until the age of pimples and puberty. But I knew the rapacious creatures were out there in the Oregon countryside of my youth, behind every rose bush or in every blackberry patch or up every white oak tree, waiting to leap out or drop upon or grab me from ambush, especially after dark.

I knew bears were there because one was picked up in the '36 Chevrolet's headlights as our family headed home from a late-night church social. I didnt see it because I was asleep, but my brothers bubbled about it the next day, using the event to terrorize their baby brother. And then there was the doddering behemoth that had the misfortune to tumble down our absent neighbors well and nobody knew about until weeks later when the odor led my father, with unerring accuracy, to its gravesite.

There was the occasional track in creekbank mud. And the rendered-out bear fat "Old Hutch" used for making doughnuts to feed a knobby-kneed kid in short pants who hiked the mile-long, brush-choked road to listen to a crippled old man's fascinating tales of cowboy days on the Owyhee and Payette and Crooked River.

Then I turned old enough to carry a rifle without dragging its muzzle in the dust. And I had my very first encounter with a savage ebony bruin that turned out not so savage as to risk facing down a budding Jim Bridger armed with a deadly single-shot long rifle in .22 caliber.

Oh, the pride of it all! Seeing that bloody-mouthed killer wheel at my approach and crash off like a runaway bulldozer through saplings and underbrush meant a coming of age. Smart, too, that bear. If he'd hung around for me to get a clear shot, his hide would have swung from my belt alongside the two digger squirrels and a sparrow already there. No doubt about it, properly armed and with an entire lifetime of mountain-man training, any tow-headed ten-year-old need no longer wallow in ursine fear—at least while the sun was up. I hitched up my overalls and swaggered on.

In the Oregon of my youth, black bears were varmints to be slain year 'round, with no license required. They could be hunted with dogs, killed over bait, trapped, or taken with the use of poison.

Given the climate of those times, one might think it strange I've gone a lifetime without killing a bear. That I would have done so had the proper opportunity presented itself (a clear shot affording a chance for a carefully-placed bullet in a mature animal) cannot be doubted.

But opportunities were too often fleeting. Or other extenuating circumstances surrounded them, such as the time on Big Oak Flats when a suitable trophy strolled in front of a big buckskin log at fifty paces. Ted and I spotted the black bear wending its way through underbrush at some distance. We crouched behind a second log and, as the bruin ambled out into the meadow, pushed our rifle barrels over the top of our log and took careful aim. Just then, a cub no bigger than a Labrador pup hopped atop the buckskin log to chase after his mother. I looked at Ted and he looked at me and we eared the hammers down on our carbines and Ted jumped up and hollered "Boo!" and the cub ran up a sugar pine and the sow ran off and left the poor little tyke to fend for himself.

The cub hung up there fifty feet from the ground and stared at us over his shoulder and cried so pitiably we couldn't even screw up the gumption to throw rocks at it like we figured he-men would.

It was off the same Big Oak Flats in another year when, in a dense copse of head-high firs, I stumbled on a bear set. First thing

I saw was: "WARNING! BEAR TRAP!" The sign was nailed to a two-foot Douglas fir. Similar signs were nailed to other nearby trees. The initial notice contained smaller print. I scanned the ground and moved cautiously up to read: "Bear Trap Site." Hand lettered in the space following was: "100 feet northeast."

Being a curious sort, I moved northeast through the screen of firs. It was what I later came to know as a "cubby" set—piles of logs stacked horizontally in a V, with rotting meat for bait inside the apex and the trap in the opening, hidden under leaves and needles.

Chills ran up and down my spine as I stared at that trap. Fully set with jaws open, the monster was the size of a double kitchen sink. Its jaws were dotted with two-inch sharpened steel teeth. Snapping shut, it was easy enough to imagine what it would do to a man's leg. A chain with links large enough to tow a loaded eighteen-wheeler led from the trap to a log fifteen inches in diameter and eight feet long.

Bear smells bait; bear steps into trap trying to reach bait; bear drags log until exhausted—pretty ingenious. Then I thought of the cub that, in another year, we'd chased up a tree not a half-mile from here. The trap was every bit as vicious as I expected, judging by the way it snapped the three-inch deadfall when I dropped it on the trigger pan.

Once I surprised a sow with two cubs while flyfishing below where a bunch of creeks come together to form the Coos River. It seemed to make little difference whether one carried a rifle or a fishing pole—humans were still objects of supreme fear. That sow abandoned her cubs, splashing, spray flying, across the river in all-out flight. I curled a lip in disdain and continued to whip a Bucktail Coachman while the cubs whimpered somewhere in the brush behind.

It was clear by my late teens that my childhood perception of ursine populations had some validity—there really were a lot of bears out there. So many, in fact, that timber companies were hiring professional hunters and trappers to eradicate the seedling-chewing pests from their private forest lands. By then I'd learned to harbor little respect for *Ursus americanus*, the common black bear. Thats why it was with some wonder that I listened to the tale a friend told of a Crater Lake National Park encounter his family had with a black bear.

"I never saw anything like it," Mark said. "The bear came right up to our picnic table. We were thrilled when he showed up at the edge of the campground. Then, when he came on in and started nosing around the camp tables, I began to wonder."

"Nobody else in the campground?" I asked.

"No. It was a cold, blustery day and snowbanks still lay around. The park had just opened."

"So what happened?"

"When he started sniffing over our way," Mark said, "we shouted and waved our arms and he ran into the woods."

"But he came back?"

"He sure did. He was gone only a few minutes when he came out of the woods from another direction and started our way. I shouted again and banged some tin plates and ran at him and he turned away. But he didnt leave the campground this time.

"We ran him off a couple more times, but he'd come back, each time a little closer. Mary got so upset she took the boys to the car and said she wasn't going to share our picnic with a bear. But I'm darned if I was going to get chased off by a black bear. So I finally pulled my double-bit axe out of the rig and stood between him and our table waving it in his face."

"Did you use the axe?" I asked.

"No, but I would have. I wasn't about to let a scrawny black bear have our lunch."

Mark Worsley's incident with the Crater Lake black bear was still on my mind when, in early July, another friend and I borrowed a horse and packsaddle for our gear and hiked thirty miles of the Pacific Crest Trail south of Crater Lake.

It was near the end of an idyllic week when we dropped from Devils Peak to Grass Lake, in a place called Seven Lakes Basin. A U.S. Forest Service packer and his boss, the district ranger, were camped at Grass Lake. Their horses and mules grazed in the meadow.

We struck up a conversation, and the kindly ranger showed me how to properly stake out a single horse to a picket pin by tying a bowline around a front fetlock. While we stood to the side admiring my handiwork, the mare threw up her head and burst away at a gallop. She must have been a quarterhorse because she was going at top speed when she reached the end of her thirty-foot picket rope. The mare's front foot was abruptly jerked from beneath her and she somersaulted, tail waving goodbye at God as she went over, crashing to the ground with a mighty thud.

I was horrified, but the old ranger puffed placidly on a crooked-stem pipe and drawled, "I'll bet she won't do that again." Then his eyes narrowed and he turned, saying, "I wonder what spooked her?"

I turned with him. A cinnamon-colored bear nosed into forest duff but thirty yards away, atop a small knoll. "Uh, huh," the ranger said. "Somebody probably cleaned their fish up there."

The bear was big, certainly the largest bear I'd seen in all my tender years. He paused to peer our way, then returned to nosing the ground. I caught myself admiring the rich brown of his coat, muscles rippling beneath. But with the biggest bear in all creation feeding only a hundred yards from my sleeping bag I wasn't into appreciating ursine finery. "My God," I said, "What'll we do?"

The ranger cast an amused grin my way, took a pull on his crooked-stem pipe, and whistled for the packer's dog. When the little tan-and-white terrier trotted up, the ranger pointed and said, "Sic em, Ben."

Ben saw the bear for the first time and took off at top speed, yapping up a storm. The big cinnamon bolted from the knoll as if careening down a mountainside at Le Mans. The sight of that football-sized terrier chasing a bear as big as a Harley Davidson, along with the noise of that dog's yapping fading into the distance—both the sight and sound are glued in my memory.

But the Oregon of my youth was changing. That Coos River country where the sow abandoned her cubs to the first flyfisherman of the season was stripped of its once vast Douglas fir forests; salmon and steelhead redds once so abundant amid the clear stream's gravel bars now lay buried beneath silt from eroding hillsides. More ominous was a scheme for the Umpqua National Forest that planned to turn even the vast Cascade Mountains wonderland into a road grid resembling the mesh on a screen door. In addition, Oregon's population was skyrocketing with transients. So this one-time country boy and his family became permanent Montana transplants.

I took employment at a new plywood- manufacturing plant located only twenty miles from Glacier National Park. It was a magical land. The Bob Marshall Wilderness sprawled a half-day's drive away. Canada loomed but sixty miles north. Great rivers drained a vast mountain country, flowing into huge lakes that teemed with fish. And wildlife. My God, the wildlife! Moose, elk, whitetail and mule deer, mountain goats, mountain lions, bighorn sheep, black bears and grizzlies—it was beyond my wildest dreams.

Right from the outset I wanted a grizzly-bear rug. Never mind that I'd never killed a black bear. Grizzly became the Number One priority despite an already well-developed affinity for elk hunting. So I listened like a mouse in a corner each time someone mentioned the mighty beasts. One fact became clear early on: *Ursus arctos horribilis* did not have the same temperament as the bears of my youth.

Area newspapers carried tales of encounters with bears in and out of Glacier Park. Some encounters were frightening—hikers mauled when they surprised a grizzly on a mountain trail, huge bears ambling indifferently through campgrounds filled with tourists. During our first year, word came that a North Fork grizzly had stalked and surprised an elk hunter west of the park boundary. One of the hunter's friends saw the attack and rushed to the victim's aid, shooting the bear several times with a heavy-caliber rifle, finally finishing it with a .44 magnum handgun. I was excited to learn that the hunters were bringing the bruin in to my company's truck scales to weigh it.

The bear was in the back of a 4 x 4 Jeep. I pushed through the surrounding crowd. "This is a grizzly?" I said. Certainly it was, but I'd seen lots of black bears that would've outweighed this scrawny specimen. On the other hand, I marveled at the size of his claws.

One of my co-workers opened the dead bear's mouth. "Look at his teeth. No wonder he was hungry." Indeed, the teeth were broken and worn almost to the gum line.

The bear weighed 265 pounds.

And this was the bear that had supposedly stalked and nearly killed a hunter? The grizzly that put a man carrying a .300 Weatherby Magnum in the hospital for weeks? I took one more look into the bears mouth and hefted a paw to peer at the three-inch claws.

The hunter who'd killed the bear stood nearby. "He's got five bullet holes in him," he said as I turned away. ∎

Richard Jackson

Chapter 3

Ephraim's Past

The first actual record of the grizzly bear is in a journal entry of one Henry Kelsey, an apprentice trader with the Hudson's Bay Company. Kelsey, though he was an inexperienced stripling of twenty, was dispatched westward from York Fort on Hudson's Bay to explore and trade with the Indians. In a journal entry dated August 20, 1691, Kelsey wrote:

". . . This plain affords nothing but short, round, sticky grass and buffalo and a great sort of bear which is bigger than any white [polar] bear and is neither white nor black but silver haired like our English rabbit. . . ."

Apparently Kelsey thrilled to the chase, for in September he wrote:

"And then you have beasts of several kinds. The one is a great buffalo. Another is an outgrown bear which is good meat. His skin I have used all the ways I can. . . ."

But by then, Kelsey had learned chasing grizzly bears might not be without risk:

"He is man's food and he makes food of man. . . ."

The young trader learned, too, that Indians held the great bears in highest esteem:

"His hide they would not preserve, but said it was a God and they should [first] starve. . . ."

Hearsay mention of grizzly bears was recorded as much as twenty-five years earlier by Jesuit missionary Claude Jean Allouez, who wrote of Indian tribes to the west (around Lake Winnipeg) who ". . . are eaten by bears of frightful size, all red, and with prodigiously long claws."

Though the good father was first to report on the supposed existence of a strange new species of ferocious bears, and the trader Kelsey was first to actually kill a grizzly and record his description, credit for having been the first European to encounter the bears should, in all likelihood, go to an unknown Spaniard laboring through the southwest: the shipwrecked Cabeza de Vaca wandering through Texas, New Mexico, and Sonora (1527-36); or one of Coronado's men, who penetrated as far as Colorado, Kansas, and Nebraska (1540-42). Or the great bear may have first been sighted from the deck of Cabrillo's sailing ship coasting along San Diego or Monterey Bays (1542).

We can never know who was the first European to spot a grizzly; his achievement went unrecorded and is thus lost to posterity. Similarly lost are any reports of encounters between the great bears and *les coureurs des bois*, those intrepid, largely illiterate canoe men and trappers of French and Indian extraction who penetrated interior North America decades before the English or Scots.

More than a hundred years passed between the journal entries of Henry Kelsey and those of Lewis and Clark. But throughout that century there was still a scant paper trail relative to the grizzly bear: a few more Jesuit journal mentions, notes in Hudson's Bay accounts, California tales of daring vaqueros roping grizzly bears. But little else.

Captains William Clark and Meriwether Lewis changed all that with their meticulous record-keeping. The only annoying creatures to receive greater mention in their Voyage of Discovery Journals are the ones Captain Clark spelled "muskeeters." Ironically, the tiny insects also exacted a much greater toll of blood from the expedition than did ferocious bears.

Though the expedition had heard much mention of fearsome bears to the west, their first actual encounter with grizzlies occurred on April 29, 1805, just upstream from the mouth of the Yellowstone, a few miles into the present state of Montana. Lewis writes:

". . . The wind was moderate. I walked on shore with one man. About 8 a.m. we fell in with two brown or yellow bear, both of which we wounded. One of them made his escape; the other, after my firing on him, pursued me 70 or 80 yards but fortunately had been so badly wounded that he was unable to pursue so closely as to prevent my charging my gun. We again repeated our fire, and killed him. It was a male, not fully grown. We estimated his weight at 300 pounds. . . ."

Grizzly bears occupied considerable of the Captains' Journal copy for the next three months as they toiled up the Missouri to the distant shining mountains. Several members of the party were attacked by the "white" bears, even as they themselves stalked the animals. The men marveled at the creatures' consistent ferociousness and, particularly, the great bears' ability to withstand punishment when wounded. And finally, though no one in the party was killed, the men of the Lewis and Clark Expedition learned to fear the animals. Captain Lewis wrote on June 28, 1805:

"The white bear have become so troublesome to us that I do not think it prudent to send one man alone on an errand of any kind, particularly where he has to pass through the brush. . . . They come close around our camp every night. . . . I have made the men sleep with their arms by them as usual, for fear of accidents."

But the men were making their mark, as well. All told, they killed forty-three grizzly bears, including one taken May 5, 1805, by Captain Clark and Sergeant Drouilliard that was the specimen on which was based the accepted classification and naming of the animal.

Forty-three grizzly bears seems a bunch, even for twenty-eight men, one Shoshoni squaw, and her infant son during the eight hundred and sixty-three days the party was in remote regions of uncharted America. Grizzlies, of course, were not the only animals taken by the Lewis and Clark Expedition. They ate hump from two hundred and twenty-seven buffalo, backstrap from three hundred and seventy-five elk, round steaks from more than a thousand deer of three species (whitetail, mule deer, and Columbian blacktail), chops from sixty-two pronghorn antelope and thirty-five bighorn sheep. In addition to forty-three grizzlies, the expedition rendered fat from twenty-three black bears.

There were scores of geese and ducks and grouse and turkeys to sweeten their pots. And to prove all hunters face adversity, nearly two hundred Indian dogs and a dozen horses were utilized to stave off starvation.

All the wild meat added up to around fifteen pounds per day, per man—and that doesn't include a few tons of smoked and fresh salmon—so much fish the party wearied of it during their months with Columbia River's fish-eating tribes. One wonders what held scurvy at bay?

For one thing, sacks of beans and cracked corn were aboard when the party began their trip from St. Louis. Too, they traded for vegetables at the Mandan villages (near present-day Bismarck, North Dakota) both coming and going. It's also known that they made acquaintance with camas roots (an Indian staple) through their Shoshone and Nez Perce contacts; and one assumes berries were consumed in quantity when available.

All things considered, an average of fifteen pounds of meat per day per person seems high—much too high even for hard-working voyageurs—leading to the conclusion that some was wasted despite Captain Lewis' assertion: ". . . Altho' game is abundant and gentle, we only kill as much as is necessary for food."

For the first time, grizzly bears faced advanced human technology. They came off second best. For the first time, the great bears experienced wanton killing by another creature.

It's difficult today for us to remember that grizzly bears once existed in great numbers from the Canadian Arctic to Sonoran Mexico, and from the Pacific Ocean into the Great Plains as far east as Kansas and Nebraska. Grizzlies were once not uncommon in the Rio Grande Valley of southern New Mexico and western Texas; they've been documented on the Platte and the Arkansas, Cimarron, Cheyenne, and Wounded Knee.

Grizzlies were plentiful in Washington and Oregon, California and Montana, Idaho and Wyoming, Colorado and New Mexico and Utah. Some estimates place their numbers, at the time of Lewis and Clark, as high as one hundred thousand.

What happened?

The last grizzlies disappeared from the Dakotas in the early 1900s, before that in Nebraska, Kansas, Oklahoma, and Texas. The last great bear vanished from Utah in 1923, Oregon in 1931,

New Mexico and Arizona in the mid-1930s. Today, for all practical purposes, Lewis and Clark's "white bears" no longer exist in Washington. And Idaho's population is marginal.

Colorado? There are persistent rumors of a reclusive remnant population in the San Juan Mountains, and indeed a grizzly was killed by mistake by a black-bear hunter only a decade ago. Do any still exist?

California's experience is, however, the most tragic. The Golden State was once thought to harbor the largest concentration of *Ursus arctos horribilis* in existence, and the state flag still carries the proud emblem of the giant bear. But the last grizzly in California was shot and killed in August, 1922, at Horse Corral Meadows, Tulare County, by Jesse B. Agnew, a cattle rancher.

It was domestic livestock that proved the undoing of the great bears in fourteen of the sixteen states where they were formerly documented. California, for instance, once paid a ten-dollar bounty for grizzly scalps. Records show that several individual bounty hunters collected money on a hundred or more scalps during a single season.

Idaho became the first state to protect grizzly bears—in 1947. But by then, the great bears were already gone from most states — dangerous vermin to be exterminated by any means possible.

Compounding the great bears' problem with man and his domestic livestock were their hereditary instincts. Until the advent of European man and his superior weaponry, grizzly bears had little to fear from human competition. They went where they wished, when they wished, to do whatever they wished. Indians, with their puny bows and spears and war clubs, were able to achieve, at best, a stand-off; at worst, injury and death.

Besides the inferior weaponry of the Indians, another factor favored the bears: many Native American tribes regarded the grizzly as a mystical creature. Thus, hunting and killing the great bears was attempted only with considerable ceremony and no small degree of courage. Otherwise, native people gave way to the touchy creatures. From the bears' point of view, why should they treat the white man differently from the red?

There is little evidence in the Lewis and Clark Journals that grizzlies, as a species, considered humans a viable food source.

Rather, the animals' fearlessness of man, particularly as the party approached the remote Rocky Mountains, may simply have indicated that the bears had little previous experience warranting wariness.

Most frontiersmen, history tells us, adopted the native point of view toward the great bears: considerable awe, mingled with respect. But in the event of an encounter, they gave little ground to "Old Ephraim." The rules were changing, and bears that couldn't (or wouldn't) change were the ones to suffer.

Early miners were even less tolerant than beaver trappers, simply because miners, as a rule, had no intention of learning to live with, instead of against, the land. Moreover, by Gold Rush times, miners were better armed, and there were lots more of them than mountain men. Fortunately for the bears, miners were usually too busy to go out of their way to exterminate the great beasts. Deliberate extermination fell to the lot of pioneers and stockmen.

All bears are opportunists when it comes to food. A roost full of chickens, a pen full of hogs, a slow-footed cow and her calf, a tied-up domestic goat, a band of idiotic sheep: to the grizzly, the arrival of these creatures was like manna from heaven. And it led to conflict with the most dangerous creatures on earth: frightened farmers living on starvation's edge and ranchers of Manifest Destiny building empires. That pair of frontier products entered the war against grizzlies with a vengeance. The only bears to survive were those retreating farther and farther from settlements and settled lands.

Like the mountain regions of Montana and Wyoming.

Like the Flathead country where our family had settled. . . . ■

Chapter 4

Ambiguous Animal Behavior

A frontier mentality was still evident when our family immigrated to Montana in 1964. Prior history of the Treasure State was one of supplying raw materials to the rest of the nation: beaver plews for hats, gold to fight a Civil War, buffalo hides for leather and meat for hungry railway-construction crews, copper for an exploding electrical-conductor market. Range grass was converted to beef and wool for eastern markets; forests went into railway crossties and mine timbers. But this was a boom-and-bust economy. When demand was high and a particular resource plentiful, Montana boomed. (Butte copper miners were the highest-paid workmen in America during the 1920s). Decline set in, however, when a resource dwindled. And during the first decades after the end of World War II, Montanans did not equally share in the prosperity enjoyed by the rest of America.

Stagnation was caused in part by dependence on one giant corporation. The Anaconda Mining Company controlled most of the state's daily newspapers and much of its economy, and reached deeply into its politics; that control proved not only despotic but debilitating. By the mid '60s, the Company was crumbling from within and Treasure State leaders, with single-minded focus, searched for other natural resources with which to supply America. They found it in vast coal deposits beneath eastern plains, water flowing from western mountains, and wood from their National Forests. Few citizens questioned prevailing wisdom.

When the gates were closed on Libby Dam in 1973, a tremendous valley was flooded for over sixty-five miles—even into Canada. Critical wildlife winter range was lost, range vital to whitetail deer, bighorn sheep, elk, bear. Too bad, can't stand in the path of progress. Without power supplied by the dam and its water releases, West Coast manufacturing plants might have to shut down. Besides, look at the jobs construction furnished. . . .

It was similar in eastern Montana where ranchers—owning surface rights to farms and ranches that had been in the same family for generations—saw their way of life disrupted and destroyed by mammoth earth-moving machines that stripped fragile topsoil in order to reach underlying coal layers sold to giant corporations by state and federal governments. If a rancher protested, he became a pariah to many Montanans. Impede progress? Are you out of your mind?

If entire river valleys and individual property rights could be trampled in the rush to develop-at-all-cost, one can imagine the short shrift grizzly bears received when their essential living space fell afoul of ambitious U.S. Forest Service logging and road-building plans supported by both state and federal governments.

One need not be a genius to understand that grizzly bears had only limited time left in Montana. Yearning as I did for a silvertip rug, I set out to learn as much as possible about the great bears. Come spring, I prowled back roads and trails searching for the animals. Black bears were common in both ebony and cinnamon color phases, but it wasn't until mid-June that *Ursus arctos horribilis* pay dirt was struck on a fire-scarred hillside.

That first grizzly was feeding on forbs and greening grasses, tearing up rotted logs and overturning rocks and stumps for bugs. Jane and the kids were along, as was a visiting family from another state. I bent to the spotting scope's eyepiece and focused.

The bear popped into view, feeding amid shoulder-high brush; big and light colored, with a pronounced hump—no doubt about it being a grizzly. The bruin fed a few steps farther into a small opening. Then a little blond cub emerged like a ghost from the brush at her side.

"Jane," I muttered, gallantly bowing her to the eyepiece.

"Oooh. It's a grizzly bear! He's so light . . . oh! Look at that. She's got a little black cub."

Others clamored to see.

"What do you mean *black* cub?" I demanded.

Just then the other lady, May, exclaimed, "Isn't the little cub a cute copy of its mother?"

"What do you mean *copy*?" her husband growled as he took his turn. "That cub would have to get whitewashed."

Jane said, "The cub is black. Why do you ask?"

"That cub is blond."

"Come on, Roland. You're carrying a joke too far."

I shoved a couple of kids from the scope to peer again through the eyepiece. The sow had moved only a little as she fed voraciously on greening ground cover. The little blond devil darted from behind a lump of what looked like huckleberry brush and playfully nipped his mother on a leg. I pushed back from the scope and turned to glare at Jane.

"Well?" she asked.

"Well what? What the hell do you expect me to say—that it's black?"

"I certainly do."

My Oregon friend bent again to the scope and said, "Black."

I snorted in disgust. Either they were blind or they made fun of me.

Our eight-year-old daughter, Cheri, had just turned from the scope and, thinking a kid would be guileless, I asked the cub's color.

"Blond." Her eyes were wide as she stared back and forth at her parents.

"Cheri!" Jane cried, shoving to the scope. "There," she said in a moment. "The cub just went up a dead snag. Now you can see."

I bent to look. "What snag? I don't see any cub up a snag."

"He was only a little way up," Jane said. "Keep looking, he'll be back."

The blond cub darted about three feet up the snag as I watched. "Ummm," I said, stepping back.

The next in line happened to be Jane's friend, May. "Blond," she reaffirmed.

Jane had tears of frustration in her eyes. "I don't care what you say. That cub is black."

The kids were arguing about it, too. A suspicion began to rise. I bent again to peer through the scope. "Well, there's the blond cub," I said. "And . . . and there's the . . . black cub, too."

The revelation about grizzly color phases was illuminating. Since that spring day in 1965, I've seen the great bears in blonde, brown, and cinnamon, as well as the more prevalent classic silvertip.

Silvertip was the color of an entire family group when next I spotted grizzlies. It was in a region near the Canadian border—a mother and three cubs. The sow was feeding on forbs growing in an avalanche path. Three cubs frolicked nearby. First one cub would bowl into another; then, while they rolled in mock combat, the third would leap atop the combatants and all three would roll down the steep mountainside in one thrashing furry ball.

But the view was brief before the sow fed across the avalanche chute and disappeared into trees, trailed by her gamboling cubs.

Next, I had a brief glimpse of a massive dark-colored grizzly some miles away into Canada. The bear was so distant I changed the spotting scope's eyepieces from 20X to 60X, but the day was warm and heat waves distorted the view at the higher power.

My next grizzly was certainly the largest I'd seen to date. A friend and I parked along a forest road where we had a view of a mountain dotted with grassy meadows peeking from a canopy of lodgepole pines. We each climbed onto the rear bumper of my Jeep wagon and set our spotting scopes on the vehicle roof. I was still fiddling with my focus when I heard Jim gasp. I looked up just as he swallowed his snoose and said, "God almighty! He's huge!"

I gauged where Jim's scope pointed and panned mine in that direction. Nothing. "Where you looking?" I asked.

"I ain't never seen nothing so big!"

"Jim, dammit, where are you looking?"

Still staring at the same spot on the distant mountain, he tried to spit. "By that tree." He bent again to his eyepiece.

"Come on, for God's sake. What tree?"

"The big burned snag. Look at him swagger!"

There were several snags on that mountain, but a swift process of elimination brought the grizzly into focus. He was indeed huge, a classic silvertip. The light-colored guard hair across his back rippled like gusts of wind swaying ripening wheat. The bear paused at a felled tree perhaps three feet in diameter, crawled upon it, and paced up its trunk as if a body builder on an exhibition runway.

"Look," I whispered. "Look at the cow elk just beyond the top of that log he's on."

Jim hawked and spit again, shuffling his feet on the bumper. "Why ain't she runnin'?"

The bear swaggered to the small end of the log. The cow raised her head, stems of grass protruding from her mouth. She chewed methodically, staring off into the distance until the last of the stems disappeared. The grizzly hopped to the ground; he and the elk appeared for all the world as though they weren't aware of each other's presence, though they could not have been more than twenty feet apart. She might have been a department-store mannikin had she not swiveled her head to eye the great silvertip as he passed, disappearing into the forest.

When she returned to feeding, my partner let out a rush of air. "What do you make of THAT?" he said, leaping from the bumper to hawk and retch on the roadside.

I lifted down both spotting scopes and said, "Better try another pinch of snoose. Good for worms."

Jim and I tracked the great bears during every free moment for three months. And, given enough weekend time, we had remarkable luck at finding them. All we waited for was the late October hunting-season opener. Then came the end of September and the first autumn snow. And though the two of us drove and hiked many miles trying to find a bear, there were none—not even blacks—in places where we'd located them all summer and throughout early fall.

"Why aren't they out there tearing up logs?" Jim asked, wiping his scope's lens.

"Or feeding on the last huckleberries?" I said.

We found our first tracks on the north slope of a densely forested mountain. They were huge, and it appeared the animal was simply wandering the road. When the tracks turned off into doghair lodgepole, Jim said, "You going in there?"

I put the Jeep in gear and drove on.

We found other tracks, all on north slopes, all near dense brush or forest. "You suppose they've changed habits with the change of seasons?" Jim said.

"I'm wondering. Maybe they're thinking about denning."

My companion and I spent all Saturday before Sunday's hunting-season opener trying to locate fresh bear tracks to no avail. Finally, just before dark, I went to Plan B.

"Tracks," I muttered, jamming on the brakes, Jeep wagon skidding to a stop. "Tracks crossing the road. See where they went up that road cut? Elk. A whole herd of 'em. They're headed into Weasel Creek."

"Elk? I thought we were hunting grizzly bear."

"We were. But I haven't figured out how yet. I know how to hunt elk."

So my intention of bagging a grizzly bear went awry that first Montana hunting season. There'd be another. In the meantime, I pursued a crash course in self-taught grizzly-bear behavior. An enormous piece of the puzzle fell into place with "The Day The Bears Go to Bed," an October, 1966 article in *Reader's Digest* on the Craighead brothers' Yellowstone grizzly research. The part that caught my eye was how Yellowstone grizzlies moved near their protected north-slope denning areas by mid-October, preparing dens and awaiting the first big snowstorm to blanket any entry tracks into their winter bedrooms.

Jim wondered why we bothered to buy the five-dollar grizzly license if hunting season for the bears didn't open until they'd already gone to bed. Good question. So I purchased a couple of horses and rounded up the necessary tack to enable me to pack into the Bob Marshall Wilderness, where hunting season opened in mid-September, before the bears moved to denning areas.

Meanwhile, I continued searching out grizzlies in order to study the animals and their habits. The glimpses, however, were all too fleeting. True, I'd learned something about individual color variations. And, as with the big boar and the cow elk, I'd discovered that relationships between animals might be far more complex than I'd imagined. But there simply hadn't been sufficient time to observe any of the dozen or so creatures thus far spotted. That's why it was a dream come true when I saw the sow and two cubs feeding near an open ridge crest.

A former hunting companion from Oregon was visiting, and we were fishing a series of beaver ponds for pan-sized cutthroats. But fish were plentiful and I got bored easily. Something caught my eye and I laid the flyrod aside to pull my binoculars from a daypack.

"Hey, Willie," I called.

The sow was turning over fallen logs and rocks, searching for bugs. The cubs scampered in play, nosing under their own stones and logs, dashing in on mom to steal anything succulent that caught their fancy. The bears fed near the top of a ridge, in an opening created by long-ago wildfire. "They're feeding," I said, my voice rising. "They'll be there for a long time."

We dashed to the Jeep wagon and drove up a cross-canyon logging road, seeking a better angle from which to watch.

It was scant minutes later when we parked the wagon and set up the scope to better advantage. "Now that's what I call a sight worth looking at, hey, Willie?"

My friend bent to peer at three grizzlies at work a thousand yards away. A slight but steady breeze blew up the canyon from our right—a crosswind to us. There was no chance the sow could sense us across the chasm.

"We can spend a whole afternoon at this, what do you say?" I grinned at the thought.

Willie moved away and I bent to peer into the eyepiece. The two cubs rolled together near where their mother tore at a rotted stump. The bears appeared to be on a well-defined game trail, paralleling but slightly below their ridgetop.

I grinned at my friend and stepped away from the scope to peel the wrapper from a sandwich.

"What the hell," Willie murmured. "They're taking off."

I snatched up the binoculars. The sow was going at a gallop directly for the ridgetop, her two cubs scrambling behind. They crested the ridge in a few seconds and disappeared.

"Why?" I stared in disbelief. "Why did they do that?"

"It sure looked like something spooked her," Willie answered. "She took off like she wanted out of there."

I panned the glasses around the area where the bears had been. "What could frighten a grizzly?"

I picked up the sandwich from the road and brushed at it in disgust, then sighed. "We may as well go back to the ponds and fish."

Before disassembling the spotting scope, I bent for one last look. "I'll be damned."

"What do you see?"

"A black bear," I said, moving away so my friend could look. "Maybe the scrawniest, scroungiest, sorriest bear you'd ever hope to see. And he's coming up that game trail where the grizzlies were."

The black appeared taller than the grizzly sow, but he'd have weighed in at but two-thirds her heft—actually looking like a cartoon caricature of a Disney bear: ears oversized, legs overlong, nose stretched out and pointed, all accentuated by his poor condition, which was surprising for an August bear who should have been rolling plump this far into the fat-storing season.

The bear appeared to be ambling without a care in the world, sniffing here, pawing there. He was, of course, traveling with the wind, so I guessed he could not possibly know that grizzlies had just been in the area he approached. I thought back to Disney adventures and how they'd implied that grizzly bears kill blacks when they have the chance.

"Boy," I said, watching the scrawny black approach the uprooted stump the grizzlies had just vacated, "he's about to get the shock of his life when he hits their scent. I'll bet he don't stop running 'til dark."

Willie grunted.

The black bear turned over a football-sized rock, then continued on to the uprooted stump in question. He nosed around in the rotted remains for a good ten seconds, then spied a log the grizzly sow had turned over, sauntered to it, sniffed around, and ambled undaunted upcountry.

"I'll be double damned," Willie muttered.

The wind was wafting from the oncoming black to the grizzly sow and her cubs. Had a grizzly actually fled from a black bear? If so, why? She was better armed, heavier, stronger, and, because of her cubs, would have fought with a ferocity the black—even in the peak of condition—surely could not have matched.

On the other hand, did the sow prefer to flee rather than risk even a winning fight? Or had the lady simply finished feeding and galloped off to her bedding ground as a hog might leave a feed trough to run to her mud hole?

How about the black—would he have been alarmed if the grizzlies had been in sight? He appeared not to care a whit about their scent. Or is it possible the black might simply have ambled

Tom Ulrich Photo

This ragged-coated, cinnamon colored black bear emerged from his den only a few weeks before. He'll continue to lose weight until mid-summer. Note the lack of hump or dish-face common to grizzlies.

past the watchful sow, somehow sensing she would not attack, as happened with the cow elk and giant grizzly mentioned earlier?

When the scrawny black disappeared, I stared at my friend for a long moment, then said, "Is any of the pap we've been led to believe about wild creatures true?"

"Or maybe," he muttered, "we just don't understand. . . ." ∎

Chapter 5

Silvertip Surprises

The bear exploded over the rock outcrop like a runaway eighteen-wheeler leaping a bridge abutment. Stan had only time to shout, "What the . . ." and it was Katy-bar-the-door as Al Joe, his nimble-footed saddlehorse, lifted off that mountainside as if from a launching pad.

It was a blur, a kaleidoscope of images: Stan's hat sailing from his head, my own saddlehorse spinning, laying about with both hind feet, clearing his own path to National Finals fame; Stan's packhorse jerking free, stampeding downslope, one sack of oats bouncing perilously askew. A saddlehorn—my own—sailed past and I grabbed it. Stan's teeth were snapping like castanets with his nimble pony's every vaulting leap. My own molars were muffled by a bloody tongue. Then I reached ahead to jerk Old Yeller's jaw to my left knee while at the same time throwing two leadrope dallies around the saddlehorn to snub the lineback packhorse close.

Stan jerked Al Joe to a standstill. He wiped a sleeve across his forehead, then craned his neck to peer through the bent and broken saplings we'd left in our wake. It looked like a battlefield. The entire melee had lasted not more than five seconds. It seemed more.

"What got into them?" I shouted.

"I don't know." Then he cried, "It's a bear."

My packhorse, Rocky, tried to jerk away to follow the disappearing Patches, but I snubbed him closer and shouted back, "A black?"

"Yeah, I guess . . . No, it's not. My God, it's a grizzly!"

From slide marks on the slabrock—a bunch of parallel scratches where his claws had skidded on the limestone—it was obvious the grizzly had tried to avoid colliding with our pack-string. And prints in the game trail, as well as flattened grass to the side, showed that the bear, after lurching over the rock edge, had not been on all fours when he crashed to the ground. But why? Had he actually crashed into the packhorse?

Why was the bear coming at such a rush in the first place? Had he heard our horses clattering over rocks and thought it a band of elk that he had a chance to ambush? Or was he merely moving crosscountry at a gallop, as I'd seen other great ursids do?

Whatever the reason for his shocking arrival, it was clear that tangling with horses and humans wasn't in the animal's game plan.

Not so clear was what occupied the bear while the rodeo rippled like dominoes through our outfit? Did he enjoy his view of the spectacle—a ringside seat in Pendleton at Roundup time? When Stan first spotted him, the creature was only a few feet beyond where he hit the game trail, heading upcountry from where we'd come.

But he should have been out of sight. Why the time lapse? Is it possible Patches had kicked the bruin on his way out of Dodge? Could that horse have stunned a grizzly bear?

Only a barbed-wire pasture fence separated Stanley Ove's place from mine. The guy had the whitest teeth and broadest smile short of politicians or encyclopedia salesmen. Moreover, the man's customary grin was accompanied by an effervescent cheerfulness that made him an ideal partner for outdoors adventure.

Stan and I searched for new hunting country, exploring a vast uninhabited land spreading across both sides of the northern Rocky Mountains, south of Canada and Glacier National Park. I'd poked into this particular area the year before, discovering what I thought might be the kind of hunting country for which I'd been searching. Now my friend and I were here to learn more.

Just getting into this spectacular piece of mountain real estate wasn't easy. Thus far we'd packed well over twenty miles, much of it fighting our way through old forest trails that had not been maintained for years: over downed trees and table-sized stones, through overhanging brush and bottomless bogs. At last we gave up, abandoning the remnant trail to pick our way cross-country, over limestone slabrock, through narrow notches and alongside towering cliffs.

Just the night before we'd camped where a spring bubbled from the ground in a tiny sedgegrass meadow. The spring was the only water along a two-mile-long, quarter-mile-wide sloping shelf that cut into some of the highest cliffs in the northern Rockies.

Mule deer bounced away like marbles dropped on concrete as our little cavalcade wound up and onto the shelf from the north. Later, as we gathered firewood, I heard Stan shout and point to the cliffs. Mountain goats clung to narrow ledges above the deer, peering down from their loftiest reaches.

Still later, while lifting a burbling pot of coffee from the fire, I asked in wonder, "How can those goats even get up there?"

Stan shook his head, then said, "You see those elk tracks beyond the spring?"

"Uh-huh. And how about the bear print in that gopher mound past the horses?"

My friend flashed his patented grin. "This might be the wildest place I've ever been, you know that?"

I shivered with the thrill.

"What I'm saying," Stan continued, "is maybe we don't have to look any further. What a view! What a place to camp!"

I said nothing, staring up at the goats, so Stan added, "And did you see the spread on that last buck?"

The white specks were scattered now, grazing on a talus slope at the bottom of the uppermost cliffs. "You might be right, Stan. This could be the place."

Then I glanced up at the pass to the south, the one I thought would lead us into the headwaters country near the center of the Bob Marshall Wilderness. "But I stood up in that pass last year and looked down here. I know there's some dandy hunting country over on the other side. And I know if we can work ponies through that pass, we can find our way to the valley beyond. Don't you reckon, being as we're here, we might as well look it over, too?"

So the next day we broke camp early, heading for the pass. The climb was a tough one. At times, game trails tailed off at rock walls, or crossed boulder fields where we dared not take the horses. But each time, we backtracked and found another way, ever clambering toward the pass and the scenic Valhalla I remembered beyond.

We rested at the top, then found we couldn't take the direct route down through a field of fallen limestone slabs. So we climbed still more, over talus slopes and through scattered whitebark pine, until we reached a grass-covered shelf sloping down in the direction we wished to go.

After resting the sweat-soaked horses one more time, we started down a game trail, following the shelf we later referred to as a "chute." The chute averaged perhaps thirty yards wide and was covered with thick soil favorable to beargrass, bluebunch wheatgrass and fescues. There were abundant flowering plants, too. Groundsel and asters still bloomed. Occasional dense patches of pines and alpine firs dotted the land.

The chute narrowed in places, with eroding layers of slick limestone slabrock either side. In one spot it steepened, flattening out at the bottom to a tiny meadow full of marmot holes. Beyond, the chute funneled to perhaps thirty feet in width. A line of small twenty-foot alpine firs sprouted in the middle. Game trails led to either side. The left-side trail looked cobbled—tough for the horses. I chose the trail fork to the right, the one that narrowed between the firs and a large slabrock formation on the right.

Twisting in the saddle, I watched my sluggish packhorse through the tight spot. He slowed, cleared it with ease, then plodded ahead. Stan's Cheshire grin flashed as I glanced beyond Rocky to my partner and his ponies.

I twisted back to study the route ahead just as Stan shouted, "What the . . ." and our rodeo commenced. . . .

Then Stan hollered "My God! It's a grizzly!" and I pointed Old Yeller up the hill and drove home the spurs, dragging the packhorse behind.

My partner stood in his stirrups, peering beyond the narrow slot we'd trailed through. His saddlehorse snorted and danced and tried to wheel our direction. But the man held him firm, reining his head back each time the pinto tried to wheel. Then Al Joe quieted and lifted his head, his ears locked forward like radar sensors, staring, staring. The horse blew softly through his nostrils. Except for the nervous blowing, he could have been carved from stone.

There! Yes, there! It was more a sense of something moving beyond the line of trees rather than a definable object. I crowded Old Yeller past Stan, past the immobile Al Joe. My big palomino's ears locked upon the shadowy movement, too; he was as reluctant as a child beckoned to a spanking. A quick glance back showed the lineback honed in, dragging on his leadrope. I nudged Yeller with the spurs.

It surprised me that we were overtaking the grizzly as he shuffled along one side of the line of trees and we moved along the other. If we continued gaining at this same rate, we'd come up on his right rear, perhaps fifty feet behind when he cleared the last trees to enter the meadow of marmot holes.

Fifty. . .forty-five. I slipped the Springfield ought-six from beneath my leg and jacked a shell into the chamber, balancing the weapon across the saddle's pommel, my thumb resting on the safety. Now the bear was beyond the trees, apparently unconcerned that we tailed him so near.

He was a classic silvertip, his dark underside shading lighter over his shoulders, hump and back. Not big—I guessed 250 to 300 pounds. By now, I'd seen more than a dozen of the great bears, all at considerable distances, all through spotting scopes or binoculars. Even so, it was easy to tell this one lacked the heft of some I had seen.

Old Yeller might as well have been tiptoeing on eggshells for all his enthusiasm for this chase. I urged him on, thrilled with the chance to study a grizzly bear close to hand.

Forty feet...

The light-colored guard hair seemed to ripple along the silvertip's back with every motion, sunlight reflecting through, as from a waving mirror. Then it hit me: *He wants nothing to do with us, but he's got too much pride to run.*

Thirty-five...

The bruin's head swung from side to side with each unhurried stride. He appeared to ignore us, but I was close enough now to see that each swing of his head seemed exaggerated; the beast was actually watching me from his eye corners with each step.

Thirty...

The grizzly stopped abruptly and thrust his snout down a marmot hole.

My saddlehorse rolled his eyes back and stopped just as suddenly. The lineback packhorse tugged on his leadrope. I could hear the bear snuffling in the hole and started to spur Old Yeller forward. Then I saw that the bear peered at me from an eye corner; that he only pretended to smell for marmots. My boots fell back into their stirrups. Was that really the sound of a grizzly bear snuffling for marmots or my heart pounding? I threw off the rifle's safety and swung the muzzle in the bear's direction.

Horses and bear stood rooted while I held my breath. Five seconds. Ten. I expelled and latched the safety back on. Then I swung the rifle to point to the side. It was still ten days until hunting season opened in "the Bob."

The grizzly lifted his snout from the hole and stared for a moment at yet another marmot burrow to his left, pausing, I thought, for effect. Then he shook himself, sunbeams flying wildly through silver hair. Captured on film, it would've been a photographer's dream.

A bee buzzed past and Old Yeller flipped his ears at a particularly annoying horsefly. I gazed off into the valley below and took a deep breath, then another. The sun beat down mercilessly from a cloudless sky. For the first time, I felt the perspiration. *Why, I'm wringing wet!*

I slid the rifle back into its scabbard and reined Old Yeller back down the hill. Stan sat Al Joe just inside the shadow of the tree line. The man's ears looked for all the world like they were about to topple into his pearly mouth. Beyond, the packhorse Patches trotted up the hill to join his equine friends, the sack of oats still bouncing precariously in loosened lash ropes.

I turned to look behind. The bear was gone. ∎

A pair to draw to.

Richard Jackson

Chapter 6

Bear Encounters
of the Third Kind

Winds whimpered and moaned along the cliff face, coming
in waves, sifting from the north, seeking cracks and crevices as if
pumped by a celestial organ, fading at last to the south, only to
reverse course, dirge rising above mournful dirge as it beat back
from whence it came in the inky night.

I leaned forward to shove another chunk of wood into the
stove. "So there he was, LaVern, too much pride to run and too
much smarts to face us down. But damn if he didn't just stop and
shove his nose down that marmot hole, sort of daring me to crowd
him any more."

My lanky friend's eye corners crinkled and he swigged his
coffee. "And that was around here?"

"Yep. Happened just over that pass to the south. As close to
a grizzly as I ever want to get."

We both cocked our ears at an eerie distant wail from the
towering heights.

"Wind picking up," LaVern said. His words still hung in the
air as ringing horsebells and horseshoes clattering across slabrock
brought us to our feet and through the tent flap. LaVern's two
quarterhorses charged in from the darkness, followed by my quar-
tet of grade nags. The herd milled outside our tent. I put an arm
around the neck of Old Yeller and stroked his shoulder.

"They appear a mite spooky," LaVern said.

I glanced at the wall above, distinguishable mostly by deeper shadow. A raft of fast-moving clouds parted, and moonlight flooded our world.

Then it was gone. But for a moment the moon was full and bright, and I thought of witches and gremlins and Druids dancing in a forest glade. Shuddering in the chill, I gathered an armload of wood and headed back to the lighted tent. LaVern's shadow played through the canvas wall as he poured another cup of coffee.

"Stan ever tell you about that Brownie Basin grizzly we got tangled up with?" he asked as I pushed inside.

I shook my head. "But it sounds like something a body ought to hear."

This, then, is LaVern's story:

The mound was full of sticks, roots, grass stems, fresh-turned earth, and remnants of dirty snow. One hunter fished under his red plaid coat for a cigarette, then dug for a wooden match in the same pocket. "What you reckon it is, Al?"

Al Framness shifted his rifle's sling strap and circled the mound on bandy legs. "Never saw nothin' like it in Alabama," he said.

The first hunter flicked a thumbnail across the kitchen match, watched it flame, and touched it to his cigarette, staring intently at the mound. The man drew deeply, then blew a smoke ring. "Pile is as big as a poster bed. *Something* made it. Any tracks?"

Al returned to his circle, this time searching the ground more carefully. "Nope. Nothing I can see, Georgie."

George Akins leaned his rifle against a spruce tree, then returned to squat on his heels. Smoke drifted from his nostrils as he thumbed his cap back. A lock of unruly graying hair spilled across his forehead. "Snow pretty much melted today. That's why no tracks."

Framness fidgeted. "We'd ought to go on. Won't do to keep our guide waiting."

Akins ground his cigarette against the toecap of his boot, then stood. He was big, well over six feet, two hundred and thirty pounds. "What we really ought to do is see what's under that pile. Something made it. Aren't you curious?"

"I'd druther get me an elk."

The big man kicked at the mound. Debris flew. "Come help me, Al. We'll get your elk tomorrow."

"But tomorrow's the last day we got to hunt."

Akins grinned. "Come on. Something's under here. I just saw hair." He kicked away more debris. "Yeah, there is. Looks brown." Another kick. "No it's not, either. Lighter colored. But it's mudded up some."

Framness said, "Aw, hell," and also began kicking at the mound. Soon, the little man laid his rifle aside and scraped with his hands. After a while, he said, "Looks like a dog."

"You're right. How could a dog get up here in the middle of the Bob Marshall Wilderness? And who'd bury it?"

The little man leaped back. "No, by God! It's a bear! A grizzly bear!"

"A grizzly bear?"

"Sure! Look at where I wiped off his back. See? It's some lighter up there than down on his side. Same color as your hair. And," he levered a leg and foot up with the toe of his boot, "look at them claws. It's a grizzly bear, sure 'nough!"

Both men heard the sounds and turned in tandem as their guide led saddlehorses into the little clearing.

"Thought you boys might be along here somewhere," LaVern said. He eyed the scattered debris and tried to rein his bay near. The mare snorted and shied, and the two ponies he led also danced away. The lanky outdoorsman swung from the saddle to tie all three horses to nearby saplings.

"There's a bear in that pile, LaVern," Al said. "A grizzly bear."

"You're joking."

"No I ain't. What do you reckon buried it?"

The guide laid a hand on his horse's rump while his eyes swept the forest glade's fringe. "Nothin' I know buries a grizzly bear, Al. Except another grizzly bear." He slipped his saddle carbine from it's scabbard as he added, "A *big* grizzly bear."

The little man stared at LaVern's gun for a moment, then snatched his own heavy-caliber rifle from the ground. His partner was only seconds behind in retrieving his .338 from where it leaned against the spruce.

The two Alabama men were hunting from Russell Fox's camp, located on Big Salmon Creek, deep within the Bob Marshall Wilderness. Two other guests shared the camp. And when LaVern brought his two hunters in around dark, Framness lost no time telling them of the buried grizzly:

"Boys, when LaVern led us into the trees and found them tracks, I'll tell the world they was big. I could stick both feet in one and do a jig. And I near melted when he showed us where the big bastard had most likely been layin' and watchin' while we tore away on his graveyard—and us six miles from camp and a hundred and six from the nearest hospital and my gun layin' on the ground and George's leanin' agin a tree. I couldn't get on my horse fast enough."

Russ Fox held out a cup of coffee with his single arm to the little man. "You boys think about taking the hide?"

"Takin' the hide? What'd I want with a mudded-up grizzly hide?"

"Maybe you wouldn't," the outfitter grinned. "But I happen to know George has a grizzly license in his pocket—I picked it up for him myself."

Akins stared blankly at the outfitter, then pulled out his billfold and sorted through it.

"A man don't get that many chances at a grizzly bear." Fox said. "They're cagey critters and there may not be as many . . ."

"Yeah," the big man broke in. "Here it is. Grizzly bear. Didn't even think about it."

LaVern Clare was raised on a North Dakota wheat-and-cow ranch. But as soon as diapers turned to denims, the lad headed for western mountains. A born horseman, the young man signed on to work with dudes for Glacier Park's horse concessionaire, and then to guide and wrangle for the same outfit during fall hunting season in what is now the Great Bear Wilderness. Gaining experience with one of the biggest dude outfits in the northern Rockies, LaVern's talents turned marketable to other outfitters.

After fifteen years, the man began ranching, gradually working his way up to a 200-cow spread of rolling pastures, sub-irrigated meadows, and a front-porch view found in few places. LaVern guided only infrequently now, when some outfitter friend got into a bind. This was one of those times; his respected, one-armed friend, Russ Fox, needed another guide for a couple of hunters from Alabama.

I'd become acquainted with LaVern through my neighbor and hunting companion, Stan Ove. Our acquaintance blossomed into friendship, and now LaVern and I were camped, during yet another elk season, near a sweetwater spring that burbled from the bottom of a towering wall of cliffs.

A stout wind gust shivered our tent walls and LaVern paused to run freckled fingers through gray-shot red hair. A dead sapling sawed against a giant whitebark pine standing behind the tent. It was an uncanny squawk that, added to the cliff-face banshees, ran chills up and down my backbone.

The lanky ex-guide grinned. "You want me to go on with the story?"

LaVern plopped to the bench by the big Alabamian. His long arm snaked out to the whiskey bottle. "Maybe we'd ought to go back tomorrow and skin out your grizzly, George. Not everybody's got a silvertip rug in front of their fireplace."

Akins leaned back against the table and crossed his legs, then nodded. "Might be worthwhile."

The guide pulled the cork with his teeth and mumbled around it: "On the other hand, maybe getting too curious about a bear cache ain't the smartest thing we ever contemplated." He took a pull, wiped his lips with the back of his hand, pounded in the cork, and added, "You reckon there's some things should be left unknown?"

Akins chuckled, winking at his partner. "Al, let's you and me go back tomorrow for that hide. What do you say?"

"What you want a grizzly hide in front of your fireplace for, Georgie? You ain't had a fire in it since you built it."

"Come on, Al. LaVern figured it was killed last night. Couldn't be spoiled yet. And me with a grizzly tag in my pocket."

After supper, when the guides commenced planning the next day's hunt, Akins said, "Russ, why don't you send LaVern to help somebody else get an elk? Me and Al want to ride back to Brownie Basin and take the dead grizzly's hide. We don't need a guide. Shucks, we know the way."

The two men returned in mid-afternoon carrying no hide. The way they told it, the dead bear was gone from the mound they'd torn apart the previous day. Deep-furrowed drag marks led from it.

They had tied their horses, slipped rifles from saddle scabbards, chambered rounds, and followed the drag trail. Three hundred yards from where they'd opened the first mound, they found a second pile of debris in the midst of a clump of leafless tag alder.

The men opened the new mound, all the while glancing about, tinkering with rifle safeties and fingering trigger guards. This time the small bear had been partially consumed and its hide ruined. "Well, that's that," Al said. "We might as well trot on back to the horses and find us some place to hunt up an elk."

George wiped his palms on his wool trouser legs and stared into the surrounding woods. "I had my heart set on taking a grizzly hide home, Al. I'd just as soon it be a big one as a little one. Wouldn't you?"

The small man shook his head. "This place gives me the creeps, Georgie. Let's get out of here."

They struck fresh tracks in a patch of remnant snow and were able to follow for a short distance before losing them on bare ground. The big grizzly appeared to be meandering. They, too, wandered for half an hour, occasionally crossing bear tracks or their own tracks in snow patches until George stopped short and pointed. Al hurried forward to see.

"Jeeesus!"

There were bear tracks on top of their tracks.

The banshees howled and our tent shivered under a particularly stout gust. I stood and pumped the lantern, then flicked the wire cleaner. The lanky ex-guide poured a dab of Windsor Canadian into the bottom of his coffee cup and contemplated it.

"And?" I prompted.

The following day, Russell Fox and his packer prepared to take the camp's four hunters on the long trek back to civilization. Russell planned to return in three days with a party from Wisconsin. LaVern and Stan Ove, the other guide, stayed behind, planning to do a little personal hunting while waiting for the outfitter's next party to arrive.

Big George Akins leaned from the saddle to shake LaVern's hand. "Take care, pardner. See you next year."

LaVern grinned. "Us and the Bob Marshall will be waiting."

Akins reined his horse away, then turned back. "There's still a powerful-big grizzly in Brownie Basin for the fellow who's man enough to go after him."

LaVern grinned. "It just might be that me and Stan, both put together, would make one good man."

An early-morning sun burned away frost as LaVern led the way along a narrow ridgetop trail above Brownie Basin. He drowsed in his saddle, as a man born to it often does when a morning sun is warm and all things are right with his world. His horse stopped abruptly. The man's eyes popped open.

Forty feet away, squarely in the trail, stood a huge grizzly. Stunned, LaVern, Stan, and their horses might have been carved from stone. The silver-dark granite block standing in the trail could have come from the same quarry.

Then, barely perceptibly at first, LaVern's horse began to tremble. The encounter seemed to go on for hours, but in reality was a few seconds as men and bear stared, and horses trembled. Thoughts of his rifle flitted through LaVern's mind, but the bear was so big and so close that he feared even to reach for the weapon. Besides, he'd have to dismount to shoot accurately, and he wasn't about to leave the saddle while a huge grizzly stood only a few feet away. From his vantage, LaVern saw the bear's eyes clearly: tiny, red-rimmed, boring a hole straight through.

Meanwhile, his horse quaked ever more violently.

Then Stan cut the silence: "I'm getting out of here!"

As if someone had tripped a starter gate, the huge silvertip whirled and in an instant crashed off down the mountain through tag alder and lodgepole pine as if the trees were no more than windrows of half-grown corn. With the bear gone, LaVern's mare stopped trembling as quickly as she'd begun, responding to the man's rein-touch, spinning to follow Stan's horse back the way they'd come.

I opened the stove door to shove another length of gnarled pine inside. A puff of smoke blew out with a sudden downdraft, prompting a fit of coughing. I waved the smoke aside and closed the door, moving up on the edge of my block of wood, then turned expectantly back to my friend. . . .

Stan lost what little enthusiasm he had for Brownie Basin grizzlies after the ridgetop encounter. Not so for LaVern. The huge bruin would be a classic trophy: dark underside and legs, turning to silver along the back and shoulders and neck, hump pronounced, and the face dish-shaped with a dark-colored "mask" around the tiny eyes.

So . . . the following morning, LaVern, alone, tied his mare to a sapling in the same Brownie Basin glade where the two Alabama men had discovered the great bear's first burial mound. Fresh snow blanketed the land, and the temperature was frigid. The man wore wool clothing for both warmth and stealth. But just in case rapid-fire was of the essence, there was no glove on his trigger-finger hand.

LaVern chambered a round in his lever-action .308 and glanced through its iron sights at the shiny front bead. Satisfied, he glided to where the hunters had told him they saw the second mound. He found it easily enough, and, as he'd expected, the big grizzly had again moved its cache.

The lanky outdoorsman created not so much as a whisper as he slipped through the snow. No breeze stirred the air. Still, the man had the eerie feeling his every move was giving him away in the motionless quiet. He had little trouble finding the third burial cache, studying it from a distance. Then he began a slow stalk through the basin, searching for tracks in the fresh snow. There were none. Though the man covered the entire basin, he found no sign, no prints, no snow knocked from branches, no melted-out bed. The big bruin simply was no longer there. The land was so lifeless not even a squirrel track marred the basin's fresh powder.

Disappointed, LaVern retraced his tracks to the mare. The horse drowsed where she stood, awakening only as the man fumbled in saddlebags for his lunch. She drowsed again as her master hunkered against a nearby spruce wondering, as he peeled the wrapper from a sandwich, what he'd do with the remainder of the day.

Twenty minutes later, LaVern licked his fingertips and wiped them on a trouser leg. He was just pushing to his feet when he noticed the mare's head, lifted and alert, ears locked forward, eyes staring intently across the glade. The horse's attitude, to a man of LaVern Clare's experience, meant something moved just beyond the ability of his own senses to identify. He eased into another position to better peer into the dark forest. Nothing. *Probably a pine squirrel*, the hunter thought. *Or a snowshoe rabbit.* Then he saw the horse's head turning ever so slowly, ears and eyes still locked upon something beyond.

What the hell is going on here? LaVern studied the set of the mare's ears and tried to see just where she was looking. Nothing. His heart beat faster. By now the mare had turned her head enough so she shifted her body to follow, snorting softly as she continued to turn. She peered behind LaVern—behind the tree where he sat. He came to his feet slowly, almost hypnotized, cradling the familiar rifle, its safety thrown off, awaiting only the touch of his finger to fire. Still, he saw nothing.

The mare shifted again. LaVern could scarcely believe she tracked movement, for the forest here was not really thick and he could see nothing. Then the mare began to tremble.

LaVern, gun at the ready, ran to her side, sighting along her head to see what she saw. Nothing! Still the horse trembled. Unbelievably, she continued to shift as whatever was out there circled them. *Why, God, can't I see it?* Sweat trickled down the man's spine, down the inseam of his undershorts. His hands were clammy on the gun. He again checked the safety.

As suddenly as it began, the mare's trembling stopped. LaVern looked wildly at her. She still stared, but now tracked movement back the other way. The man ran forward thirty feet to peer farther into the forest. Nothing. He threw a quick look back at the horse. Her head continued to swing to the right, but she seemed more relaxed.

Soon, one ear flicked back and forth. She swung her head to stare at LaVern. Then both ears flared back and the animal's head drooped as she fell to dozing. . . .

"So what did you find?" I asked when it was clear that my friend had finished his tale. "What kind of tracks were out there in the snow?"

Shadows played on the man's angular, freckled features as his eyes caught and held mine. "I never looked." An embarrassed grin spread. "Me and the mare galloped most of the way back to camp, and I ain't been back."

He paused, then added, "I'm never going back, neither." ■

Chapter 7

The Puzzle Continues

It turned easy to find grizzly bears. Plunk yourself down in mountain country where a few of the creatures roam, devote so much time to finding 'em the kids wonder who's sticking his feet under the kitchen table on the few occasions when you're home for supper, kiss your wife and your job and your sanity good-by. Do that and anyone could find the big beasts. By 1970, I knew enough about grizzly habits and habitat—at least during the summer foraging season—that I was willing to make bets I could find one on any given weekend. One might ask if such familiarity bred contempt.

Hardly. Though I was still yearning for a silvertip rug as a symbol of outdoors skill and savvy, my admiration for the animal was rising. But there was frustration, too. After six years trodding some of the wildest land in the northern Rocky Mountains, I had yet to see a grizzly bear during hunting season. Put a rifle in my hand and *Ursus arctos horribilis* turned as scarce as Hottentots before a slaver's whip. When I was without a weapon, it seemed I had to kick wildlife—all wildlife—out of the way.

I wondered: Does man-the-hunter emit some sort of recognizable behavior or odor or sound that alerts animals? Documentaries demonstrated that herds of antelope or wildebeests or zebras would stand and watch well-fed lions trot through a grazing herd with nary a glance right or left. But let one of those lions appear on a distant horizon while hunting and the entire gaggle of grazers would be off at a gallop. Why? How did they know?

Am I a carnivore? While on the hunt, I'd seen a species that was not in season stand and watch me pass—deer during elk season, for instance. Two weeks prior, while they were fair game, those same deer would have leaped for the next county.

Is that the way of bears, I wondered. Did they simply yawn and return to digging glacier lilies, ripping up rotted logs, or grazing on clover if someone eyed them through a spotting scope? But did they take the fast train to Memphis if someone lined up a rifle scope? Did game wardens provide them with a calendar on which opening day of hunting season was stenciled in? Were they psychic? Did they have a D.E.W. Line system to warn them each time my Jeep wagon headed for hunting's hinterlands?

I grew careless while traveling in the great bears' domain. The Night of the Grizzlies changed that. That was the infamous night (August 13, 1967) when two girls were killed and devoured in separate Glacier National Park backcountry campgrounds by different grizzly bears. That was the night that forever put to rest a prevailing wisdom that unhunted bears view humans through the same prism as hunted bears. Plain unvarnished fear is why I turned around while hiking the Harrison Creek Trail and beat it back to join my companions. . . .

Harrison Lake is well known for its trophy cutthroat and bull trout. But the lake is in one of the most isolated and seldom-traveled portions of Glacier Park. We'd packed into Harrison Lake over the Fourth of July weekend and had the place pretty much to ourselves. But I grew bored with fishing and swimming, and decided to hike farther up Harrison Creek from the lake's inlet. The other guys in my group preferred to fish, so I went alone.

I found the old park trail easily enough. Just as I'd been told, the path had not been cleared in years. But exploring new country is high on my priorities list, so I set out whistling and singing through the big spruce and brush-filled bottom. Platter-sized leaves of devil's club and thimbleberry hung over the trail, obscuring it. I'd not gone far when I slipped in the first pile of bear dung. From its size, I took it to be from a grizzly.

Moving more cautiously now, I spotted other scat piles, then came upon huge grizzly tracks in the mud. Another track.

Another pile. More tracks—these of differing sizes. The volume knob on my senses cranked to broadcast when I smelled my first bear.

Bears (at least some bears) emit an acrid odor peculiarly their own. I've been told it's generally limited to older bears, usually boars, that have fed on fish or carrion. I'd smelled the odor before, always where a grizzly laid up in a thicket.

There was no wind on this day and the forest was so dense that visibility was limited to less than twenty-five yards. I faltered. No gun. Two, perhaps three miles from my companions. In a section of Glacier National Park so remote it's visited perhaps once per decade.

I crept on, parting thimbleberries and devil's club to do so. Another pile of dung. Another slip. More tracks. The overpowering, acrid odor again.

At last I lost my nerve. *But what's this? Shadows are long. How much time before the sun sinks beyond western ridges? If only I could see out of this dense tangle! Can I climb a tree to see how much time is left before dark? Don't be silly, Roland! Don't run! Are you out of your mind, running in grizzly country? Slow down. Walk. Watch that pile; you slipped in it on the way up-trail.*

I stepped up the pace, nevertheless, slipping and sliding in the mud and dung. The odor again. I spent more time looking behind than ahead. At last, the lake. No one fishing. Must be at camp. I paused to take a deep breath, then sauntered up to the fire just as night fell. Trout sizzled in a pan.

"See anything?" one of my friends asked.

"Nope. A little grizzly sign is all."

The outdoors bug romanced me more assiduously than any of my contemporaries and I applied for an outfitter's license. In the beginning I intended, while on vacation from my lumber-company employer, to guide one or two hunting parties. There was just one hunter in 1971, a party of four in '72, two parties in '73. There was also little time for me to hunt.

So I did what might seem logical to folks flirting with golden sunsets, wind soughing through spruce trees, streams burbling down a staircase bed of gentian and monkeyflower—I relinquished clockwork paychecks to spend more time amid God's finest.

Valerie Chambers came into our lives in late June of '73. Valerie was an exchange student from Australia who became sister and best friend to our sixteen-year-old daughter Cheri and big sister-advisor to eleven-year-old Marc.

Valerie, who hailed from humid Queensland, had two dreams: to feel snow and to see a grizzly bear. Our family took Valerie on a horseback packtrip into Glacier Park within a week of her arrival. As we crossed the crest of the Rockies, we stopped the stock truck at a snowbank, then drove on, at last packing six miles to a campsite near the Belly River Ranger Station.

Belly River country is prime habitat for grizzly bear. I'd learned that on a visit to the area the previous year when a ranger advised me not to venture into the isolated Mokowanis Basin

Tom Ulrich photo

Minding his own business.

without a "smoke pole" for protection. Though my companion and I had spotted considerable evidence of bears (tracks, dung, excavated hillsides where they'd dug for marmots), we actually spotted only one grizzly, a large male on the far shore of Glenns Lake.

I wasn't there to view grizzlies this time, however—not with my family in tow. Instead, I'd brought them to see some of the most beautiful lands God ever made. If Shangri La exists, Belly River's that place. The entire upper valley and its multi-glacial basins are surrounded by stunning sky-scraping crags that might stem from a landscape artist's imagination. There are outsized lakes of the purest clarity snuggling in basin bottoms—lakes so large that whitecaps are common amid gale winds sweeping from snow-clad peaks. Inlet and outlet creeks from those lakes would rate as major rivers throughout most of America—and would be dammed for power or drained for agriculture. Belly River waters, home to several native trout and char species, are so clear one cannot accurately guess the depth of multi-colored bottom rocks and so tasty most folks would pay to belly down for an honest drink. Several stunning waterfalls lurk amid those waters, miniature Niagaras of the northern Rockies with names like Dawn Mist, Gros Ventres, and White Quiver.

There are vast meadows in the Belly River country with grass waving at stirrup level to a tall horse. There are lush forests of lodgepole pine and Englemann spruce. And the wildlife! It's all such a panoply of creation I would've been derelict had I not led my family there.

The two girls loved it. Marc and Jane, as it turned out, were appreciative but also commodity-oriented—they wanted fish for supper. Or rather, Jane wanted fish for supper; Marc wished only to *catch* fish for Jane's supper. Fortunately, there were beaver ponds nearby where brookies danced atop the surface.

It was late afternoon when the three kids and I galloped our ponies through rolling foothill country to a low ridge overlooking the nearest beaver pond. The grizzly was the first thing I saw.

He fed on sedge near the pond's dam of sticks and grass and mud. Though we were but a hundred yards away and had thundered up on horseback with kids shouting and laughing, the bear appeared unaware of our presence.

"Stay on your horses," I commanded.

"What is it?" Valerie asked.

"It's a bear," Cheri replied. "Dad, it's a grizzly, isn't it?"

"Mmmhmm."

Our ponies keyed in on the bear, too, and either stood motionless, watching, or pranced about wanting to get out of Dodge.

"Are we gonna get to fish?" Marc asked.

I laughed. "Let's wait and see, boy."

This was ideal rangeland. The rolling uplands where we sat our horses was sagebrush and bunchgrass covered with perhaps a half-dozen beaver-pond and willow wetlands amid the folds. Belly River itself flowed through grass-filled bottoms but a quarter mile to the south. Between this pond and the river stood the only forest nearby, perhaps eighty acres of spruce and lodgepole and alpine fir.

"Look," Cheri said. "He's moving toward the trees."

She was right. The grizzly, a classic silvertip with the standard hump and broad head, was nearer the forest, still feeding, still seemingly blind to us humans.

Fifteen minutes passed while the bear inched toward the forest. Then the animal disappeared.

"Can I fish now?" Marc asked.

Good question. Dare I let the kids dismount? Was the bear gone? Or was he merely out of sight, as intently studying us as we had been eyeing him?

I said, "I'm going to ride down to the river and see if he comes out of the timber on the far side. You kids stay on your horses until I get back." With that, I jammed spurs into my saddlehorse, Buck, a quarter-thoroughbred mix who was capable of traveling faster than I was able to ride.

Buck skirted the forest fringe at a high lope and, within a couple of minutes, cantered up to a high bank overlooking the river. The silvertip was already wading out on the river's far side. The bear shook himself like a dog, sunlit spray flying into ten thousand tiny rainbows, then took off like the hounds of hell were in pursuit, rushing across the first meadow, racing through trees and dashing across a second meadow at express speed.

I stood in the stirrups and waved my hat in salute as the bear disappeared into the distance.

"He was already across the river," I told the kids as Buck and I cantered up.

"That means he had to run, doesn't it?" Cheri said. "He knew we were here all along."

"He . . . he was beautiful!" Valerie said.

"Can I fish now?" Marc asked.

It was the summer of '75 when I scheduled my first fishing party on a week-long horseback-in, river-float-out, wilderness trip. I took a packtrain in with stock feed and heavy inflatable rafts before the actual trip took place. Our son, Marc, now thirteen, helped out.

We planned for the Michigan group to fish Big Salmon Lake during their first three days, and I needed to select a campsite where we could store our gear and be out of sight of other visitors to the lake. We looked over one spot that appeared adequate, but I wanted to check out another point of land a mile up the trail. The August day was shirtsleeve weather. The packstring trailed along behind, moving well.

"Lots of huckleberries," Marc, said, pointing to the side of our trail.

We rounded another trail bend and Buck stopped. Perhaps fifty yards farther on, a grizzly stripped berries. I beckoned to Marc, hoping the bear wouldn't dash away before my son could see him. Marc reined to my side and whispered, "Is it a grizzly?"

I nodded.

His berry patch was a good one, and the bear had hardly to move to shovel them into his mouth. After a few minutes, the packhorses became restless and I said, "You seen enough?"

"Yep. Let's get to where we're going and unload these horses."

Incredibly, the bear still hadn't heard us. So I shouted, "Shoo, bear!"

He continued to feed. I spurred Buck up the trail a few feet until we were in plain sight. The bear turned to face us, then sat down in the middle of the trail to shovel in more berries with his forepaws while staring clearly in our direction.

I glanced back at Marc. "You know, after pondering on it, I think I like that campsite we passed earlier."

"I know I do," the boy replied. ■

Chapter 8

Surviving on Insects

I studied the bear for an hour while he redesigned his living room of charred or rotted stumps and logs and billion-year-old stones. From the looks of the ransacked hillside, he'd toiled in the area all afternoon. The bruin rolled a log, then began taking mammoth bites. Shadows stole across the distant peaks as I clambered stiffly to my feet, dusted my trousers, and folded the spotting scope into its knapsack.

The reverse took place the following morning as sunlight kissed the mountaintops while I stood on the vandalized hillside. As expected, the grizzly was nowhere in sight—gone for hours by now.

It was a mystery to me how an animal as large as a grizzly bear could expend vital energy in pursuit of beetles, grubs, and ants. Yet I'd watched bears turning rocks and logs, then pouncing in delight when a bug was exposed. How could it be?

Only remnants were left of what had been a bucket-sized ant nest in the rotted log the grizzly had rolled. A few eggs were scattered about. Perhaps a dozen survivor ants were stirring in the morning chill, lugging their few precious eggs to an unknown safe house. I wandered on around that hill, investigating each rock and log and stump the bear had overturned or torn apart, a layman searching for behavioral clues. There were other, smaller ant nests, also vandalized. Then I stumbled upon a world-class pile of grizzly scat.

It was enormous, stacked up in a not-so-neat pile in the middle of a game trail. What the hell? I'd been poking into everything else this bear did—why not? The scat was mostly composed of rotted wood. It was mixed with a little offal from other sources for binder, but mostly it was just rotted wood packed into Polish-sausage-sized rolls deposited to nourish the land. Spreading it apart with a stick, I also made out an occasional ant leg and an antenna or two.

So that's how grizzlies can spend time and energy going after insects, I thought; they not only eat the bugs, but gobble up their houses, too. With grizzly jaws waiting, there can be no hiding place for a grub. No way. Not with the entire parlor, playroom, and pantry going. Then the parlor passes through the bear's intestines while the grub adds insect protein and fat to bear muscle and bone.

Squatting on my haunches, hands dangling over knees. I pondered this: an ingenious, energy-effective method of insect transferral. Had I not then confined my layman's research to the on-the-ground variety, I might have learned that better-trained, better-equipped, more properly funded researchers were not only interested in the same topic, but were also actively engaged.

Interest was spurred in ursid insect-feeding by an August 3, 1932, observation by John Romer, while climbing McDonald Peak in the Mission Mountain Range of western Montana. Romer encountered a group of twelve grizzly bears in a high, rocky basin just below the 10,000-foot summit. He observed the bears for several minutes as they overturned rocks and fed on what he concluded were ladybird beetles, present in large numbers amid the rocks.

Romer returned to McDonald Peak many times from 1932 to 1956, observing "literally hundreds of grizzly bears," mainly females with young, feeding on ladybird aggregations atop the lofty mountain. He estimated that concentrations of the insects were so great that, on occasion, five to ten gallons of beetles could be collected per day. Romer's estimate of ladybird concentration attracted commercial interest, spurred by the fact that in certain parts of the country, ladybird beetles were being collected and sold for release in orchards as a means of controlling marauding aphids and other insects.

Romer's observations were validated by longtime Mission Mountains guide Bud Cheff, who reported observing grizzlies on McDonald Peak as early as the 1920s, usually in August, feeding on insects and grazing amid surrounding alpine meadows. Concentrations of ladybird beetles atop high ridges have long been observed throughout the mountain west. Research indicates the insects migrate to high altitudes for hibernation beneath heavy mountain snowpacks. With gallons upon gallons of beetles available, grizzly bears must be attracted to ladybird concentrations as we're attracted to steakhouses.

Hearing of the phenomenon, John Chapman visited McDonald Peak in late September, 1952, to gather grizzly scat samples for analysis. Chapman's research, afterward largely verified, led to unexpected results—microscopic examination revealed the remains of army cutworm moths, not ladybird beetles. Chapman's findings launched a new wave of research aimed in several directions.

Much of today's fertile analysis of cutworm-moth/grizzly-bear connections comes from several mountain sites around Yellowstone National Park. To understand the essential nature of those connections, it is first necessary to understand something of the dynamics of cutworm cycles—just now becoming understood.

Each fall, adult female moths lay their eggs throughout the Great Plains in the soil at lower elevations. Cutworm larvae emerge in early spring, feeding on leafy plants, including commercial crops such as wheat, barley, oats, sugarbeets, alfalfa, etc. Cutworm depredations are often so severe that pesticides are utilized to reduce crop damage. After feeding for several weeks, the larvae enter a beneath-the-soil pupal stage, emerging as adult moths in early summer. Shortly after surfacing, they migrate *en masse*, sometimes for hundreds of miles, to distant alpine habitats where they spend summer nights feeding and pollinating a variety of wildflowers.

During their summer-long stay, cutworm moths convert flower nectar to body fat—from 30 percent of abdominal body fat when they first arrive in the mountains to 70 percent by fall migration. That high fat content produces high energy, compared to other available bear food.

The moths are entirely nocturnal, feeding on wildflower nectar during the night and taking shelter from heat, rain or snow under various rock formations—usually talus from nearby cliffs, cols, or aretes—while metabolizing nectar. Research indicates that moths tend to aggregate in large clusters, distributed randomly throughout the talus, gravel, and boulder fields. Those moth concentrations serve as pot roasts to a host of predatory pillagers: black bears, coyotes, ravens, American pipits, mountain bluebirds, owls, bats. And, of course, systematic excavations of the cutworm army's bivouac by grizzlies.

Temperature affects the moths' ability to escape when they're exposed during excavations, according to an excellent report; *Grizzly Bear Use of Army Cutworm Moths in the Yellowstone Ecosystem*, by French, French, and Knight:

"Moths exposed near the rock surface had to flap their wings several seconds before flying away, but those exposed farther down where it was cooler had to spend more time warming up before flight, and as a consequence, usually fled by crawling deeper into the rock interstices. This mode of escape concentrated moths at the bottom of the excavations when they were prevented from going down farther by rock or ice."

According to ongoing research in the McDonald Peak area of western Montana, both ladybird beetles and army cutworm moths are present in and on talus slopes at high elevations. With ladybirds above ground and visible while cutworms hide amid talus rock during the day and emerge only at night, one can at last understand how initial observers erred in naming the insect of the bears' collective focus.

How important are these moth concentrations to bears? Very—especially to females with young who (according to a report entitled Grizzly Bear Use of Alpine Insect Aggregation Sites, Absaroka Mountains, Wyoming, by O'Brien and Lindzey) "have higher nutritional needs."

O'Brien's and Lindzey's findings are echoed over and over again. According to French and Knight:

"They [moths] also appear especially important to adult females since each moth-feeding area contained from 1 to 3 distinctive family groups throughout each moth feeding season during this study. . . ."

". . . And finally, moths are important because they are available during hyperphagia, a metabolic stage that begins in mid-July when grizzly bears increase their feeding activity to accumulate fat reserves required for winter hibernation."

My question had been: How can animals as large as bears spend energy in pursuit of tiny insects? And the answer: They go for insects in volume. Consider these observations: "Bears meandered back and forth on the talus fields and appeared to locate moth clusters by scent. They spent several minutes excavating and eating before moving on to search for another moth cluster . . ."

The real kicker, of course, is how many moths are available?

". . . Approximately 65 percent of their time was spent eating and only 22 percent excavating. Review of film records revealed that bears commonly continued to feed on moths while excavating. Therefore, somewhere between 65 percent and 87 percent of their total activity was spent eating during their pursuit of moths."

How many bears are working these talus slopes for cutworm moths? French and Knight reported that they "observed 51 different grizzly bears feeding at 4 of the 10 moth-feeding areas on a single morning in August 1991."

Their observations disclosed remarkable social tolerance between bears at moth dining tables:

"It was common for several grizzly bears to feed on moths at the same time in close proximity. . . . Females with cubs routinely fed in the presence of adult males. . . ."

The largest concentration of bears observed at one area was twenty-three, nine within an area thirty yards in diameter. Such concentrations resulted "in a continuous intermingling among all age and sex classes."

Such social tolerance among animals that make solitude their life work is indeed a revelation to me. My assumption was grizzly bears routinely become enraged if anything approaches a winter-killed elk carcass claimed as their own, or put the run on another bear feeding unobtrusively along the edge of a hundred-acre huckleberry patch. So why the camaraderie at cutworm banquets? The reason lies in the abundance of the banquet. Research discloses that bears usually feed for a couple of hours twice each day, usually in early morning and late evening. Though moths congregate for a two-to three-month period, individual bears come and go, sometimes wandering away for days, perhaps to valley bottoms or berry-rich hillsides to sweeten their diets. Some bears are known to show up at other moth-filled talus slopes to shoulder up with strange bruins in pursuit of protein. And it's that protein they must have to survive another winter's sleep.

Other extraordinary sources of essential protein are tapped by bears to ensure survival. One with overtones as evolutional as the annual cutworm orgy is that of spring carrion. Vast herds of grazing animals—bison, antelope, bighorn sheep, elk, deer—roamed the Great Plains to their interface with the Rocky Mountains. An annual process of survival of the fittest took place among those grazers. That process is called winter—the instrument of choice for nature's selection of the fittest, the survivors.

Winter selection took place like clockwork as harsh weather wound down just when wild ungulates reached their limit of endurance. Many North American Indian tribes called March the "Hunger Moon" for good reason. It was then that bears began emerging from their dens in search of the animals who didn't make it. And in the following weeks, foraging bears depended upon that carrion source for nourishment until the abundance of summer.

Mike Madel is a soft-speaking, slow-drawling western man, shaped by wind and heat, snow and cold, mountains and grizzlies. Especially grizzlies. A trained wildlife biologist employed by Montana's Department of Fish, Wildlife and Parks, Mike has spent the bulk of his professional years in research. Now he's a Grizzly Bear Management Specialist. Mike's duties are manifold: quick response to problem bears; providing useful information on grizzlies to the public; developing proactive actions to correct human/bear problems before they occur. He's a guy who finds common-sense solutions to the problem when grizzlies hang around ranchers' lambing sheds or calving grounds. But dang it, he's slow to write a report about the affair—just the kind of guy most folks find easy to admire.

"Bears have always fed on spring carrion along the Rocky Mountain Front," Mike told me on a typically raw, blustery spring day. A tuft of black hair whipped about his forehead with each gust. He tipped his wool cap back, sliding a forefinger to tuck the errant lock. "Formerly it was herds of wild grazing animals, buffalo, elk, deer. Now its cattle and sheep. But the point is, carrion is a traditional—and vital—food source for grizzly bears in the spring."

Tumbleweeds trapped in a nearby fence corner rattled a dirge, signaling a change of seasons.

"What about now?" I asked. "The buffalo are gone."

"Every rancher has losses, Roland. Even with domestic livestock and controlled feeding, there's still the potential for loss during blizzards. Then there are losses during calving and lambing, both with young and old. There's disease and deaths for unknown reasons. The point is, there's still carrion, and bears still depend upon it. But the really important point is where they get it."

"I don't understand."

"Most every rancher has a 'boneyard' located someplace to dispose of his dead livestock." It's in connection with those boneyards that Mike Madel made his most lasting mark in improved relations between ranchers and bears.

The major problem with ranch boneyards is often their location. When nature struck down weakened ungulates, it was at random, scattering carcasses along the entire Rocky Mountain Front. But when man disposes, it's usually in a few concentrated, bear-attracting piles. Sometimes those boneyards are close enough to farm or ranch calving grounds or lambing sheds to be within nose distance of a hibernation-hungered grizzly. If the rancher is a trifle dilatory in his carcass disposition, bears have been known to take on the job by carrying carcasses from ranch corrals.

Such contact with humans has a dangerous influence on grizzly bears. How many steps is it from raiding ranch complexes for carcasses to raiding for live, easy prey? What's the risk that rancher or wife or children will blunder into a foraging bear?

It was to address this danger that Mike Madel came up with his carcass-redistribution scheme. The plan is so simple it makes one weep at all the unnecessary decades of conflict between man and beast. Mike and his crew pick up carcasses from cooperating ranches and distributes them along a hundred miles of remote lands of the Front, choosing locations where the possibility of conflict between humans and bears is negligible.

The plan has proven so effective for eight years that many ranchers and farmers who were less than infatuated with the big bruins are now supporters, recognizing that the bears themselves are indicators of whether their way of life will vanish under developing America.

Mike Madel has been instrumental in devising other schemes to reduce conflicts on the Front: electric fences around beehives and sheep bedding grounds; quick response to potential problem bears roaming so far out on the prairie as to constitute danger amid human living space—trapping those bears and relocating them into remote areas.

The biologist estimates carrion represents twenty to thirty percent of spring food for the estimated fifty to sixty grizzly bears roaming the Front. His innovative method of emulating nature may be the only way grizzlies can continue to survive in a wild and free environment first reported during Meriwether Lewis's and William Clark's Voyage of Discovery.

So we come to the big question I asked of the grizzly specialist:

"Some folks say there might be a connection between bears learning to feed on livestock carcasses and turning to predation on the living. Has there been any research on that question?"

The answer was short and crisp: "Yes. And we've found no correlation."

Madel has been so successful at reducing human/grizzly conflicts on the east side of Montana's Rockies, that he was invited as an advisor to Japan, where conflicts between brown bears and people are epidemic on the northern island of Hokkaido. The Japanese government is paying Mike's expenses and he's going with the blessing of his immediate boss, Mike Aderhold, Fish, Wildlife and Parks Region 4 Supervisor, who says: "I can't say enough about Mike's work and what it has done for grizzlies and people along the Front."

The Supervisor told Madel his visit to Japan is the chance of a lifetime. It's also recognition that Montana has a grizzly-management program that is working.

Aderhold added, "More people need to know Montana cares about their grizzly bears, and we're willing to put both money and effort into the bears' survival."

Madel's experimental proactive program has been so success-ful that the Department added two other Grizzly Bear Management Specialists in other regions of conflict: Kevin Frey, working out of Bozeman, addressing bear problems in the high-profile area north of Yellowstone; and Tim Manley, responsible for resolving conflicts west of the Rockies, outside of Glacier National Park and the Flathead Indian Reservation. It's my good fortune that Manley lives but a mile from my home. I count him as a friend.

Conflicts are markedly different where Manley and Frey work than in Madel's prairie ranching community. Both Gallatin and Flathead Counties (Bozeman and Kalispell) are among the

Mike Madel, Rocky Mountain Front Grizzly Bear Management Specialist, at work checking predator utilization of carrion from FW&P's carcass redistribution program.

most rapidly growing sectors of Montana. Conflicts most often come from improper rural garbage disposal and from subdivision development amid grizzly habitat. Giant strides are being taken, however.

"Education is the key," says Manley. He's identified a need for better bear-proof dumpsters at garbage-collection sites. As a result of working with county commissioners and private organizations to develop funding for improved collection dumpsters, the incidence of bears hanging around garbage-collection sites is diminishing.

Although garbage is unquestionably a high-protein food source for bears, Manley is quick to point out there's nothing "natural" about it. Continued access to human food is certain to habituate bears to humans, leading to an ever-increasing cycle of conflict.

Tim works with homeowners to reduce other bear attractants. "Many people dwelling in remote locations simply don't know that a sack of dog food on a porch, or bird seed in a feeder, can attract grizzly bears."

The litany goes on from there: hunting-season deer carcasses hanging in open garages, horsefeed stored improperly, overflowing home garbage cans—the sheer volume of problems must be frustrating to Manley. Yet the man exhibits no evidence of burnout, and he is succeeding. Public awareness of grizzly needs is slowly changing from fear to tolerance.

Even more certain is Manley's contribution to solving the grain-spill conundrum.

There were several train derailments during the 1980s along Burlington Northern Railway's main line. Carloads of corn from the Midwest were repeatedly spilled near the mountains' Continental Crest, with only half-hearted efforts at cleanup. The tracks, paralleled for much of the distance by U.S. Highway 2, run through prime grizzly habitat, bordered on one side by Glacier National Park, on the other by the Great Bear/Bob Marshall Wilderness complex. It soon became obvious both grizzly and black bears were attracted to the spilled corn. Also obvious was the fact that bears were falling like dominoes in collisions with trains and automobiles.

Burlington Northern train crews were dispatched to bury the grain. In subsequent years, corn excavated by the bruins not only continued to be a prime source of protein, but fermented through burial and decomposition. Bears digging at the corn spills turned into a spectacle for tourists driving U.S. 2. Officials worried not only about the potential for conflict, but simply how to keep intoxicated bears and metropolitan tourists apart. They closed several miles of highway to parking or stopping or camping. Still, bears continued to be killed or injured in highway and railway crashes.

In December of 1993, yet another train was derailed. A car loaded with wheat scattered grain for a mile and a half before discovery near the west entrance to Glacier National Park. Then, on March 28, 1994, a train derailment occurred three miles east of West Glacier. Twelve cars left the tracks; six spilled approximately one million pounds of wheat along the tracks and into the Middle Fork of the Flathead River.

Up to this point, seven grizzlies had died as a result of the spills and frustration mounted, not only among the general populace and professional wildlife managers, but among the Burlington Northern staff. A commitment to cleanup, orchestrated in part by Tim Manley, was made and an agreement reached. An informal group, composed of railroad, Glacier Park, Flathead National Forest, Montana Department of Fish, Wildlife & Parks officials, and Middle Fork citizens, was formed to monitor cleanup and make future recommendations.

Finally, Montana's Fish, Wildlife & Parks lifted the stopping or parking restrictions for highway travelers, and the U.S. Forest Service re-opened a campground in the area. Flathead Forest Supervisor Joel Holtrop said:

"Prompt cleanup of this year's smaller grain spills and the lack of bears at the older grain spills show the group is being effective in controlling bear problems."

At the height of the bears' grain smorgasbord, bruins from as far as fifty miles away were known to visit the sites. That's the way of bears, you see—opportunists to a fault. During times of mountain berry shortages, they've been known to raid lowland

orchards, seek out juicy suburban garbage, or steal deer or elk carcasses hanging inside rural sheds. Each incident leads ultimately
to conflicts between man and beast. As with the grain spills,
death to bears is the usual result when man instead of nature provides the protein.

High-fat-and-protein food sources have attracted bears since
pre-history, and in many cases are essential for ursine survival. But
the information contained in this chapter was still unknown to
me when, during the beginning of the "Reagan Revolution," I
squatted on my haunches to examine bear scat and ponder how
grizzlies could survive on an insect diet. ■

This Lubec Hills marsh, near East Glacier, is an excellent example of prime bear habitat found in the foothills of the Rocky Mountain front.

Chapter 9

Talus Griz—Dream Come True

By the fall of 1976, I'd lived and hunted in Montana for a dozen years. For half of those years I had worked as a licensed outfitter and guide, leading others to adventure in the heart of what is often accepted as the wildest wilderness of the northern Rockies. But my one great dream of taking a grizzly-bear rug was still unfulfilled. In fact, though I'd encountered dozens of the animals during those dozen years, I had yet to see a single griz during hunting season. I made a joke of displaying my years of unused licenses to friends.

Some might say my problem in obtaining a bear rug was that as a full-time guide, I had little opportunity to hunt on my own. And there was a thread of truth there. But our outfit was not known for its success in taking bears, largely because the country we hunted in September and early October, while bears were still feeding voraciously to store winter fat, was too high and too open and had too little vegetative cover to be good bear habitat. And though the late-season area had numerous blacks and grizzlies, we pulled back to that lower camp in November, after the bears had gone to bed. As a result, I usually advised our hunters not to purchase bear licenses, though I always carried one.

Some of our hunters did buy licenses, however, and a few of them took black bears, usually in the cinnamon color phase. Grizzly bears were much less common, but occasionally hunters would see a rare silvertip. For instance, two Wisconsin hunters and their guide spotted a giant grizzly walking the crest of the "Chinese Wall," the massive fault-block summit of the Continental Divide that is the most prominent feature in all the Bob Marshall Wilderness. However, the proper mix of licensed hunter and blundering grizzly never merged.

I was content to slide the personal goal of my grizzly rug onto a back burner. Then came a week in early October with no guests scheduled. I used the time to take a packstring loaded with hay to hunting camp—twenty-seven miles through splattering mud and bog, clambering over logs and stones, clawing up through a high pass and down into the valley beyond.

It was dark by the time I'd unloaded, unsaddled, and grained the packstring. More time passed before I could slip between the satiny folds of my sleeping bag. The next thing I knew it was daylight.

Since the trail into camp was so long and grueling, it was standard procedure to rest the ponies before trailing them back to civilization. That meant I had an entire day with little to do. I

Author relaxing near location where he first spied the grizzly of his dreams.

yawned, grinned at the unaccustomed luxury, slipped into trousers, and kindled a fire in the cookstove.

After the breakfast dishes were washed and copious quantities of stout coffee consumed, I sauntered from the tent whistling. First it was stack the hay brought in the evening before, then fold the canvas manties (pack covers) and ropes in preparation for tomorrow's trail out. I thought about cutting wood, but the pile we already had split and stacked by the cooktent was more than enough to last out the season.

I poured another cup of coffee and glanced at my watch. Mid-morning. I strolled from the tent to stare up at the square-topped mountain behind camp, sipped my coffee, and thought, *Why not?*

Ten minutes later, I ambled from camp, my familiar Springfield '06 slung over my shoulder and pair of binoculars tucked inside my shirt. I was mostly just killing time, but if preparation meets opportunity . . . hey, our family could use a winter's supply of elk meat.

The creek-bottom forest and the basin at the drainage head were as familiar to me as most folks' backyard. After all, I guided hunters here often. There were moments spent staring into tiny pools, searching for the silver flash of a cutthroat trout spinning from the entry ripple with a late-hatching gnat in his mouth. Other minutes passed while exploring an outcrop of oil shale. (Better keep this secret or Exxon will be pressuring Congress to "explore" for oil and gas here.)

I found fresh elk tracks in the mud of a game trail near where the two creeks joined, about where I expected. I cradled the familiar old Springfield and licked a finger, holding it up to test the wind. The drift was still downhill, in my face. Good.

It was easy enough, since I was in no hurry, to slip along the game trail without a sound. It took an hour to reach the top of the first hogback. That hour was interrupted for several minutes by the sight of a pine squirrel harvesting cones and by the haunting glimpse of a pileated woodpecker ebbing and flowing in waltz-flight through my spruce forest.

The elusive elk appeared to be wandering, so I wandered too, gradually working up to their mainline trail near the bottom of a line of cliffs that border the basin on its entire south side. The day rapidly warmed in the noonday sun, and wind currents turned fickle as rising ground air collided with sinking drift from high above. It would be barely an hour until the thermal rise won out and the winds settled into a steady up-canyon breeze. Then I could begin a hunt back to camp.

I dozed, leaning against a big spruce, only to be awakened by the raucous cries of whiskey jacks fluttering through treetops 'round about. I grinned good naturedly and bit into an apple, eyeing the cliffs towering above.

There was a high, wild and broken chunk of land above those cliffs. We called it the "hanging basin" because the cirque was suspended above the wall, hanging from the gigantic mountain that guarded this upper river valley. I'd climbed into the place three or four times previously, and had even spotted elk traveling through. But there was little food amid the jumbled rocks and alpine heights and, as a result, little game to be found there. Naturally, I clambered through a notch in the cliff, into the hanging basin.

I saw what I expected—only a few scattered deer tracks. So four o'clock found me sitting atop the cliff, gazing across the untamed land still the way God made it. I peeled the wrapper from a candy bar, leaned back against a boulder, and wriggled my butt into the soft cushion at its base. How many people, I wondered, have ever sat upon a carpet of alpine tamarack needles? I looked up at the rare misshapen tree above and smiled in delight. What a great place to be! There was Larch Hill to the east and lofty Silvertip Mountain to the north—one of the most dominating peaks in all the Bob Marshall Wilderness.

I glassed across the broad valley, across our "long ridge" at what we called "the chutes," hoping to spot animals moving. There were a couple of deer, too far away to tell buck from doe. Then I studied what we called the "high plateau" in the middle foreground. It was an expanse of raw, broken limestone slab with tiny pockets of soil stocked with verdant forage, often containing a remarkable panoply of wildlife that seemed always to pop up when least expected. None moved on the moonscape this day. A golden eagle soared on air currents in the basin below. I hadn't a care—or even a thought. I laid the glasses aside and again dozed.

How long the grizzly had been there I haven't the foggiest idea. It must have been the dirt and stones flying between his hind feet that led me to him when my eyes popped open. Or, if not soil and stones, the silver fur rippling in waves as the bear tore furiously at the ground would have attracted my attention. He was big—not as big as some I'd seen—but one powerful bruin, nevertheless.

I blinked and wiped my eyes. The bear was in a brown-tinged color phase, shading lighter across his shoulders and hump. The hump wasn't as pronounced as I'd expected. But then I realized I'd never before looked *down* on a grizzly bear from above. There! He had something in his mouth; it was gone in an instant. The bear paused, staring straight ahead at the base of my cliff. No mistaking that broad head and dished face. Then he returned to moving earth with a passion, dirt and gravel and football-sized stones flying.

I picked up my binoculars to study both the bear and the ground he excavated. Was he after a colony of hibernating ground squirrels scattered in holes in tundra-like soil on an old talus slope? The bear broke off digging to wander to a broken rock the size of a footstool. He turned it over with the flip of a forepaw, sniffed beneath, then returned to dig once more amid the squirrel or marmot holes.

Again he stopped excavating to wander about the talus, flipping rocks and nosing beneath, apparently searching for remnant bugs. He entered a circle of dried and rustling cow parsnips and dug at his leisure. Mixing parsnip roots with ground-squirrel protein?

I came to my feet slowly, intending to parallel his movements below the cliff—and stumbled over my rifle. I ducked and froze as the bear lifted his head at the sound of metal clattering against rock. But I was a good three hundred feet above him, and I'd shrunk instinctively with the noise. Fortunately, the afternoon breeze held its upward drift. Soon he returned to digging.

I picked up the rifle and leaned it against the same rock, then began creeping to a spot directly above the bear where I could study him at a better angle. With a start, I whirled back to stare at the rifle, then down at the grizzly. My heart began to throb. I shrank away from the cliff edge and dropped down to crab-walk back and pick up the weapon. I examined its sights carefully, knowing the front bead and Redfield peep to be nearly indestructible. *No, they're unmarred by the limestone, still in place. I can drive nails with this gun.* I peeked again over the lip of the cliff. *He'll never know what hit him! This is it!*

When I again peeked at the bear from almost directly overhead, he'd lain down in his cow-parsnip bed with hind legs beneath and head resting on a mound of excavated talus gravel. I studied the animal through a hunter's eyes, hefting the rifle from palm to palm. His coat was in full fall splendor—perfect for a rug.

The eagle sailed along the cliff, this time between the bruin and me. Ravens called back and forth on the long ridge, and a flock of sparrows flitted through stark branches of the deciduous conifers above my head. I squatted and rested the barrel on a boulder, took aim . . . and sighed.

Shadows stole across the land as I trotted along the cliff ledge, hurrying to reach the dangerously narrow strip of trail before fading light took both courage and coordination. When I left, the grizzly still snoozed, head resting on his excavated mound.

I ran a thumb under the Springfield's shoulder strap and clambered up to the next level, then trotted on. ■

Chapter 10

Confusion Reigns

It was a watershed in the evolution of my attitudes and priorities that I had not killed the talus grizzly even after all the stars aligned.

When did I turn the corner from hunter to wildlife observer? One thing seemed clear as I trotted along that cliff ledge: There would never be a grizzly rug to evoke the envy of my hunting contemporaries.

I slowed to a walk, then a crawl as the trail narrowed to ribbon size across the dangerous chute, trailing fingertips along the wall to my right while, only inches from my left boot, nothingness yawned. *Don't look down, Roland, for God's sake! Watch your step. Just a little more. Another step. Another. Sweet Jesus! What a great feeling to be back on the ledge! No need to hurry now. Let's see, what was I thinking? Oh, yes, grizzlies.*

Though my feelings toward the great bears had altered, the animals themselves soon made plain I shouldn't consider them as cute and cuddly teddies. The first example of ursine dissuasion was visited upon a spike camp set in a deep and gloomy spruce forest seldom reached by sun. Large numbers of elk often found refuge within the thickets and blowdowns. That bears of all types and sizes also called the hell-hole home was already known. But had I not unilaterally declared a truce between bear and man? There was nothing to fear, right?

The first site chosen was a tiny sylvan glade only a little larger than the tent. A clear and cold mountain stream chuckled nearby—it was as close to a cheery place as one could find throughout the entire gloomy drainage. But the spike camp proved too far for early-morning approaches to licks, wallows, and rub lines frequented by elk in the rut. So we moved the tent the following year to an unwholesome, brush-choked place near the bottom of a mainline game trail cutting across the dense forest from east hills to west cliffs.

Bears had sniffed out our first campsite, circling the tent and, because there was no stored food or carelessly handled garbage, moving on. But that second camp must have broken some immutable bear rule—perhaps it was an intrusion akin to an urban newcomer throwing up a summer cabin across a hiking trail used by the locals.

My wife Jane and I worked industriously for an entire early September day, clearing and leveling a spot for the brand-new ten-by-twelve tent of lighter and expensive nylon material. We finished by setting up the combination heating and cooking stove. Then, just before we left, I single-bucked blocks of firewood from a felled spruce while Jane pulled up the tent walls so a bear could, in our absence, wander freely about without making his own entrance and exit holes.

Two days later, I was back at that spike camp with a pack-string loaded with hay. The tent was in shambles. Several guy ropes had been jerked loose or chewed off, one of the side walls was hanging in tatters, even the tent roof had been ripped.

I set the shelter back up as best I could, covering the roof and sidewall holes with an extra canvas pack cover, then stacked the hay under a plastic tarp.

I returned with a couple of hunters a week after the mid-September opening of hunting season. The plastic hay cover looked as though it had been through a paper shredder, and the bales had been ripped apart and knocked askew. And though the tent was still standing, it had an angry bear's signature of muddy footprints and fresh rips in the fabric.

"Boy, Roland," one of my guests said, eyeing the rag-tag camp, "don't you think it's about time you spent some money and bought a new tent?"

The spike camp proved to be in a strategic location for elk hunting, though. So the next year we set up the same (albeit patched), tent alongside the same trail in the same place. And we got the same results from—judging by the tracks—the same grizzly.

"What's with this damned critter?" I asked Kenny Averill, my veteran guide, as we sawed blocks from the felled spruce. "He's tearing up this camp for no reason I can see. There's no food here, no grain. He's never around when people are here. Why's he doing this?"

The old guide stared at me, through me, as his arms moved rhythmically with the crosscut saw. Then his face broke into a crinkly grin. "You suppose the camp is in his territory? Walk up and down that game trail yonder and you'll see claw marks on trees. I believe they're territorial marks. Maybe he's mad because somebody is moving into his territory."

"What's he think this is? South Chicago?"

We lifted the saw as the block fell free and moved up the log to start another cut. Kenny grinned. "Might be safer," the old man said, "to muscle in on Capone than to go nose to nose in a territorial scrap with a grizzly bear. Especially if he's packing a chip on his shoulder."

I laughed. "Any grizzly that lives in this God-forsaken hole has got to be mean."

At last we abandoned the Wall Creek spike camp as a losing proposition. We didn't abandon the camp because of constant grizzly depredation—though I breathed a sigh of relief when we took down the tent for the last time—we abandoned it because none of our hunters cared for hunting the gloomy canyon, no matter how many elk might be in residence.

I continued to purchase a grizzly-bear license for several years, though I no longer intended to hunt the creatures. My reason was, in case of a grizzly raid, I could legally protect my camp or guests. But since the giant bears proved more circumspect about respecting my territory than I had been toward theirs, I finally stopped buying the license. Eventually, though averaging upwards of fifteen hundred trail miles per year through some of the wildest real estate in North America, I quit even packing a weapon for bear defense. Except for the time I found myself pointing a pop-gun at the Pentagon Grizzly. . . .

The Pentagon Guard Station is near the headwaters of the Spotted Bear River in a seldom visited part of the Bob Marshall. Bears, both grizzly and black, use the area extensively. We used it, too, hunting elk from a nearby tent camp during November's late season. But our hunters arrived after the bears have gone to bed.

We'd packed into the Pentagon area over Labor Day week-end to set up camp and cut a couple cords of wood. My partner was Al Reid, a retired lumber-mill manager who'd made a living during his youth by felling trees and cutting saw-length logs with crosscut saws. My wife was also along to keep the hard-working men fortified with fuel. We spent the remainder of the first day setting up the tents. Then, from early morning of day two, we fell bug-killed spruce trees and bucked stove-length blocks from them.

The day was hot, and sweat streaked down faces and soaked shirts, shorts, caps, gloves, and trousers. Often we'd have to clear brush out of the way in order to swing the saw in rhythm. Jane came from the cooktent to roll blocks three feet in diameter nearer the woodpile. Block after block after block.

I wanted to quit before the sun passed beyond the western horizon, but the old-time wood cutter wouldn't hear it. Five o'clock came and went, then five-thirty. Finally, at ten minutes to six, the last block rolled from the saw and Jane, bless her, was there with a saving cocktail for each of us.

At supper, table conversation turned to bears, and I told the story again of the sow bear that charged me—the one I told about at this book's beginning.

Al asked, "On the Whitefish Divide? Just this summer?"

"July 16 to be exact. Reason I remember is because it was my birthday. You know, it's really something to know you can stand up to a charge. Ever happen to you when you were sawing in the woods?"

"I always had a tree to climb."

A contented silence fell between us as we became lost in our own thoughts of bears and times past. I mentioned that for the past several years, we'd spotted a big black bear working the river bottoms about this time of year. I told Al the bear had repeatedly broken into the Forest Service cabin a few hundred yards upriver. Since it wasn't yet dark, I asked him if he'd care to walk up and take a look at the guard station.

He was game. Since grouse season had opened the day before, I picked up the little .22-caliber revolver loaded with birdshot that Jane carries during bird season and whistled for America's best grouse dog—our Brittany spaniel, Hunter.

Evening was beginning to steal into the canyon bottoms, and the woods were silent. Hunter stalked two paces ahead, nose lifted, sniffing the motionless evening air. We were about a hundred yards from the cabin when an eerie, ripping, tearing sound—like a huge wrench turning a rusted bolt—rent the stillness. The hackles on Hunter's neck stood and a low growl welled in his throat. I grasped the dog's ruff and exchanged a puzzled glance with Al.

Again the screeching noise rent the early evening silence. Hunter slapped out one bark before I jerked him up short. Then it hit me. "Bear!" Both of us sprinted for the guard station's parallel-log corral fence, where we planned to hide and watch a black bear in the act of breaking and entering a cabin.

Black bear, hell! It was a grizzly! And he wasn't breaking and entering the cabin, but tearing two-inch-thick planks from the corral's feed-shed door to get to the molasses-flavored rolled oats within.

Not only was it a grizzly, it was a *giant* grizzly that must have measured at least two axe handles between the eyes. Perhaps he'd heard Hunter's single bark. Whatever his reasons, the monster decided a strategic retreat was the better part of valor, and he lunged for the very spot in that corral fence that we were sprinting toward.

The first thing we saw was a mammoth blur coming out of the corral's gloom: a great toothed head, followed by neck and hump and shoulders and torso and hind legs and huge feet as the grizzly hurdled the fence in a mighty bound, heading our way. We skidded to a stop and he, too, slid to a halt—no farther away than the distance to a Little League pitcher's mound. Hunter's nose crowded into the back of my knee as though he wished to hide. I didn't breathe.

The bear, for his part, stood as still as the cabin, staring directly at us. He was BIG, bigger than any bear I'd yet seen. The claws alone looked as enormous as ice teeth on a road grader.

I remember thinking, *My God, I don't know if I could stand up to a charge from this bear!* If my knees hadn't been too rubbery to move, I would have flinched.

Our stand-off seemed to go on for hours. Then the monster swung his head to the side and galloped off. We heard him tearing through brush, crashing up the nearby mountain like an infantry brigade in full rout.

Al expelled the breath he'd been holding and turned to look at me standing in rubbery shock. "What in hell you figuring on doing with that friggin' little popgun? Make him mad?"

I didn't hear him at first. I was thinking how I stood up defiantly to a small grizzly's charge earlier this summer but would have broken for the nearest tree had this brute continued our way. "Huh? What'd you say?"

"I asked if you figured to make that bear mad with that popgun." He pointed to my fist.

I looked down. The Ruger .22 loaded with birdshot was on full cock.

I thought of that Pentagon Grizzly's outsized fingernails when Jane found her own private grizzly claw at the supposedly bearproof forest service building known as the Black Bear Cabin. My wife was struggling to lift one of the two heavy, bear-proof plank panels from the ground. I helped by lifting the top one for her. Sandwiched between the doors was a single three-inch grizzly claw, curved like a Saracen sword and rapier-sharp. Scattered on the bottom panel, near the claw, were several droplets of dried blood. Losing a claw must have enraged the bear because the aftermath of his breaking into the supposedly impregnable U.S. Forest Service cabin was plain to see.

The first of the scattered cans popped up as we crossed the meadow, two hundred and fifty yards from the cabin. As we approached the building, the place looked more and more like the

Houston dump. Empty cans, cardboard cartons, and plastic sacks lay about the picturesque cabin as if scattered by a typhoon. Then we saw the plank bear-proof doors lying askew. The thin inner cabin door had its center punched into the building.

He must have been mad, so thoroughly had he demolished the interior. Cupboards were ripped from the walls and torn open. Two-and-a-half-pound ham cans had been opened with one bite. At least seven hundred dollars worth of canned goods had been liberated from that isolated cabin's shelves, then crushed, ripped, folded, spindled and mutilated by an enraged grizzly with a sore finger. The heavy plank table was upside down. Dishes lay scattered and broken. Remnants of torn flour sacks were draped about, syrup cans were punctured and spilled, salt containers broken and dumped into the debris. To top it all, the grizzly had shoved the cookstove across the floor and its stovepipe collapsed, shooting its clogging soot to the far wall, across the wreckage.

After exacting vengeance for his lost claw, the bruin apparently decamped for parts unknown.

The Black Bear Cabin is the most splendid piece of forest craftsmanship I've ever seen. It was originally constructed of hand-hewn logs, selected and prepared on site. Those logs were double-dovetailed by an old German craftsman who used no mortar. I'm told those logs fit so perfectly a mouse can't find his way inside. In addition, the cabin is perched in the most beautiful spot in the world.

Not so that day.

I told Jane, "I sure hope that grizzly with a chip on his shoulder isn't heading where we're going."

Do I leave the impression that I was confused about the great bears? I'd made a conscious decision that I really didn't care as much for a grizzly rug as for the thrill of watching the magnificent creatures. But the animals themselves swiftly rebutted any notion that they'd abide by a truce. And my regard for the animals bounced about like a yo-yo.

First my attitude was uneducated fear, then armed disdain that eventually led to unarmed, unreasoned fear. From there it was transformed to unbridled admiration that led to what approached blind homage for the cuddly creatures. Then it turned into grudging respect, and probably a creeping suspicion that I really didn't know what to think about an animal that was edging deeply into my soul.

Then came yet another revelation.

I wasn't alone in my confusion. ■

Chapter 11

Surrounded By Controversy

It's probable some ancient philosopher taught that wisdom first lies in the admission of ignorance. Perhaps such profundity initially surfaced in the teachings of Socrates or in Hammurabi's Code or in the writings of ancient Chinese scholars. But for me, it came with the admission that after two decades of intermittent association with *Ursus arctos horribilis*, I really knew little about the creatures. Ahead, the great bear's trail forked.

One fork was a broad and beaten path of blissful ignorance traveled by an array of folks ranging from wildlife managers operating with inadequate information and training, through sensationalizing authors and journalists, through opinionated lay people, to arrogant individuals embracing a "Shoot, shovel and shut up" attitude toward all bears. The other fork led to data-gathering and education. Its path was barely discernible, traveled rarely, and then only by pioneer researchers rewarded usually by the chance to pursue a labor of love that often put them at cross purposes to managing agencies with agendas that might be more political than scientific.

So it was with Frank and John Craighead's Yellowstone grizzly research. The Yellowstone Grizzly Research Project began in 1959. It was the first in-depth study of *Ursus arctos horribilis* ever undertaken. Theirs was a pioneer effort in large-scale trapping, drugging, and monitoring grizzlies utilizing space-age technology. Craighead teams followed bears to denning sites, delineated "home" and "transitional" ranges, and monitored behavioral habits in relation to other grizzlies, as well as people. They observed mating and followed family groups virtually from conception through birth (and sometimes death) until their study was terminated by action of the National Park Service in 1971.

Craighead teams developed definitive population estimates based on hard science, including population breakdowns by sex and age groups. They pioneered computer modeling of birth and mortality rates and wound up with a surprisingly accurate ability to predict grizzly bear population dynamics on the Yellowstone Plateau.

Frank and John Craighead are today considered scientists' scientists. And that may have led to their program's undoing by their inability to accept that political or social factors can sometimes preempt scientific conclusions. So it was when Park administrators closed the Yellowstone's internal garbage dumps after grizzly bears with prior access to human garbage killed two young women in widely separated portions of Glacier National Park on the same night in August, 1967.

Though not averse to closing the dumps, the scientists opposed abrupt closure without first weaning away grizzly bears who had for decades been conditioned to find a significant portion of their diet therein.

Predictably, the Yellowstone administration took offense at the intrusion of science into management. They, in turn, accused the study team with delaying critical information on grizzly habits and habitat that should have been available in a more timely fashion. That's a charge often leveled—sometimes with merit—at scientists who prefer to have every research "i" dotted and every data "t" crossed before releasing information to lay folks who, in their opinion, may not have proper training for interpretation.

The real losers in the Yellowstone affair were, of course, the public and the bears.

Much of today's modern grizzly research owes both methods and materials to the Craigheads' pioneering work. But the brothers' own major research ended abruptly, just at a time when many Americans wondered if the great bears would survive beyond the 20th century. The loss to America was severe, for public awareness of grizzly population dynamics was the greatest legacy left by

Doctors Frank and John Craighead. Unlike most researchers, the Craigheads were also good publicists. News stories, articles, film footage, and photographs highlighting their research and its individual bears so tweaked America's consciousness that a genuine groundswell of interest in the great bruins' plight arose. That groundswell led to this important question: How many grizzlies are out there? The silence was deafening.

Dr. Charles Jonkel was on the scene early, attempting to find an answer through his Border Grizzly Project. Jonkel, already world-renowned for his Montana black bear and Hudson's Bay polar bear research, led a team of biologists trained in trapping into a vast area encompassing northwestern Montana, the Idaho Panhandle, northeastern Washington, southeastern British Columbia, and southwestern Alberta. Jonkel's mission was to estimate numbers of grizzlies inhabiting an interrelational area and develop recommendations for management to sustain that population. Border Grizzly Project funds came from an amalgam of sources: industry, universities, and state and federal wildlife agencies.

Glacier National Park, perhaps still smarting from criticism as a result of the Craighead Yellowstone research controversy, declined to become a player in the independent Border Grizzly Project, even though the park contained one of the larger concentrations of the great beasts within the study area.

It was thanks to the Border Grizzly Project that I had my first opportunity to observes biologists in actual trapping operations. The time was early May. I was relaxing in my end-of-the-road travel trailer after stockpiling horse hay for future wilderness packtrips when a pickup truck rolled to a stop alongside the trailer and a young man climbed out carrying a hand-held radio. I went to the door.

He introduced himself as Terry Werner and said he led a team of grizzly researchers working the South Fork of the Flathead. Since my horse corral was located in an area sometimes utilized by bears, and my trailer was usually parked in the same spot for several months, the man asked if I'd ever had any problems with bears.

I told him there'd been one incident when a bear left muddy footprints on my door and pushed out a small window in the rear. "But," I said, "from the size of the prints, it was probably a black."

Werner nodded and I asked him in for a cup of coffee—and to question him about the Border Grizzly Project. A half-hour slipped away as he told of trapping and radio-collaring grizzly bears throughout the South Fork. Suddenly his radio began beeping. He walked outside for better reception and I heard him ask, "Where is it?" Pause. "Oh, that one again?" Pause. "Yes, I'll be right there."

Terry switched off the radio and turned. "We've got a bear in a snare. It's a cinnamon-colored black that we've caught twice before. I'm going up and help with the release. You want to ride along?"

The bear lay a few feet back from the top of a six-foot road cut. The animal was in shadow, beneath the drooping canopy of a big spruce tree. His head was up, ears forward, to all appearances resting. Two team members leaned against their own pickup truck. One of them grinned at Werner. "We may have to move this set if we're going to keep that one out of the snare."

Terry's reply was a good-natured smile. "Drug ready?"

The man produced a five-foot stick pointed with a needle and syringe.

Meanwhile, I studied the bear from fifteen feet. It was lying motionless with hind feet beneath, nose on forepaws. Only the animal's eyes moved, tracking each human. Orange ribbons hung from each ear.

Behind the bear, up against the bole of the tree, was a lean-to of limbs and poles laid in a V, open in front. The lean-to's interior was just large enough for a child to sit in. The ground in front was torn, stripped of vegetation, dirt pushed into furrows.

"Where's the bait?" I asked.

"Ate it," one of the men said. "We think he's decided it's worth getting caught, just to get the bait."

The team leader asked me to move nearer the truck, then approached the bear gingerly with his stick-syringe. The bear's eyes followed the man, but otherwise the animal made no move. The stick's point poised over the bear's left thigh, then darted down with Werner's thrust. The bear jerked forward, then fell back into place. In that instant, I saw the cable around his right rear leg.

Werner ambled back to the road, handed the stick to one of his crew, and, while waiting for the drug to take effect, questioned the biologists about other trap sites they'd checked.

After only a few minutes, the bear's eyes drooped. Terry waited a moment more, then poked the bruin with a tree limb to make sure the animal was comatose. The men worked rapidly, releasing the snare and checking the bear's gum where a tooth had been pulled earlier.

"If this was a new bear, we'd go through all the steps," Terry told me over his shoulder. "We'd snap a numbered tag and identification ribbons in his ear, pull a tooth in order to age him, and weigh him. But since he's a repeat, there's no need to do it again."

"You do this with black bears, too?"

"Everything except the radio collars. They're too expensive. But otherwise we gather as much data on blacks as possible."

One biologist pulled up an eyelid. ""He's showing some signs. Maybe five minutes." The other biologist smeared disinfectant where the snare had worn through leg hair.

Werner walked with me back to the road and the pickup truck. "How much did that bear weigh when you first trapped him?" I asked.

"A hundred and sixty-three pounds."

"What!" I turned and looked back at the cinnamon black. "He looks a lot bigger than that."

Terry smiled. "That's what most people think. And he'll weigh two-fifty, maybe two-seventy-five in the fall. What's deceptive to you is, just after coming out of hibernation, his pelt is so luxuriant. But until a couple of weeks ago, that bear had nothing to eat for perhaps five months. And pickings are still pretty slim."

The biologists were hurrying down the bank. "He's fluttering," one said.

"Roland, why don't you move over by the door," Terry said. "I think he'll run the other way when he comes fully awake. But you never know."

The bear raised his head, then lowered it for a moment, only to raise it again. His eyes appeared clouded. Then he rolled up until his legs lay beneath. The eyes slowly cleared. Suddenly, as if launched at Cape Canaveral, the bear popped to his feet, leaped down the bank, and sped across the road, diagonally away from us. We heard him crashing through brush until the noise faded into the distance.

"Shall we reset the snare, Terry?" one of the men asked.

Werner nodded.

The man pulled the lid from a foul-smelling fifty-five-gallon steel barrel and lifted out a pungent portion of a road-killed deer. The other biologist put the trap site in order, smoothing the dirt, scattering needles and branches about the surface to appear more natural.

Fifteen minutes later, when we all drove away, the place would have fooled me. The spring-loaded cable snare's loop was entirely hidden just in front of the lean-to's entry, ready to snap closed at a touch. Inside, a pungent deer's hindquarter lay beckoning.

"Will you catch that same bear again?"

Terry smiled. "Might. Might get him there, or in one we've got set up the road. On the other hand, tomorrow might find the biggest grizzly God ever made in that trap."

Prompted by public concern over the fate of America's last grizzly bears, the species was listed as "threatened" under the Endangered Species Act and was thus afforded some federal protection. Montana still allowed limited hunting, however, on the premise that it's an effective method of eliminating troublemaking grizzlies who lose their fear of humans and become a threat to human life. Dr. Charles Jonkel, authoritative head of the Border Grizzly Project, also thought removal of problem bears might be a factor in overall survival of the species in a world increasingly filled with humans.

But, with U.S. Fish & Wildlife Service direction over grizzlies increasing under the Endangered Species Act, was it possible for any state to regain management control? Federal officials responded by establishing criteria for ultimate delisting (removing the grizzly from the "threatened" classification). Those criteria included proof of recovery by verifying numbers in age and sex classifications. Shawn Riley, a far-sighted wildlife manager in Region One of Montana's Department of Fish, Wildlife and Parks, came up with a plan he sold to his superiors: Montana could begin its own research program to determine actual numbers, including age and sex classification. The ambitious ten-year South Fork Grizzly Project got under way in 1988, at about the time when funding for Jonkel's Border Grizzly Project began to fade.

The concept of the South Fork Study was to do far more intensive trapping, collaring, and monitoring—much of the tracking by regular aerial overflights—than was ever before accomplished. The plan also called for data-gathering over a much longer period than had been attempted since radio telemetry had hit its stride. Riley's plan targeted the weakness of any management program related to grizzly bears—the paucity of data concerning the species. Besides more regularly scheduled radio monitoring, the Project also planned to utilize hidden trail cameras triggered by motion sensors to record images of bears. One outcome of utilizing both trapping and remote camera images might be, by cross-referencing, a more accurate analysis of bear numbers. And a goal of the frequent aerial and on-the-ground monitoring was more detailed information on habits and habitat.

Other Montana research was initiated during the 1980s. Some, such as that conducted along the eastern Rocky Mountain Front from U.S. 2 south to the Dearborn River, resulted in changes in management techniques. Others, such as studies of both the Cabinet Mountains and Mission Mountains grizzly sub-populations, produced gloomy conclusions: Mission numbers were declining and the Cabinet population was approaching collapse.

Both the Blackfeet and Flathead Tribes employed biologists for their reservations. Though tribal biologists were responsible for management of a broad array of reservation wildlife, investigating the dynamics of grizzly-bear numbers was high on each tribe's list of assigned priorities.

Meanwhile, U.S. Fish & Wildlife Service biologists provided advice and support where requested by National Forest and tribal researchers. Perceiving a research hole regarding grizzly dynamics amid rapid human development along the North Fork of the Flathead, USFWS teams began yet another study.

Meanwhile, Glacier National Park pursued its own grizzly-bear research objectives, the details largely withheld from public scrutiny.

From little or no research along the northern Continental Divide in the 1950s, '60s and '70s, grizzly-bear biologists pervaded the system by the 1980s and '90s. Many Montana natives complained that research itself—the trapping, drugging, and radio-collaring of the animals—might be altering bear temperament and habits. Even some scientists seemed to agree.

Dr. Jack Stanford, respected scientist, Professor of Ecology, and Director of Flathead Lake Biological Station, believes radio-collaring as a tool in wildlife biology has a tendency to be overused. Stanford told me:

"I don't have any reservations about using radio collars. The point is, there are many ecological questions that require careful observation of animals in their natural environment, functioning as naturally as possible. And in many of those cases, it's probably best not to radio-collar."

I asked Rick Mace, Team Leader for Montana Fish, Wildlife & Park's critical South Fork Grizzly Study, about the necessity for trapping and collaring bears:

"There's simply no way we could obtain the kinds of data we need without . . ."

"But, Rick, the implication here is these bears are no longer wild, free-ranging animals when they're being tracked by radio transmission. What about that?"

"Why don't you ask Jack Stanford if they've got wild, free-ranging fish when his teams net and tag lake trout in Flathead Lake?"

But it was the thoughtful Tim Manley, Grizzly Bear Management Specialist responsible for ameliorating problems between grizzlies and people, who may have provided the most definitive response:

"There is no question that radio-collared bears are more likely to have their movements interrupted. But it's doubtful the kinds of data we're obtaining from those bears could be acquired by other means."

Manley paused to stare at a distant mountain peak. "And even if it were possible to track bears visually, discover their food habits, denning preferences, seasonal movements, relationships with people and other bears, it's probable that would require such a volume of human presence, that type of monitoring would have a more detrimental effect on the bears than tracking with telemetry."

Stanford conceded that in cases where "information is needed on how far the animals are ranging, what sorts of habitats they're using, and the frequency of use, there's very little alternative to radio-collaring."

Kate Kendall, a biologist with the National Biological Survey stationed in Glacier National Park, is less sanguine about radio-tracking. She says, "I'm sympathetic to not collaring and handling grizzly bears unless there's no other way."

Kendall suggested that collared and beribboned animals are a visual form of pollution. And she feared tourists visiting Glacier to view wildlife might be turned off by that form of research.

So I asked if the park had any kind of data on numbers of grizzlies in Glacier? The lady said they compile bear sightings into their record base. But when I raised the question about the authenticity of "sightings" compiled on the say-so of tourists with little experience and no training, she said it's still the best source of data the park has.

That's why I found a March 16, 1995, news story especially interesting:

"Glacier National Park has been criticized by the General Accounting Office for failing to adequately collect scientific data about Park wildlife."

The criticism came during testimony by James Duffus, GAO director of natural-resource management issues, before House and Senate subcommittees that oversee the National Park Service.

The General Accounting Office is not the only critic of Glacier's information gathering. State, federal, and tribal biologists responsible for managing bears outside the Park perimeter have expressed frustrations about their inability to obtain reliable information from Park personnel on bears ranging in and out of Glacier. One biologist said:

"The Park Service will someday be forced to recognize that Glacier's bear population does not exist in a vacuum."

Kendall thinks it's a waste of time for people to worry about grizzly bears in Glacier National Park. She asks, "How can you ask if grizzly bears are doing all right in Glacier? Where else is there such a tract of land still in its natural state? Why wouldn't bears be doing well here?"

It's an interesting question. Is Kendall's confidence that her bears are receiving the best possible protection justified? Consider this: Million-acre Glacier Park annually hosts over two million visitors. The two-million-acre Bob Marshall-Great Bear-Scapegoat Wilderness complex to the south annually receives perhaps ten thousand visitors—one half of one-percent of Glacier's human visitation on twice the land size. National Forest wildlands outside classified Wildernesses receive even fewer visitors. That's the reason I find it odd that Ms. Kendall is dismayed that folks might be interested in data relative to Park bear numbers and habitat.

Still, Kendall says, "In my mind, I'd rather monitor bears somewhere else."

With the possible exception of woodland caribou, Glacier National Park is still home to all the wildlife species originally found there. Does this mean the park's management policies and procedures are above reproach? Let's look at a few problems associated with maintaining that array of wildlife amid the hordes of annual visitors from Poughkeepsie or Portland, Dallas or Detroit. ∎

Chapter 12

Bears and Humans— Knitting or Raveling?

The road is called "Going to the Sun," and it's considered by most of Glacier National Park's two million visitors to be the most scenic highway in America. Some also think it the most terrifying.

Stunning ten-mile-long bodies of water anchor each end of Going to the Sun. Between St. Mary Lake (most photographed calendar scenes in America) on the east to Lake McDonald on the west, the highway snakes up and over the Continental Divide through spectacular alpine meadows lush with wildflowers and wildlife. During the journey, the traveler passes through a timeless land of geographic features with such evocative place names as Sunrift Gorge, the Garden Wall, Golden Staircase, and the Weeping Wall. Roadside pullouts are numerous, providing distant views of active glaciers, thousand-foot waterfalls, and heart-stopping mountain peaks kissed by dawn and tucked in by sunset.

Logan Pass visitor center is perched in a huge expanse of alpine country, right where the road crosses the continental spine. The center's parking lot easily accommodates a hundred cars. But it's not at all unusual to find the lot jammed and vehicles spilling over for hundreds of yards in both directions, into roadside parking.

Congress first appropriated specific money for "Glacier National Park's transmountain road" in 1921. It was an idea that progressed no further than birth throes for over ten years. Construction along the steep mountain portions was not completed until autumn of 1932, when the first automobile navigated its entire fifty-one-mile length. Obstacles to completion included sheer cliffs, short construction seasons, sixty-foot snowdrifts, avalanche danger, and tons of rock—some loose, most solid. Survey work alone was so challenging that one crew suffered three-hundred percent labor turnover during a single three-month survey period.

The road was officially dedicated on July 15, 1933. It's name, "Going to the Sun Road," came from nearby Going To The Sun Mountain, said to be named by the Blackfeet to commemorate a deity, Sour Spirit. Final paving of Going To The Sun Road was not completed until 1952.

Millions of Americans have driven this highway since its completion. Each year, vehicles passing over the road exhibit license plates from all fifty states, plus Canadian provinces and foreign countries. Those vehicles carry people from eastern inner cities, and high-plains wheat farms, Michigan factories, and California lettuce fields. Some are outdoors enthusiasts. Others have experienced little exposure to sun, wind, or rain. Most know little of grizzly bears. A few do not care.

Robert Frauson was Eastside District Ranger for his twenty years in Glacier, retiring in 1982. Frauson is a big man, lithe and muscular, a former Tenth Mountaineer combat veteran from the Italian Apennines campaign of World War II. He's a no-nonsense sort of guy who, one believes, embodies physique, temperament, and experience necessary to handle any problem, rise to any occasion.

It was on an August day in 1966, as a merciless summer sun softened the macadam of the highway, when Ranger Bob Frauson, returning from Logan Pass to his District Headquarters near the Park's east entrance, spotted a crowd of people gathered at the tourist facility of Rising Sun. In Bob's words:

"It was a big bunch of people milling around between the store and the gas station. The lady manager there was trying to get people back away from the building, where there was a grizzly bear."

Bob joined the effort. "I tried to push the people back, but it wasn't working too good."

The ranger said people were running to the scene from the cabin area (up the hill) and from the campground (across the creek). They had the bear surrounded. For its part, the grizzly was confused and exhibiting signs of frustration and anger (laying back its ears, stamping a front foot). The ranger feared that an explosion was imminent and several people would be injured. He ran back to his vehicle and jerked out a rifle. "More and more people were coming from every direction," he said.

To Ranger Frauson there was but one responsible alternative left—a field decision to destroy the bear. "I finally maneuvered into position where I could shoot without endangering human life, and I—shot the bear."

After making sure the bear was dead, the ranger left to call his fire guard for a truck to haul the animal away. When he returned minutes later, the still-warm carcass swarmed with tourists. Some had knives and were cutting out claws for souvenirs.

The disgusted ranger tried unsuccessfully to shoo the crowd away; "I finally went and pulled people off the bear, then stood on the carcass until the fire guards arrived and we could load it out."

Bob Frauson tells of another case when he received a call about a bear problem at Many Glacier—another instance of primal instincts seizing a crowd. A large group of people had a young (but mature) grizzly cornered right above the hotel, by the horse corral. When Bob received the call, the crowd was stoning the bewildered bear.

The pack continued hounding and stoning the bear—out of the parking lot, down past the caretaker's cabin at Swiftcurrent Lake's outlet, and up to the hillside beyond. Bob said:

"That was the most tolerant bear I've ever seen. He could have killed some of them. Or all of them."

I looked up from my notes to murmur, "Should have."

"Should have," the ex-ranger echoed.

Glacier Park's philosophy of bear management has, over the years, caromed from elimination of all problem bears to restrictions on disposing of any bears. More aggressive bear management became policy after the August, 1967, deaths of Julie Helgeson and Michelle Koons in widely separated bear attacks during the same August evening. But by the mid-'70s, amid a spreading controversy over crashing grizzly populations in Yellowstone (caused, some said, by a management policy of too-aggressive "cleansing," Glacier philosophy again flipped poles.

Policy shifts aren't always clear to those who are responsible in the field, however, as evidenced in a July, 1974, incident at Logan Pass when Ranger Frauson was again faced with hordes of camera-toting tourists surrounding and harassing an irritated grizzly bear. Frauson says:

"It was a midsummer day, and there must have been dozens, perhaps hundreds, of people there. I would move people back one way and here they would come in from another direction. Others would park cars along the edge of the road and come running with cameras. The bear was just running around, back and forth."

Mount Clements, thrusting above a fog bank, basking in the early morning sun. Clements is one of the guardian peaks towering over Logan Pass, where several of the grizzly/human incidents mentioned in this chapter occurred.

It was clear that an explosion might occur at any moment. He explained:

"My decision was based entirely on human safety. I had to control the people or the bear. Try as hard as I might, I couldn't control the people, so the bear had to go."

This time, however, the ranger ran afoul of shifting policy, both public and park. A Park Service naturalist stationed at Logan Pass was enraged at Frauson's decision to dispatch the young grizzly. Never mind that the naturalist shouldered no responsibility for controlling the public. Never mind that he shared none of the ranger's duties. The naturalist solicited bystanders to write letters to park administrators decrying the "unnecessary" destruction of the bear. Frauson's punishment for dispatching the cornered grizzly was that he had to answer each letter, many of them from the very people who were harassing the bear and whose lives he may have saved.

Bob Frauson is unbowed yet today, defending both the necessity and responsibility for on-the-ground personnel to make field decisions affecting a balance between human safety and wildlife integrity. And he's outspoken in his contempt for administrators who fail to support the subordinates who must make difficult field decisions.

I asked Bob if the naturalist who complained tried to turn people from harm's way.

"Not that I'm aware of. But that's not to say there aren't many fine naturalists out there. Did I ever tell you about the black naturalist who led people from danger above the visitor center?"

I shook my head, amused at the ex-ranger's tact.

"This naturalist was hired as part of the National Park Service's affirmative-action plan," Bob said. "He wasn't a particularly good naturalist, but he certainly demonstrated courage and an ability to think the day a grizzly took to a patch of stunted alpine firs up near the overlook to Hidden Lake [a popular walk for casual tourists]."

This time, apparently, there was a role reversal. A group of people was trapped on the overlook with a bear that became agitated. The animal thrashed in the brush and clacked his teeth each time someone approached. The naturalist finally eased past the bear's hiding place to reach the people, then courageously led the group out, posting himself at the point of danger and talking soothingly to the animal until every onlooker was safely beyond.

"Someone easily could have been hurt if that naturalist hadn't acted swiftly and properly," Frauson concluded.

The ex-ranger tells of yet another incident when he was called to the Logan Pass parking lot to assist a woman naturalist struggling to keep bear and people apart. "They weren't paying much attention to her," Bob said, "possibly because she was a woman. But with my bullhorn, I was able to clear the lot of both people and cars, and then we hazed the bear away."

He said the most tiring day he ever spent was when he had to keep hordes of people hiking the boardwalk from the visitor center to the Hidden Lake overlook away from a grizzly bear feeding in the area. The boardwalk spans a mile of fragile alpine grasses and flowers, and hundreds, perhaps thousands of people hike that trail each day. The retired ranger shook his head and sighed:

"Keeping those people on the boardwalk and out of harm's way was all I could do. Most of them just have no idea. . . ." The big man's voice trailed off.

Experience with grizzly bears is no survival guarantee in a face-off with an enraged sow protecting her cubs. Charles Gibbs, an experienced outdoorsman and a budding wildlife photographer with an affinity for bears, died in such a face-off. It was late afternoon on April 25, 1987, when Gibbs and his wife Glenda, hiking from Glacier Park's Ole Creek, spotted three grizzly bears feeding on a shoulder of Elk Mountain. The couple split at that point, and Glenda continued on to their vehicle while Charles climbed to get photographs of the bear family.

Night fell. When four hours passed, the now frantic woman drove to the Walton Ranger Station to report her husband missing. Ranger Charlie Logan hiked into the area and fired three rifle shots without eliciting a response. Logan had no choice but to discontinue the search until morning.

Gibbs's body was discovered soon after daylight at the 6,000-foot level, approximately a mile from the trail. The man lay crumpled on a hillside of scattered trees and dried grass. He had bled to death as a result of puncture wounds and slashes from tooth and claw. No wounds were found on his back—Gibbs died facing his adversary.

From the evidence, the photographer had tried to climb a small tree but had been pulled down. Grass clumps beneath the tree were ripped up, soil churned, graphic evidence of a titanic struggle. A Canon camera with a 400mm lens was found nearby. Film had been exposed through the seventeenth frame. A .45-caliber semi-automatic Colt handgun lay on the ground near the camera. There were five live rounds in the weapon's magazine and one in the chamber. The gun had not been fired.

Later development of the film disclosed that Gibbs had systematically approached the grizzlies, shooting frames from close range and different locations. The photos clearly proved that all of the bears were aware of the man, the sow becoming increasingly angered, lowering her head and flattening her ears. There was no exposed frame indicating a bear in an attack.

Glenda Gibbs said of her husband, "He had a great love and respect for grizzly bears and accepted any risk involved when in their territory. He was proud to live in a state that still has enough wilderness to support these magnificent animals."

Glenda asked that Glacier Park officials not destroy the grizzly that had killed her husband. "His wish was that no harm would come to the bear."

Glenda Gibbs's sentiments echoed those of the Peterson family from Des Plaines, Illinois, who surprised a grizzly while hiking to Grinnell Glacier on August 7, 1975. The attack took place about 8:30 in the morning, roughly a mile from the picnic area, below the base of Glacier Park's largest active glacier. Harold and Donna Peterson and their daughter Karen, 11, and son Seth, 7, were bound for the glacier when they rounded a trail bend and the bear exploded from nearby bush.

Seth was knocked askew first, with the bear only momentarily pausing before charging into the rest of the family. Mrs. Peterson apparently swooned and was unharmed, but Karen was savaged around the head and face. Her father, in a moment of fantastic heroism, jumped astride the bear and tried to pull it from his daughter.

According to Ranger Frauson, who investigated the attack and interviewed the family in their hospital beds: "The bear bit both of Harold Peterson's arms, breaking them. [News reports said the left forearm was shattered.] Then the bear ran back to the boy, who was beginning to stir, and roughed him up before charging back uphill to the girl. The father, even with broken arms, picked up a big stone and slammed the bear on the head, driving it from his family."

Aside from Harold Peterson's notable acts of heroism, perhaps the most impressive part of the story comes from Frauson's interview with the family in a Cardston, Alberta, hospital:

"Karen, the girl, pleaded with us not to hurt the bear. She said, 'It was only doing what it felt it must do when surprised.' And you know what the father said?" Bob asked.

I shook my head.

"He pleaded with the media not to put the incident on the wire services. 'If it's printed across America that we're lying in an Alberta hospital, thieves will break into our house in Chicago and steal us blind!'"

An entirely different attitude toward grizzlies was expressed by a man who phoned me from his hospital bed, wanting me to take him grizzly-bear hunting. It was the second week of September, and we were preparing for our first elk hunt of the season, deep into the Bob Marshall Wilderness. "I beg your pardon?" I said.

The guy repeated his name, then asked, "Do you know who I am?"

"I believe so. Aren't you one of the folks who were just mauled by a grizzly bear in Glacier?"

"You got it. We were minding our own business and this beast roared out of nowhere and tore us up for no reason. I'm not done with it yet, and I want to get even. Will you help me?"

"You can't hunt in Glacier National Park. Surely you know that."

"I know. But they tell me you're the best guide around. You can find me a grizzly bear somewhere."

I took the phone from my ear to stare at it in dismay. The voice seemed to come from the bottom of a well: "Hello. Hello! Mr. Cheek, are you there?"

"Let me get this straight," I said into the mouthpiece. "You and your lady friend have been attacked by a bear in Glacier Park, and you want to get even with the species by killing one a hundred and fifty miles away in the Bob Marshall Wilderness?"

"I'll be doing my part."

I stared wide-eyed at my wife. She poured a mug of coffee, plainly curious as to what had flummoxed her husband.

"Dammit, I want to do my part," the man repeated.

I sighed. "I reckon you'll just have to do it without me."

Attitudes about bears differ among people, and so also, it seems, attitudes toward humans differ among bears.

Mary Patricia Mahoney of Highwood, Illinois, a University of Montana coed, was the first person—according to a National Park Service Board of Inquiry—ever to be killed by a grizzly bear while camped in a major auto campground. Mary Pat, still in her sleeping bag, was dragged from the Many Glacier Campground at 6:30 on the morning of September 23, 1976. She was one of a party of five college girls on an outdoors outing.

Other findings from the Board of Inquiry were:

"The five girls in campsite number 74 had a clean camp and also followed or exceeded the precautions one would take in avoiding conflict with bears."

In what may have been an attempt to sidestep responsibility, the Board also found:

"It is questionable whether the fatal attack on Miss Mahoney could have been avoided."

Consider these prior incidents, also occurring in the Many Glacier vicinity:

It was just a few weeks before Mary Pat Mahoney's tragic death when Pam Sue Wise, 17, and Pamela Benda, 18, of Minneapolis were hiking toward Ptarmigan Falls on their way to Iceberg Lake. One of the girls spotted a grizzly bear following them on the trail. They dropped their packs and climbed a tree. The bear followed, stood on his hind legs at the tree, growled, and moved off, then returned to scratch and growl, finally leaving the area.

The encounter with Miss Wise and Miss Benda was the third of the season between grizzlies and humans on the Iceberg Trail. Fortunately, none resulted in injuries. Iceberg Lake is but a two-hour hike from the campground where Mary Pat Mahoney died. Ptarmigan Falls is half of that.

Then there was the two anglers at Fishercap Lake, Kerry O'Dell and Donald Brurud, who were chased into the lake by two grizzly bears, one of which grabbed the toe of Brurud's waders before abandoning pursuit of the yelling, kicking fisherman. One of the bears, more aggressive than the other, had earlier chased O'Dell up a tree, then climbed a short way after him.

Fishercap Lake is a short distance from the campground where Miss Mahoney was dragged from her tent. Even more frightening is the fact that the incident at Fishercap Lake occurred just four days before the young lady was killed and partially eaten by—you guessed it—*two* grizzly bears.

Perhaps the most chilling detail concerning all the incidents was the fact that Park Rangers had, on the same day as the Fishercap Lake incident, received a report that two grizzlies were reported in Many Glacier Campground. Seasonal Ranger Fred Reese toured the campground and discovered, according to a press report: "Two mature grizzlies, about 250-pounders, likely three-to-four year-olds. They went through the campground without incident except to get some garbage that wasn't fully disposed within a can."

Mary Pat Mahoney was sleeping in a tent with two other young women. Another tent containing two classmates was nearby. The attack took place within a hundred yards of a park ranger station. Of the 117 campsites within the campground, nineteen were occupied by upwards of eighty people.

None of those at the campground, nor the rangers responding, thought they were dealing with two bears until Rangers Bob Frauson and Lloyd Kortge followed the drag trail to the partially consumed body of Miss Mahoney and shot first one, then a second bear.

Repercussions from the tragedy at the popular campground, located in one of the most favored sectors of Glacier National Park, was intense. Indeed, all America was shocked. Park officials scrambled for a solution. They decided to install a chain-link fence around the campground *to keep bears out!*

Novel idea. Keep bears from re-arranging a Mustang in search of an igloo. No more popping-down of pop-up tents. Now tourists can sleep secure.

There have been better ideas. What happens, some campers asked, if the last tourist in for the night leaves the gate open for a wandering bear? The animal will then have all the humans

On the trail to Elk Mountain, near the spot where photographer Charles Gibbs was killed as he stalked a sow grizzly with cubs.

trapped. What a grizzly smorgasbord! Wouldn't that redefine the term "mummy bags?"

Despite complaints, the fence stayed up until the campground was visited by high-level personnel from the Park Service's Washington office who, it is assumed, personally felt the discomfort of humans being penned in a cage in a National Park. The fence was dismantled.

National Park Service policy fluttered like a moth to a candle flame. It would be unfair, however, to categorize NPS bear management as *laissez faire* when all America thought of grizzly bears as virtual teddies until the "Night of the Grizzlies"—that August night in 1967 when two widely separated bears turned killers the same evening. On the other hand, it does seem fair to expect more from that same Park Service than short-term, ill-considered management driven by emotion and politics.

The listing under the Endangered Species Act in response to accelerated demise of the great bruins resulted in a bounce in the other direction, which led to growing public intolerance of the bears' increasingly aggressive behavior, which led to. . . .

Meanwhile, the National Park Service offers no proof that bear numbers are either rising or declining in Glacier, even while criticism is being leveled by federal, state, and tribal agencies for their failure.

Fortunately for the policy-potholed Park Service, other agencies—and not a few individuals—had clearer ideas about what constituted proper behavior for both bears and humans. ∎

Chapter 13

Adopt a Grizzly

Despite occasional wind gusts that billowed jackets and rattled dead leaves from tag alder clumps, visibility was still so crisp it looked as if one could reach out and touch the magnificent peaks rising on all sides—the sort of day to make a man stand on a ridgetop and pound his chest in exhilaration. Off in the distant south and west, dark, heavy-bellied clouds drooped below mountain tops.

It was in October, 1974, and the two couples were car-camping in Glacier National Park. On this day they'd chosen the popular loop trail to Granite Park Chalet, but they'd not encountered other hikers, perhaps because it was late in the season, perhaps because the weather seemed unsettled.

Pat O'Herren and his friend John hiked just out of sight, ahead of the girls. Pat tells the story:

"We heard noises from an alder thicket above the trail—sort of woofing, bushes shaking. Suddenly the thicket exploded and a cinnamon-colored bear—a grizzly—hurtled toward us!"

Pat turned to look at his companion, who was fleeing back along the trail. Then he was struck a mighty blow that knocked him tumbling from the trail, skidding through alpine timothy and autumn-dead stalks of groundsel and daisy and penstammon. He lost consciousness. When he came to his senses, he lay curled amid the alpine plants in a fetal position. He blinked, shook his head, and looked about.

"The bear was walking back up the trail, clacking her teeth, saliva dripping. I lay still for several minutes, then climbed to my feet and called softly for John. I didn't know if he'd been injured or not."

Pat found his terrified companion back with the girls; all were about to flee to the road in order to report the bear attack.

I asked Pat what went through his mind at the time of the encounter.

"It all happened so fast, I never really had time to think. After I was knocked from the trail, I can't really remember much. I suppose she had cubs." He chuckled. "I'm not even sure she was a 'she'."

It took ten years before O'Herren screwed up the courage to hike again to Granite Chalet. But somehow in the interim, the man became detached enough from the trauma of his grizzly encounter to cross a watershed of his own, coming to believe the big bears belonged in wild country. He wanted to help other folks to somehow understand, and he wanted to help the bears, as well. But how?

At first the idea was no more than a vague dream. But as he shared it with friends, he discovered that others, too, wished to do something for the bears. Primarily because of the academic and artistic backgrounds of O'Herren's friends, they focused on education as their best potential vehicle for change: perhaps an educational program to teach primary-level schoolkids who dwell in occupied grizzly habitat how to co-exist with the big bears? Thus, in 1989, fifteen years after Pat O'Herren was swatted from Glacier's Highline Trail by a grizzly bear who was possibly protecting her cubs, Brown Bear Resources was founded as an all volunteer group offering educational, technical, and research assistance. Seldom has brute battery led to such positive profit for the perpetrator. Right from the first, the school children displayed their curiosity and eagerness to learn:

> "Thank you for coming and talking about being safe around grizzle bear and black bears."
>
> Cody M.

*"I hope I learn more about bears. I love animals. I
really enjoyed what you taught us."*

-your friend, Desiree

In the beginning, Pat and his wife Amy contributed most of
the organization's seed money and shouldered the entire administrative load. But they were not without competent colleagues.

"People with specific talents or professions were recruited,"
O'Herren said, "in order to develop a well-rounded professional,
scientific, and artistic program we could present to kids."

Recruited talents include: An educator specializing in artistic perception of wildlife and their values; a university adjunct
professor teaching movement and dance; an undercover state fish
& game enforcement officer; an art and education instructor with
the state teachers' association; a biologist and author providing a
bridge between science and the creative; a freelance journalist
with major credits who specializes in stories about undercover
investigations into illicit trafficking in wildlife; a biologist with
the U.S. Fish & Wildlife Service; a journalism graduate student
contributing as editor for *Silvertip Tracks*, the newsletter for Brown
Bear Resources.

*"Thank you. I liked the play that you did. Also, I liked
the art that we did."*

- Your friend, Seth

Because Pat and his staff believe a successful educational
program needs several years in order to develop sensitivity among
kids, Brown Bear Resources committed to a nine-year effort with
their first school, Swan Valley Elementary, located in an isolated
valley between two remote mountain ranges. BBR named this
pilot program *Adopt A Grizzly.*

Adopt A Grizzly, according to a flyer on the group's activities,
allows teachers, students, and parents to follow the activities of

specific Montana grizzlies. The program teaches the vulnerability of the bear to natural forces (such as avalanches) and to human activities (habitat loss and direct mortality). In addition, suggestions are offered on how humans can best live and travel in grizzly country (better garbage-handling techniques, camping methods, moving in groups, making noise).

Via cooperation with various agencies, Brown Bear Resources receives information on bears currently radio-collared and tracked. This information is passed on through periodic updates to enrolled schoolkids so they can follow "their" grizzly through spring, summer, and fall. Summer updates are forwarded by the students' teachers. Bears are in hibernation during winter.

I asked O'Herren how his group avoids providing a false picture of bears.

"By telling the truth. Even when a bear they've adopted engage in acts that lead to its trapping or destruction, the children are told the truth about their bear's behavior."

"How do you keep the kids from becoming attached to a bear they've adopted?"

Pat shrugged. "I'm sure it happens to a degree, but you'd be surprised how realistic most of them are. We were surprised at the kids' minimal reaction when two cubs of an 'adopted' female [Jessie] were taken out [the previous summer in the Spotted Bear area]."

The children name their adopted bears. Swan Valley schoolkids chose "Jessie" for their first bear, a female ranging the mountain high country just north of the Bob Marshall Wilderness and daughter of the first bear trapped in the South Fork Grizzly Study. With Jessie as their first, it seemed natural for the Swan Valley kids to select "James" as their second adopted bear. James is a large male, also calling the Swan Range home territory. "DJ" is a female from the Yaak, "Bart" a Yaak male, "Marie" a female with a home range spanning the border between the upper Yaak and British Columbia.

There's an unnamed female in the Cabinets who just emerged from her den with a cub at her side and, finally, an unnamed female from the Swan that is being regularly monitored and included in the updates. DJ and Marie have been adopted;

the others are all waiting to find an interested and deserving bunch of kids from some yet uninvolved grade school.

The kids' notes were printed on hand-made, carefully crayoned cards addressed to Patrick O'Herren, Director, Brown Bear Resources. More legible (if less charismatic) was the letter from John Hargrove, Superintendent of the West Yellowstone Public Schools:

> *"I would like to . . . thank you and your staff for the excellent program presented at West Yellowstone Public Schools on January 13th, 1993. The programs were well received by students and staff. Please keep us on your list for future programs."*

In addition to the long-term *Adopt A Grizzly* project, Brown Bear Resources also provides a one-shot *Be Fair To Grizzly Bears* program involving music, dance, art, biology, and storytelling in a manner designed to teach children about the real life of grizzly bears.

"We go into a school with an average of a half-dozen people," O'Herren said. "Each one presents a one-hour segment to a portion of children, then they switch. We're at each school for an entire day."

Other educational efforts by Brown Bear Resources include the quarterly newsletter *Silvertip Tracks* and a *Traveling Grizzly Library* containing books, videos, posters, and brochures designed for loan to schools.

What's the charge for these services to elementary schools located in occupied grizzly habitat? Nothing.

Success is not without its cost, however, as Brown Bear Resources apparently heads into uncharted territory. Despite an original intent merely to provide educational programs to schools throughout much of mountain Montana, schools from distant places are also interested.

"We identified what we thought was an unfilled niche and moved to fill it," Pat O'Herren says. "But what we didn't sense was how big that niche is."

The first hint that the niche might include all America came when an elementary school from Milford, Connecticut, asked Brown Bear Resources if they could adopt a grizzly and receive periodic updates on their adopted bear. Milford Elementary offered to pay whatever costs were involved. The Connecticut school was soon followed by one in Sand Springs, Oklahoma. O'Herren is astonished by it all.

It seems clear that folks with Brown Bear Resources are making a difference. That difference is increasingly apparent to resource managers from federal, state, and county agencies. But in the process, the physical and fiscal resources of the all-volunteer group is being stretched to the uttermost.

BBR officers have served as National Park staff instructors, made National Forest campground presentations, sponsored interns to work on an individual basis with people dwelling where grizzlies live, co-produced and distributed brochures, sponsored brainstorming resource meetings for various levels of government, and worked to preserve habitat vital to the great bears' future.

In addition, the organization has completed a comprehensive survey of attractant sites in the Northern Continental Divide Ecosystem which may reduce bear mortalities and translocations.

The group offers rewards for information leading to the arrest of poachers. And they're presently expanding into research programs to benefit private landowners dwelling in bear habitat.

Brown Bear Resources enjoys unparalleled communications with agency personnel at all levels, brought about by a commitment to be non-controversial. As a matter of fact, the group's bylaws preclude involvement in litigation—a strategy paying enormous cooperative dividends.

Committed as BBR is solely to education and research, it's doubtful that any other group of volunteers can or will achieve so much with so little. Still, there are questions to be asked about the group's efforts. How practical is their approach to classroom instruction? Research? Human development? Overall educational efforts? Community outreach?

Who dares criticize volunteers, whether they're untrained but willing workers manning a rural fire station or a Pee Wee baseball coach who knows little about the game but gives freely of his time so your child and his can play? It's even more awkward—

perhaps reprehensible—to criticize an aspect of Brown Bear Resources' educational efforts when they're staffed with such an array of educational experts. They are, however, not infallible.

Some think their educational message drifted beyond the practical with an October, 1994, *Adopt A Grizzly* report sent to Swan Valley Elementary School children about their adopted bear, James:

> *"James found apples in an area where the residents were asked to clean up their orchards but failed to do so. As a result, James was lured into the site and has been eating the apples for several days. . . ."*

Despite the report's implications, there are no special rules applying to orchard owners relative to keeping fruit out of reach of bears. In fact, there's near-unanimous opinion among experienced growers that such a rule would be impossible to implement. Yellow Bay orchardist Bill Collins, a committed conservationist, chuckled when I asked if it was possible to maintain an orchard in a way that would not attract bears.

"I've seen bears feeding from my trees before the fruit even ripened." Then the man mused, "Picking [the fruit] itself is a pretty sloppy process."

Bill said he's seen bears stand up and reach eight feet into a tree. "Commercially pruned trees are developed to keep fruit as close to the ground as possible. Our new trees—the ones we've just planted—are dwarfs designed to grow no higher than eight feet. There's really no way you can keep an orchard clean."

But it was my turn to smile when the Yellow Bay orchardist said he tries to keep spoiled apples picked up and thrown on the compost pile.

"And where is your compost pile?"

Bill saw my smile and he, too, grinned. "Behind the house."

Why was misinformation sent to impressionable schoolkids in Brown Bear Resources' Adopt A Grizzly report? I asked Pat O'Herren, but his answer was vague—that of a man who may be too close to academic theory. Unfortunately, it sends the wrong message about the polemics of a volunteer organization to which I would otherwise give the highest marks.

Are other Adopt A Grizzly reports to schoolchildren flawed? Let's hope not. Here's a better report, dated December 18 of the same year:

> "James has excavated a den at the 6,600-foot level for his winter home. He traveled approximately 50 air-miles from the spot where he was relocated to a slope with a northwest aspect. While he is now safely in the den, one question remains: Did James expend so much energy returning to his home range to den that he now lacks sufficient reserves to survive the next several months without food? We will not know the answer to that question until spring. . . ."

Pat and Amy O'Herren say their personal goal is to recover the bear and drive Brown Bear Resources out of business. It's a long step from here to there, however. And as Pat said earlier, they had no idea how big the niche they chose was. The man shows his strain and one wonders how much more blood can be squeezed from an all-volunteer turnip?

A recent issue of Silvertip Tracks provided a breakdown of BBR revenue sources: one grant of $10,500; three additional smaller grants; fifteen individual donors of $100 or more; a contribution from Cub Scout Pack 86, who gathered aluminum cans to help. . . .

I stared across the table at Pat O'Herren. The guy appeared exhausted—as would anyone holding down a steady job and facing burnout from a volunteer commitment with no end in sight. "How much time do you put into this program, Pat?"

"You mean hours? Lots."

"So is it worth it?"

"It's something I *have* to do."

But what about Brown Bear Resources itself? Is the group having an effect on human/grizzly relations?

A resounding yes! Through dedication and effort, those volunteers have taken recent technical research material and information about grizzly bears throughout history and distilled that material to a level grade school children can understand.

How well is it taking? I went to the Swan River Elementary School to find out. Tabby, a first-grader, tells what she'd learned about grizzly bears:

"We had this big bear in our backyard and we tried to stay away from him—my sister and brother and me. And he kept just going over to the huckleberry bushes and eating the huckleberries."

"He ate the huckleberries?" I asked.

"He ate all of them."

"All of them?"

"I just found one on the ground."

Jennifer, also a first-grader, said, "When they're hungry they eat ladybugs."

Second-grader Kristi said, "They have big tracks and they growl."

I didn't talk to a single Swan Valley Elementary School child who didn't know at least something about grizzly bears—an important point when one remembers these rural schoolkids could encounter a grizzly in their backyards.

Pat O'Herren's attitude toward grizzly bears changed. The ripples from that metamorphosis may ultimately reach far beyond Pat's modest dreams. ■

Prime grizzly habitat. Marion Lake, west of Essex, in the Great Bear Wilderness.

Chapter 14

Bear Aplomb and Human Chagrin

I looked in the mirror and one day saw that some of my hair had turned gray and the rest loose. There were turkey-track squint lines at my eye corners and age spots on sunburned cheeks. Others must have observed my aging, too, and misinterpreted it to assume a man who'd spent most of a lifetime outdoors knew something about things wild: rivers, mountains, horses, elk, grizzlies.

I wouldn't want to disillusion them; but I've sometimes had cause to wonder how much I knew. Take the time I brought a party of Pennsylvanians out over Bungalow Mountain and spotted a dead elk at the bottom of an avalanche fan. The climb to the top of Bungalow is a grueling one of two-thousand feet in seven miles—hard on horses. I've made it a habit to pause at a stunning overlook in order to give our stock a breather. Besides consideration for the ponies, we've often spotted elk or deer in the basin below.

It was the second week of August. Our guests had "oohed" and "ahhed" all morning at the ride, the scenery, the wildflowers still blooming in profusion. "Now if we can just spot an elk," I told them as we edged toward the vantage point.

Fortune smiled; an elk was there. Except that its belly was bloated and legs thrust straight up and out. This elk was dead.

"What do you suppose happened to it?" my dairy-farmer guest asked.

Good question. But the animal lay at least five hundred yards away, while we stood at the top of a thousand-foot cliff. With the guests already tiring and a long ride yet ahead, I could hardly trot down and investigate.

"I don't know, Foster. But it died of natural causes."

"Why do you say that?" June prompted. "You don't think someone shot it?"

I shook my head. "No way. It's still a month until hunting season, and there's not a half-dozen people travel this trail each year. And no poacher is going to get this far from a road."

"Then what do you mean by natural causes?" her husband asked.

"Disease, old age, tired blood. Hell, I don't know."

"Looks like it was fat when it died," the farmer muttered, staring through binoculars.

"Or it could have been killed by a wild animal—lion, bear."

"No sign that anything's fed on it."

"Or maybe it was killed in a fall. If we had time, I'd look for a way down and find out. But there's still ten miles to our next campsite, and then it's tents to set up, wood to gather, and horses to care for."

I glanced at the sun, then at each guest in turn. June slapped at a mosquito. Horses stamped while fighting flies. I knew all three of the people standing at the overlook were game to investigate. Foster would probably go with me if I decided to clamber down the cliff. Perhaps Ken, too. And June would volunteer to stay with the horses and watch us from a distance. But the trip down and back would add a couple of hours to what was to be an already long day. I shook my head.

"Mount up. We'll eat lunch on top, at an old lookout site."

The dead elk was still in the back of my mind when guide Dan Cherry and I packed a load of hay into the White River camp a week later. And when we pulled out of the remote camp to return home, I looked back at the fast-walking, lightly loaded packhorses and shouted to Dan that if it was okay with him we would take the longer, steeper Bungalow Trail in order to check on the dead elk.

"The carcass should have ripened long enough now so as to pull in a bear," I told Dan as we tied the packhorses to stunted trees at the top of the Hoop Basin overlook.

But when we crept to the edge of the cliff to peer over, I muttered, "That's strange." I swept the dry arroyo and avalanche fan with binoculars. "There's no sign of it. Ought to be at least a few bones and scraps of hide."

"Where was it?" the guide asked, tugging his hat down against a sudden gust of wind.

As I pointed to the arroyo forks and the rock outwash, a movement two hundred yards to the right and farther out in the basin caught my eye. I whipped up the glasses. "There he is, Dan! A big silvertip!"

This was the young man's first sight of a grizzly. The bear galloped through stunted alpine fir and limber pine. Had we not had an eagle's-eye view from above, there's no way we could have followed his route through the trees.

"Did we spook him?" the lad asked.

"Could be."

"But we didn't make much noise."

"Might have been shifts in the wind. He didn't see us, that's for sure."

Horses stamped and shuffled behind. A fly droned by. The distant bear slowed to a walk, coming out into a long meadow studded with scattered whitebark pines. In choosing his route through the basin, the animal made a sweeping arc until he now shuffled at ninety degrees to us. He dropped into an arroyo, angled up it a ways, then clambered to the top and ambled into a dense patch of spruce timber.

"Dan, that bear is circling."

We could catch only glimpses of movement through the denser forest, but sure as God made little apples, the animal was turning in our direction. "If the wind will only hold. . . ."

Ten more minutes and the big bruin strolled out onto the rock outwash near the arroyo forks, where the elk had been. He ducked his head and tore at a mound we'd missed when we'd first searched for the dead elk—a cache buried under dirt, sticks, rocks, and clumps of grass.

I glanced at the guide and grinned. "May as well pull up a bleacher seat, boy. We'll be here a while."

We sat for an hour watching that grizzly, sprawling on his belly across his delicatessen, tearing off great chunks of meat from the decomposing elk. Occasionally, he would lift his nose high into the air and gulp down a long strip. Or he might idly rake the cache with a paw, in order to expose a particularly choice cut. Though I had watched dozens of grizzlies by then, this was my first chance to watch one of the great bears feeding on carrion.

The sun beat mercilessly down as our packstring shifted and stamped and fought flies. By the time I called quits to our giant nature video, we had but ten hours until dark and still had ten hours of riding time ahead.

"You were right," Dan said as we tied our packstring together, nose to tail. "There was a bear on the carcass."

I felt smug about being such a repository of outdoor knowledge. It was false security, and I should have guessed that bears have a penchant for taking presumptuous outfitters down by degrees. It was but a few days after watching the Bungalow griz in his dining room when our packer dropped my wife Jane and me off at our Pentagon campsite. It was our very own annual idyll, where we spent a few days alone together, setting up hunting-camp tents and cutting firewood.

As I've mentioned, camp set-up is grueling work. But even after thirty-five years of marriage (forty-two as I write this) Jane and I are still very much in love. And frankly, we looked forward to a few days without guides or guests underfoot.

It was at the end of day three when the two of us, cocktails in hand, retired to what she called her "grotto"—a secluded river nook.

Our Pentagon hunting camp was within a few miles of the headwaters of the Spotted Bear River. The river rises in the high basins near the crest of the Continental Divide, falling rapidly into forested bottoms of huge Englemann spruce and lodgepole pine. Red osier dogwood and willow choke the riverbank throughout much of its length.

Three miles below our camp, the river gushes over Dean Falls, marking the upper limit of fish migration. The lack of angling opportunity above the falls translates into little human use of the river's upper reaches. Travelers are few, and the U.S Forest Service trail in this sector is located three hundred yards from the river. With no chance of being surprised, my wife and I felt at ease skinny-dipping at the end of a sweaty day. And that's where Jane's grotto came in.

The river there is but twenty-five feet wide and varies in depth from shallows to five feet. The bank nearest our camp was brush-choked, but the south side kissed a cliff. A narrow ledge sloped at an angle from the water's edge to a level section four feet above the river. There was just room on that ledge for two people to sit and hold hands and, with cocktails perched nearby, watch the sun shimmer in kaleidoscopic patterns upon rippling water. First the plunge and swim, then the clamber to the ledge to drip-dry. Delicious! No one around. Be as uninhibited as is possible for a couple of aging wood sprites. . . .

That's why I felt like snatching up moss to cover our indecency when the bear ambled out of the brush to eye a buckskin log that spanned the river some fifty yards below. I hissed at Jane.

That bruin had us! Oh, he had us dead to rights—both without so much as a stitch of clothing near, pinned on the ledge! The nearest tree, climbable or otherwise, was either across the river or atop the cliff.

At first I thought he might not be aware of our presence as he plodded head down across the log. A gentle breeze blew upriver in our direction; there was little chance he could wind us. I gripped Jane's arm and shook her gently when she leaned forward to whisper.

The bear reached the log's midpoint, stopped, and swung his head to stare directly at us. I felt Jane stiffen. My mind flashed back to a few years earlier, when a giant grizzly stared me down at the nearby ranger station. That incident happened about this same time of year, too.

Time stopped. If there's such a thing as ursine "candid camera," we were on it!

At last the bear had seen enough; swinging his head forward, he ambled on across the log. The last we saw of him, he picked his way into dense brush, moving downriver.

Another case of a bear not caring about or seeming to react to human presence happened at My Lake. My Lake is not my lake. "My" is the proper name for a gorgeous spring-fed jewel perhaps ten acres in size, near the north end of the Chinese Wall. We had a group of hunters from California who'd hunted hard for several days and wanted a break. I suggested we spend a day riding to view "the Wall." They were game. All told, eight guests and crew made the trek.

As mentioned before, the top of the Chinese Wall is also the summit of the Continental Divide, and rain falling there runs to both the Atlantic and Pacific Oceans. From the summit east, though the area is yet within the Bob Marshall Wilderness, it is also the Sun River Game Preserve. So before we left camp, I explained to the hunters that it was open season to the top of the pass, but once we passed through and began riding on the east side of the Wall, they could no longer shoot an animal, even though they had a license for the species.

We spotted mountain goats feeding on cliff ledges and saw several mule deer. Many of the riders exposed roll after roll of film, capturing one of the most gorgeous mountain lands in all America. By the time we pulled up to the shore of the tiny, picturesque My Lake for lunch, we'd already climbed two thousand feet and ridden over twelve miles. The guys dug lunches from saddlebags and sprawled in the grass. It was a bright sunny day, and soon most of my party was snoring. I strolled to the lake's upper end, habitually casting for tracks in the wet ground.

I was surprised to see the bear track. It was big, very big. But the claw marks weren't clear enough to judge if it was a black or a grizzly. The bear solved that question only minutes after I spotted his track, strolling from stunted firs, ambling around the far side of the lake. He was black.

I dashed back to my companions, slapping their boots and pointing as I trotted by. Some ran for their binoculars or cameras. Others merely sat up and stared across the tiny lake. One yawned and lay back in the grass to continue his nap.

The bear, though black, was big, packing a full winter's supply of fat. "It's impossible he doesn't know we're here," one hunter said.

The bruin paused, staring up at the top of a ten-foot alpine tamarack. Then he turned, backed his butt against the sapling, and reared on his hind legs, stretching nearly as high as the tree.

"My Lord!" one of the hunters gasped.

Reaching over a shoulder, the big black seized the upper end of the tamarack in his teeth, then began sawing back and forth.

After a moment of stunned silence, there was a babble of voices:

"He's scratching his back!"

"Will you look at that!"

"Mike, you're stepping in front of my camera!"

The bear dropped to all fours, still ignoring us, and walked on a few steps before repeating his back-scratching maneuver with another sapling. At last he disappeared into a finger of trees along a low ridge.

"By God, that sight was worth the whole price of the trip," one man said, stuffing his empty lunch sack into a saddlebag. "But right now I'm ready to get back on the other side of the mountain so I can hunt again."

I don't know what makes bears tick, especially grizzly bears. Moving toward four decades of off-and-on association with the great beasts, it's clear I know enough to predict *some* of their actions. But the simple truth is, I don't know enough about the mighty bruins to bet the farm on that knowledge.

So how about what the animals themselves know or don't know? Are they as confused about us? Does a three-year-old bruin expect every human to run off screaming just because the first homo sapiens he encountered did so? What if the next is a shriveled up specimen with graying hair and a crackling voice who looks him right in the eye and talks in a gentle tone while easing slowly away? Or how about the milky white couple with enough aplomb to splash around in a river in the middle of grizzly country while bears are about? Or was that bruin smart enough to know we had neither nose to smell nor ears to hear—nor enough sense to practice avoidance in the presence of danger?

Or was Jane's and my grotto bear mildly curious, while Bob Fullerton's aspired to graduate status in human understanding?

Fullerton was a Glacier Park naturalist out on a bushwhack climb to remote and trail-less Falling Leaf and Snow Moon Lakes, south of Many Glacier. It was midsummer and the day was warm. Fullerton stripped down, laid his clothes in a neat bundle, and plunged into one of the lakes. It was while the man paddled around in the ice-cold water that the grizzly emerged from nearby brush, strolled over, sat down on Fullerton's clothes, and proceeded to study the man treading water.

Wouldn't you love to know what was going through the bear's mind? Or Fullerton's, for that matter? Did flashbacks of encounters with other grizzly bears come instantly to the naturalist's mind, as happened to me at the grotto? And might the grizzly have spent moments recalling incidents with humans from his past?

One thing seems clear after all these years: grizzlies are smart creatures. They do think. I believe they have the ability to reason. Some of them, like humans, may be better at it than others. The ability to reason may sometimes be clouded by short fuses or belly aches or hangovers. Obviously they operate from a different set of guidelines and instincts. Above all, grizzly bears are different. They're different from you and me and different from each other.

That much I'd learned after spending decades in on-the-ground, seat-of-the-pants study. But how far had my knowledge of the big creatures really advanced? Was I not just now at the primary-school level? Advanced education into bear behavior, so it seemed, must come through another venue.

Fortunately, the South Fork Grizzly Study was advancing in the mountain range filling my home's picture window. It's in those Swan Range Mountains that Montana's Department of Fish, Wildlife & Parks was engaged in a ten-year study clearly demonstrating what I'd already come to believe—that enormous differences existed among individual bears. I began hanging out around the men and women conducting this research. ■

Chapter 15

Trapper's Nightmare

My career as a Montana wilderness outfitter and guide ended with our final November hunting party in 1990. It was a great twenty-one years, full to the brim with excitement, challenge, physical elan, romance with nature, and friendships developed across America. No one could have enjoyed life more, but it was time to move on.

The reasons were many, but one truth became more and more apparent—that the demands of adventure leadership in the wildest lands in the northern Rockies belong to younger, more physically able men and women.

Another reason for retiring from outfitting was that my career as a writer had reached a crossroads; it was time to get in or get out. The decision was relatively easy. Odds were I could write many more years than I could cope with the rigors of loading and leading ten-horse packstrings across remote mountains.

Besides, Jane and I thought it might be fun to explore wild lands without the responsibility of guiding others.

So it has been. We've trekked through distant valleys and traveled trails I'd not visited during all the decades we were guiding guests into the same country. Since retiring from guiding, we've re-visited places with names like Jewel Basin, Tuchuck Mountain, Spruce Park, Granite Chalet, Grinnell Glacier, and Trinkus Lake. And we've stumbled into hidden spots we'd been unable to visit before: Boulder Pass, Turquoise Lake, Daughter of the Sun Mountain, and Angel's Bathing Pool.

All of those places are vistas where bears roam. You see, my interest in the great bears remains undiminished, and a land where the grizzly is unwelcome cannot seem as welcome to me. Most of all, as a full-time freelance journalist, I now have time for in-depth research regarding *Ursus arctos horribilis.*

I began extended research where I felt it would most count— by researching the researchers. And of all bear research, none in the Rockies matched that spilling from Montana Fish, Wildlife & Parks' South Fork Grizzly Study. . . .

The camera lay upon the ground, dented with tooth marks. Part of the frame was missing where the bear had ripped open and sprung the door, its film cartridge gone. The carefully prepared "set" was vandalized: logs and rocks overturned, brush flattened, snares tripped. The bait—a road-killed deer carcass hung in a tree—was gone. The Mud Lake Bear had struck again.

"It's his modus operandi," Rick Mace said as he handed me the camera, a compact Olympus Infinity stamped No. 12. "He usually appears at night and always rips up our trap site."

I turned the camera over and over, staring at the tooth marks. Johannes Brahms could not have tuned into a Beethoven symphony with more rapt attention than I honed into Mace's sonata.

"We suspected the Mud Lake Bear, of course, but can you believe it? We found the film cartridge off to one side, smashed, but we were able to develop enough film for a positive I.D."

Mace gets paid for trapping and monitoring grizzly bears. He prefers trapping grizzlies, but sometimes gets a black bear by chance. A trained biologist with almost two decades working grizzlies behind him, Mace is project leader for the South Fork Grizzly Study, the ten-year program designed to gather detailed information on the habits and habitat of one of America's most concentrated populations of grizzly bears.

Years before, when Rick was still a graduate student, he'd asked me to pack him into the Bob Marshall Wilderness so he could do a quick analytical overview of mid-wilderness grizzly habitat. Now our roles were reversed. He was a veteran study leader, and I, with hat in hand, was an aspiring journalist eager to learn more of grizzly bears.

Focusing on the north end of the Swan Mountain Range in northwest Montana, the study-area boundaries include Hungry Horse Reservoir on the east, Flathead and Swan Valleys to the west, south to the Bob Marshall Wilderness, and north to Columbia Mountain and Bad Rock Canyon. It's a region where project trappers place their remote cameras and cable snares, and where they radio-collar grizzly bears.

Bears trapped in the study area, do not, of course, restrict themselves to such artificial boundaries. They range far and wide—to the south deep into the Bob Marshall, across the mountains to the eastern plains, west to the Missions Mountains and, sometimes, even out where lots of people live, into Flathead Valley. They can be unpredictable in other ways, too. But of the fifty or more different bears thus far trapped, tagged, collared, and subsequently monitored, none has been as uncooperative as the Mud Lake Bear.

The Mud Lake Bear is officially known as No. 146 in the South Fork Study. He picked up his nickname because he spent much of his life roaming into the Flathead Valley south of Echo Lake—more specifically, in the dense forest and marsh area around Mud Lake.

Number 146 first came to the attention of humans when he tagged along with his mother and sister on forays onto the plains near Dupuyer. Though neither he nor his sibling was directly implicated in livestock depredation, their mother was destroyed for her indiscretions.

Captured in a culvert trap in September, 1985, at just 19 months of age, the half-grown orphaned cubs were fitted with ear tags and radio collars and released along the east side of Hungry Horse Reservoir, well over a hundred miles from their home country.

The female cub cast one look around and bee-lined home to the Rocky Mountain Front. But the young male apparently found a forested setting not unappealing and settled in for the duration. The South Fork Grizzly Study had not yet begun and, though the immature bruin was radio-collared, comparatively few monitoring attempts were made. Thus, information is scanty about the bear's movements until later, when the South Fork Study really got under way.

The young bear discovered Mud Lake and the Flathead Valley as a "long two-year-old" and drifted as far out as the mouth of Ashley Creek, just two miles from the County Courthouse in downtown Kalispell—the area's commercial center of about fifteen thousand population. Shawn Riley, former Region One biologist and architect of the South Fork Study, said, "We always wondered if this particular bear thought the open, expansive Flathead Valley was part of the eastern plains where he was born."

Whether he felt at home or not, the growing young grizzly spent daylight hours near dense riverbottom thickets and nights foraging wherever he wished. This went on for two weeks until a hog farmer happened on his track in a plowed field. About the time the alarmed farmer got on the phone to Fish, Wildlife & Parks headquarters to ask questions, the young bear packed his bags and took a direct flight to Swan Range high country. That was in May, when most red-blooded grizzly males go on the lookout for compliant females.

In the spring of 1987, about the time when Riley's proposed study got off the ground, the coming four-year-old lost his collar. And it wasn't until the following spring, as veteran biologists (who learned grizzly trapping via Chuck Jonkel's Border Grizzly Project) swarmed into the area, that the now nearly grown, unusually dark-colored grizzly was again captured.

It was a near-thing. The process used was a cubby set, a pile of logs stacked into V-shape. The bait is laid inside the tip of the V and a snare is placed in front. The dark-colored male was held by just four toes.

The growing bruin was tranquilized by a dart, then aged, weighed, and fitted with a radio-transmitter collar. Finally tags, bearing Number 146 were clamped to the bear's ears.

In less than a month, they caught Number 146 again. This time, according to Rick Mace, the young bear fell afoul of an approach snare to another cubby set while keeping love-sick company with bear Number 97, an old female on the far side of twenty. Unknown to biologists, the youthful, dark-colored bear was developing a distaste for traps—and anything associated with them.

In early autumn, Number 146 was radio-tracked to the Flathead Valley, and he remained in the Mud Lake vicinity for two months. Now nicknamed the Mud Lake Bear, the young grizzly clambered across the Swan high country to his denning site, entering in mid-November.

Biologists snared the Mud Lake Bear for the last time in June of 1989. This time the mature bruin blundered into a blind trail set. It completed the bear's education, a doctorate in trap distaste. He began writing his thesis within the month.

By August, Number 146 had returned to the Flathead Valley. He paused only briefly at Mud Lake before continuing across Highway 35 into rich Creston farm country. Moving always at night, the big bear was radio-tracked through landmark Gatiss Gardens to a tiny patch of woods a scant distance south of the Creston fire hall—and the Creston school. Because of his near-school hideout location, a decision was made to trap and move him. Fat chance.

Biologists wheeled a culvert trap into position near the woods and baited it with their ripest road-killed deer. During the

Remains of camera "eaten" by Mud Lake Bear. Note tooth marks and sprung gate.

FWP remote camera photo

1. Mud Lake Bear Sniffs blood dripping from bait (road killed deer).

2. Looks up, spots bait. Bear has already triggered surrounding snares.

FWP remote camera photo

FWP remote camera photo

3. Ambles over to see if this is the right trap station? Yep, number 85. (Note the yardstick enabling biologists to estimate size from remote photos).

4. Returns to try for bait.

FWP remote camera photo

5. Becoming angry! Night has fallen. Final two photos are flash lighted.

FWP remote camera photo

FWP remote camera photo

6. Success! Note rope securing bait in corner (upper left) of all photos in sequence.

night, the Mud Lake Bear tripped the trap's gate without entering. Again the device was set. The following night the bear turned over not only the heavy culvert, but its trailer, too, making no attempt to retrieve the bait. Again the trap was set. On the third night, Number 146 pushed the awkward contrivance through two barbed-wire fences and, tiring of the sport, decamped for the Swan Range's high country.

Grizzly Number 146 had only just begun getting even. Soon, he began sniffing out other trap sites, vandalizing and pilfering from them. One biologist said, "He must view the baits pretty much the same way Willie Sutton ogled greenbacks in a bank vault."

Number 146 denned in late November of 1989, again digging a hole near the area where he'd bedded the winter before; always in dense brush at a high elevation and on a north slope. The Mud Lake Bear emerged in mid-March and bee-lined for Mud Lake. He found company.

One important discovery during the South Fork Study's years was how much the big bruins use the vicinity around Mud Lake—prime spring bear country. In fact, *several* grizzlies are known to have roamed surrounding woods and marshes at the same time. Perhaps it was chance that brought a male later known as the Rottweiler bear down from his usual high-country fastness into the valley bottom nearby. The Mud Lake Bear had competition. Project leader Mace tells the story:

"According to the Mud Lake Bear's radio collar, he wasn't moving, so I went into the area to see why. It's really spooky in there!"

I nodded. The country east of Mud Lake can be dense.

"Well, I followed radio signals until I found the collar. It was lying on the ground in a tiny glade and, boy, things were torn up around there—brush flattened, rocks overturned, small trees knocked over, grizzly hair! There'd been a hell of a bear fight."

When I glanced up from my notes, Rick nodded and reiterated, "A grizzly fight. And within three feet of the collar was a dead dog . . ."

"A dead dog?"

"Yeah, a terrier type, and it was all ripped up."

"Go on."

"The first thing I do is look to see if the collar has been cut off. That'll tell if humans had anything to do with it. But it didn't look like it. Instead, it looked as though it'd been yanked off in the fight. Well, I edged around—getting spooked by the minute— the dead dog, the collar, the fight, the brush. And you know what I found about twenty yards from the collar and the dog?"

I shook my head.

"An arrow sticking in the ground!"

"An arrow?

"Now I don't know if the arrow or dog had anything to do with it. Anyhow, a few feet away, here was an ear tag ripped from Number 144. Those two big males had been in a hell of a fight!"

I wondered aloud if the tiny dog tried to break up the fight. And what was the significance of the arrow? There was no answer from the project leader.

The real significance of the incident, of course, was that biologists no longer had a tracking device on the Mud Lake Bear. And that was about the time the big bruin really swung into high gear on his one-bear vendetta against man's traps.

"We flag—hang orange flagging ribbon—on our way from a baited set so we can follow the trail when we return to check it," said biologist Tim Manley, then a Study trapper. "We could always tell when the Mud Lake Bear was there ahead of us. Every piece of flagging ribbon was down. We put up plastic signs, too, warning people away from the sets. And those signs would be ripped down. He'd invariably trigger our snares, steal the bait, knock over the remote cameras, and generally tear up the site."

Shawn Riley claimed the Mud Lake Bear "ate cameras." And if the Olympus that Rick Mace showed me was any indication, it certainly appeared so.

"It was his standard operating procedure," Mace said, "to come to a set during the night and tear it up. He always left a trashed trap site as his calling card."

All through the rest of 1990 and 1991, biologists returned to their carefully planned and constructed sets to find them ripped asunder, the bait stolen. When 1992's spring and summer trapping season opened with the same results, Mace turned his men loose on their nemesis.

"I told them their number one priority was to catch that bear. I said the Mud Lake Bear could tell us a lot about bear behavior and use of the area—if only we could put a collar on him. But he was too smart. He wouldn't just avoid a set, he'd destroy it. Then we'd have to start all over planning the set and laying it out."

"And you never caught him?"

The project leader shook his head. "We never got him. We'd make a cubby set and put other snares around it. When he trashed them, we began making trail sets leading to our bait. At one time we had twenty-two snares set around one bait that was hanging from a center tree. And Number 146 triggered every single snare and got the bait anyway."

When I shook my head in disbelief, Mace said, "Roland, it looked to us like he picked up rocks and limbs in his mouth and dropped them on the triggers. Sometimes he pushed a sapling into a snare to spring it. However he did it, he tripped all twenty-two snares, then took the bait at his leisure." The man shook his head again and repeated, "We never did get him."

"So how about this year?" I asked.

The answer was subdued. "He's not out there."

As of September, the Mud Lake Bear hadn't destroyed one 1993 set. Neither did the study team have a heat-sensor-triggered photograph of an unusually dark-colored grizzly taken by remote cameras. For study purposes, Mace at last declared the Mud Lake Bear "dead."

If he really is dead, the grizzly died at age ten, the dominant bear in the study area. Without a radio collar, it's unlikely his fate will ever be discovered.

What lessons, if any, have we learned from the Mud Lake Bear?

"He seemed smart beyond his years," Mace mused. "Right from the outset—to come over here from the east side and do so well. He was sort of exploitive. He was a tester, he liked to test extremes of grizzly behavior. And he liked to explore. A flatlander who moved into a forested mountain setting and thrived."

Was the Mud Lake Bear hostile to humans?

Research people know of no encounter. Yet the big bear must have been exposed to humans often; his forays into the valley proved that. And it would be impossible to believe, in many cases, that Number 146 wasn't just around the corner, out of sight in the brush, waiting for trappers to leave so he could begin destroying their increasingly sophisticated attempts to capture him. All the same, there is no record of confrontation between the Mud Lake Bear and humans.

Before he left the Department of Fish, Wildlife & Parks to pursue a Cornell University PhD, Shawn Riley may have provided the most insightful analysis regarding what we may all learn from the South Fork Grizzly Study:

"It's proving they're here—perhaps more of them and nearer than we thought. We're approaching a crossroads where we must either accept that fact as desirable, or we must change this place so it's like every other place."

It seems the Mud Lake Bear had something to say about the insistence of *Ursus arctos horribilis* on being a player as the future is dealt out. And yet the big male grizzly with the "Don't Tread On Me" style is no longer available to sit in nature's game. What now?

Fortunately, the trapper's nightmare is not the only dominant male grizzly walking the woods. Nope, there's another—a bruin with many names, but best-known as the Dairy Queen Bear. Survival is his game. ∎

After guiding elk hunters to wilderness adventure for over two decades, I left the profession to devote more time to learning about grizzlies and writing of the outdoors.

Chapter 16

The Dairy Queen Bear

They call him the "Dairy Queen Bear." A charismatic name is appropriate for a charismatic bear.

He was assigned Number 22 by trappers who first snared him in the South Fork Grizzly Study. But even those professionals immediately referred to him by a descriptive nickname rather than an impersonal number. They called him "Digger."

Only the ears protruded above the trench as biologists Tim Thier and John Waller approached the snare they'd set the previous day. As grizzlies go, nervous digging when trapped isn't unusual. But this bear's pit was larger and deeper than most. And unlike other bears, except for the hole, this one hadn't thrashed about or savaged his immediate surroundings. In fact, Number 22 proved remarkably docile.

He was trapped and radio collared at age three in what biologists refer to as the "core" of the Grizzly Project's study area, the northern Swan Range from near Columbia Falls south to the Bob Marshall Wilderness boundary. From the beginning, Number 22 stretched parameters of recognized grizzly behavior.

He acquired yet another alias when kids at the Swan Valley Elementary School, participating in the Adopt-A-Grizzly program of the *Brown Bear Resources* "adopted" the young male and gave him the name "James." Tranquilized, measured, weighed, aged and radio-collared, Number 22 was released and monitored thereafter. First captured in mid-June, 1989, the young bear wandered for a couple of weeks in the mountains west of Hungry Horse Reservoir, then swam the mile-wide lake and clambered over the Flathead Range, dropping to the Flathead's Middle Fork near Spruce Park. Only a day or two later, he'd found the corn spill along U.S. Highway 2, near Marias Pass.

Climb mountains, swim lakes, all to discover delicacies attracting gaggles of grizzlies, but that he could in no way have known about. How could a young bear, only a season after being evicted by his mother, find his way over thirty miles and two mountain ranges to fermented grain spilled years before in a railway derailment?

"If you find the answer to that question," said research specialist Tim Manley, "let us know, will you?"

Even more amazing is the fact that during subsequent seasons, Number 22 never again visited the fermented corn. An alcoholic, Digger is not.

That first year after being trapped, home was where the bear's heart was. First he was attracted to huckleberries along Twin Creek, then, in late November, to an elk carcass in a Logan Creek clearcut. There he stayed. And stayed. As late as December 13, when other bears were already long-denned, Number 22 was still active. When Manley last flew over the area three days later, Digger had finally gone to bed.

Mid-December seems late for any grizzly to be out and about. I asked researchers if Number 22 delayed his denning in subsequent years and was told that in 1990 and '91 he entered hibernation by early November—typical bear behavior in northwestern Montana. The following year, however, Digger's biological clock again stuck when he became enamored by the glitz of Bigfork.

Bigfork is a quaint unincorporated village of around a thousand people located where Swan River spills into Flathead Lake. With its superb location—ready lake access and surrounded by stunning river and mountain backdrops—the community has developed into a retirement center and is becoming the cultural center for Flathead Valley.

There's considerable support amongst Bigfork's business community to maintain the village atmosphere, though occasional national franchise operations succeeds in establishing a foothold—like Subway Sandwiches and Dairy Queen.

Though Number 22 was leading a reclusive, more or less typical male grizzly existence, replete with wanderlust and few time cards to punch throughout ages four and five, he still managed to put his own spin on bear behavior—like returning to the same den for hibernation. Research indicates that *Ursus arctos horribilis* never uses the same den twice. But the one Digger dug in 1990 apparently was so comfortable he re-booked for a second Swan Range hibernation visit in 1991.

It was in 1991 that Digger first ventured over the western mountains into Flathead Valley. His sojourn was brief—a few days in late April while grazing the greening skunk cabbage and digging the bulbs of spring beauties and glacier lilies in the bottomlands that abut the Swan Range. Then it was back to his home range on the west side of Hungry Horse Reservoir as his biological clock ticked off the days until mating season.

Number 22 emerged from his twice-used den on March 13, 1992. By March 26, he'd floundered across the Swan's deep snows to feed again in the greening Flathead Valley, but returned again to his home range by mid-May. Research trapper Tim Manley, hiking in Wheeler Creek on May 13, had a face-to-face encounter with him at a mere 30 yards:

"He's very shy around humans," Manley said. "As soon as he became aware I was there, he wheeled and crashed away."

In early September, wanderlust (and perhaps hunger, since huckleberries failed because of a high country drought in 1992) drove Number 22 once again to the Flathead Valley. This time he roamed out across the Swan River near the mouth of Swan Lake, entering settled country. By September 21, Digger had moved into urban Montana, zeroing in on apple trees along the west side of the Swan Hills, just outside of Bigfork. The next evening, the bear was radio-tracked to within two hundred yards of the Bigfork Dairy Queen, prompting his latest nick-name.

He hung around for a week, then crossed the River to work along Flathead Lake as far south as Yellow Bay. He was back to his Swan Hills apples by mid-October, and there he stayed. And stayed. Few settlement residents were aware the shy nocturnal bear was around, but Fish, Wildlife & Parks people sweated, knowing a grizzly roamed close to quantities of people. Among those who knew a grizzly was in the neighborhood, opinion was mixed.

At the time of the bear's first Bigfork visit, brothers Art and Jack Whitney were eighty-three and seventy-six years old, respectively. The brothers live in adjoining homes only two blocks from the heart of Bigfork. Between them, they own four hundred acres spreading east and north from their homes into the Swan Hills. Art Whitney purchased his place 53 years ago. He recalls when it wasn't uncommon to find evidence of grizzly bears on his property. Both Whitney brothers have a wealth of outdoors experience, Art as a professional forester, Jack for over sixty years as one of the state's premier bowhunters.

Whitney apples evidently turned out to be Number 22's favorite treat as he spent most of his Bigfork sojourn on property belonging to the Whitneys. I asked Art if the bear had damaged his apple orchard.

"Oh, he broke down a few old trees, but it didn't bother me. He can have any he can get."

When asked how he felt about trapping and removing the bear, he said, "He didn't bother me, and I was hoping they'd let him stay around to go away on his own. But when I heard he was threatened—."

Art's brother Jack and his wife are partisan to the bear Jack calls Gentle Ben. Jack and Ursula Whitney are among the very few residents to actually see Number 22: "There he was," Mrs. Whitney said when I interviewed her weeks later, "right by the corner of the house! He was so—so beautiful!"

Jack cut in to say, "He was heading down to Arthur's [home] and I didn't want him to get among people, so I [opened the door and] hissed at him and, boy, did he take off!"

Jack says Gentle Ben is an exceptionally shy and timid bear. "When I saw him here at forty feet, I realized I wouldn't have any fear of him."

But when I asked Jack what he thought of Number 22's future, his answer was abrupt:

"None!"

Earlier, he had expressed the exasperation of many Montanans who resent interference from outsiders with no experience with grizzlies trying to tell them what to do:

"I don't like traffic, but I'm not going down to California and tell them to get rid of their freeways. And I don't want people to come up here and tell us to get rid of the things we have."

Mr. and Mrs. Jim Lafever's views are diametrically opposite those of the Whitneys. The couple live on Swan Hills Drive, a county road serving several small tracts and penetrating the Hills from the north. The Lafevers have lived in the Bigfork area for over twenty years. He's a carpenter; she operates Rosie's Hair Corral in their home.

Like Jack Whitney, Jim Lafever is a hunter who spends lots of time outdoors. He, too, expressed exasperation, but of a very different kind:

"I'm very much against that particular bear because he was here where kids are running around on this mountain and no one knew he was here. My wife was afraid to work in her flower garden."

He went on to say, "Rosie doesn't walk any more because she's afraid of bears and cats [mountain lions]."

Evidently Number 22 had raided the Lafevers' garbage can on two widely spaced occasions. "That's when I started hauling out our garbage every day on my way to work."

FWP Photo

#22—Digger—as four-year-old. Photo taken with Fish, Wildlife & Parks remote camera set.

Jim Lafever said he doesn't necessarily believe in the three "S's" ("shoot, shovel and shut up") where grizzly bears are concerned, but he thinks they "should stay where they belong—in Glacier Park and the Bob Marshall and Great Bear Wilderness areas."

I gathered up my notes and thanked the Lafevers for sharing their opinion. Jim's parting words were, "I'm not moving out so the grizzlies can move in!"

Quotes by the Whitneys and Lafevers were collected for a *Montana Magazine* article shortly after Number 22's visits to Bigfork were widely reported. After deciding to include a chapter on the Dairy Queen Bear for my book on grizzlies, it seemed prudent to seek out additional opinions from Bigfork-area residents. Surprisingly, from the vantage—that is, the distance—of two years' time, anti-bear sentiment was difficult to uncover. On the contrary, people I interviewed were obviously intrigued by occasional presence of a grizzly bear in their midst.

Dave Coe is a retired air traffic controller who says, "To me, it's a gift to live in a country so rich in life's quality. You can have a million dollars, but no one can buy such a gift."

Dave's wife Marlies said of the Dairy Queen Bear: "Oh, I would have loved to see him."

The Coes live but a few hundred yards north of Bigfork's Dairy Queen, in a wooded subdivision called Peaceful Acres. It's not unusual, according to the couple, to see wild animals: deer, turkey, even black bear. "Marlies had a black bear come up while she was picking strawberries," Dave told me.

"What did she do?"

"She gave up her strawberry patch to him. What else?"

"Did it bother her to give up her strawberries to a wandering bear?"

"Not at all. Seeing the bear, having him around, was a thrill to us."

Coe, though born and raised in Cleveland, Ohio, isn't exactly a newcomer, having lived for thirty of his last thirty-two years in the Treasure State. He loves to hunt and fish and says of his first assignment to Montana in 1963:

"When they came and asked if I would transfer to Great Falls, I treated the assignment like a bear nibbling apples." He still feels that way and said so emphatically: "We can maintain that quality of life here if we can learn to live with the animals."

I found that the community's response to the great grizzly invasion of 1992 had initially been mixed. The first reaction upon learning a giant grizzly roamed the byways of Bigfork was horror. Then, as days passed without incident, horror changed to humor, then quiet pride.

On September 25, Fish, Wildlife & Parks issued a press release about the grizzly frequenting the Bigfork area, then breathed a sigh of relief as the genial giant left for points south, into the boondocks of Crane Mountain. From there, they expected him to head east toward the Swan Range and his winter den. Instead, the bear returned to Bigfork and the Whitneys' apples.

The debate at Fish, Wildlife & Parks headquarters must have been fierce: Do we put out another frightening press advisory that the bear is in town? Or do we trap him and move him far away? What if he's too smart for us? What if we can't get him by trapping? What then?

FWP personnel finally snared Number 22 on November 14, nearly two months after he first came to town. At the time, the Dairy Queen Bear was the largest grizzly ever caught during the South Fork Project—650 pounds at age six. They captured him outside the study area, amid civilization.

That, you see, seems the most surprising oddity about the Dairy Queen bear. Here was a gargantuan grizzly who could take anything he wanted from anyone he wanted at any time he wanted—but didn't. When an alpine huckleberry famine brought him slumming among humans, he remained shy and retiring, nocturnal, doing everything a grizzly must do to survive amid mushrooming humans.

There are some individuals who feel Fish & Game blinked. Officials knew precisely where the bear was, knew how, when, where, and why. Perceiving that the bear was retiring around people, they hoped he'd move on to den in the rugged Swan Range high country. But, according to critics, they made the wrong choices when he was slow to do so: first with the press advisory that a grizzly bear neared Bigfork, then with the decision to trap and remove.

But perhaps we ought to consider what pressure must have been upon those responsible. After all, their debate was about a grizzly bear amid people. Under the wrong circumstances, it's an animal that can maim and marinate all in one lazy motion. Imagine the hue and cry if the Dairy Queen Bear had chosen to open up the Dairy Queen, either during or outside working hours. What if a child was injured?

For that matter, what if some frightened property owner shot the bear? Was the decision as much for the bear's sake as for the humans surrounding him? After all, biologists did allow the bear to roam the roads of Bigfork for nearly two months. How much blood are responsible managers and biologists expected to sweat?

"Take the bear's radio collar off," one interviewee said. "They can't worry about his being here if they don't know."

Fish, Wildlife & Parks trappers transported the giant bear nearly one hundred and fifty road miles from Bigfork. They dropped him off near the Continental Divide, south of Glacier National Park.

Apparently confused after release, Digger wandered over the Divide, into waters that flowed to the Atlantic. Biologists radio-tracking the bear worried that he might stray beyond the moun-

FWP Photo

Digger, also at Mud Lake. Photo taken by FWP remote camera, April 25, 1992.

tainous part of the Two Medicine drainage into ranchland border-
ing the Rocky Mountain Front, or even onto the Blackfeet
Reservation.

But he's a traveling bear, that Digger. Both the Flathead's
South and Middle Fork drainages are over a hundred miles long.
Mountain ranges tower between. Yet clambering twenty miles
over ten-foot snowdrifts and eight-thousand-foot mountain peaks
took Digger little more effort than one evening's stroll.

At last getting his compass set, the big bear turned from the
eastern plains to homing strains. He journeyed through ever-
deepening snow, over two mountain ranges, to his old stomping
grounds, to a mountain thrusting to the sky east of Hungry Horse
Reservoir. There he dug his den beneath the roots of a huge
spruce tree on the shady side of the mountain. Digger entered the
den for his winter's sleep on December 14, 1992.

A widely accepted truism about grizzlies is that when an
abundant food source is discovered, a bear never forgets its location. Biologists fully expected Number 22 to hone in on Bigfork
upon emerging from his den in the spring. Instead, the bear confounded his trackers by remaining in the mountains surrounding
Hungry Horse Reservoir clear through and beyond the May/June
breeding season. It wasn't as if the Dairy Queen Bear had difficult
choices to make; 1993 proved to be a bumper year for huckleberries everywhere. And it wasn't until mid-July that the big bear
wandered over the Swan crest to work his way through one huckleberry patch after another, down to the valley floor.

Moving always at night, the secretive giant made a swift
August trip through his relished haunts of the previous year, then
resolutely set his nose to the east for the alpine huckleberries he
preferred over the still-green jonathon and winesap apples growing in the Whitney orchards.

In midsummer of 1994, I asked Rick Mace, South Fork
Grizzly Study team leader, what facts subsequent radio-tracking
had disclosed about Digger.

"Actually, he's been pretty boring."

By 1994, Number 22 (alias Digger, James, Gentle Ben, the Dairy Queen Bear) was considered by biologist-trappers to be the dominant male in the study area. Huckleberries, though spotty, were generally adequate. And though he twice ranged into the foothills and fringes of Flathead Valley—once in the spring and again in the fall—the bear proved to be as reclusive as ever.

"Why hasn't he gone back to the apple orchards around Bigfork?" I asked.

Mace smiled. "Maybe—just maybe he hasn't had to. Maybe he never really wanted to be there in the first place. Maybe he fed there to survive."

Maybe, maybe not.

I want to believe this bumbling giant is really such a consummate survivor. After all, he's nearing eleven years of age as this chapter is being written in the spring of 1996—as old as the crafty Mud Lake Bear when he disappeared; as old as most male grizzlies live to be in the wild. Maybe this is one male grizzly who is taking care of himself so well he'll exceed the normal dozen-year life span of his contemporaries, to approximate the twenty-five-year cycle of the females.

This big aging bruin has been trapped many times and shows not nearly the ursine aversion to the experience. As batteries fade and his neck size expands, he's been fitted with many radio collars, and he's been pinpointed with more radio-location fixes than any other grizzly in the study. Through the close monitoring of his movements through those fixes, Number 22 has provided a plethora of information about bear behavior previously unknown to researchers. During his long life he has often encountered humans, but hasn't been killed because he somehow senses when to retreat. Evidently, the huge bear knows when to hold them and when to fold them.

The incident with the dead horse up on the Red Owl Road is a classic example. Apparently some person or persons unknown abandoned a horse carcass near the end of a forest road. An innocent deer hunter rounded a bend and came eyeball-to-eyeball with a mammoth grizzly lying across the horse carcass. Hunter and grizzly stared at each other for several seconds while the man's knees turned to jelly. Then, showing none of the rage displayed by many bears to a perceived threat to their food source, the giant bruin rose to his feet and ambled into the brush while a panting hunter leaned on his rifle and took great gasps of air so sweet only one experiencing close encounters of a bear kind can ever know.

A swift call to Fish, Wildlife & Parks and a quick telemetry check pinpointed Digger on the Red Owl Road, near the dead horse. The carcass was removed, and doing so removed another threat to a bear that's becoming legendary.

Take 1995:

It was another year of mountain huckleberry failure. This time Digger didn't even bother to rotate between high and low country; after all, it was in the lowlands that he found his best foodstuffs. Now, however, the genial giant wasn't alone in his forays to farmland, for trackers monitored a four-year-old male whose radio signals matched locations with Digger's. An apprentice was learning the ropes from the master! Then came the bear invasion. There was the sow with cubs, raiding bird feeders and rural garbage cans in the foothills area between mountain and macadam. And another four-year-old male was trapped behind Mountain Brook School. And a pair of three-year-old twins were trapped from the Swan Hills. What the hell was going on here?

But Number 22 was — and is — seldom seen, his passage hardly known.

FWP Photo

Dairy Queen Bear after capture, prior to being trucked to distant release site. At the time, number 22 weighed 650 pounds—the largest bear trapped during the study. He'd spent the last couple of months feeding on Whitney's apples.

Royce and Ruth Satterlee are Jane's and my hiking companions. They know. The Satterlees live on a narrow isthmus of land between two glacial pothole lakes, Loon and Horseshoe. The isthmus appears to be a favored travel route for the Dairy Queen Bear, and it's not uncommon for the giant to leave his calling card—a mammoth dump in the middle of their driveway. My wife and I are usually among the first to hear about it.

"Have you any information about Digger?" Royce will ask, knowing I'm often in contact with biologists.

"Has he been around your place again?"

"Night before last. He left his mark."

Yet neither the Satterlees nor any of their neighbors have ever seen the genial giant.

There's little doubt Number 22 is an ursine anomaly. Supposedly, bears always return to abundant food sources, yet Digger seems erratic. He visited the grain spill, yet never returned. He found abundant apples during a time of hunger, yet did not return until a second huckleberry famine occurred. Does he have reasons for his untypical behavior? He's used the same den twice for hibernation—extremely rare among grizzlies. Instead of flying into a rage when his horse carcass cache was threatened, he abandoned it without resistance.

Thus far, the Dairy Queen Bear has proven unusually opportunistic, extremely canny and star-crossed lucky. One wonders, is it possible Number 22 is a bear of the future? Has the Dairy Queen Bear exhibited exactly the type of behavior all grizzlies must adopt to survive amid the mushrooming human populations that are predicted to double within the next sixty years? Who can say.

I can say this, however: I hope the riveting drama of Number 22 is far from over. ∎

Richard Jackson

Curious bear.

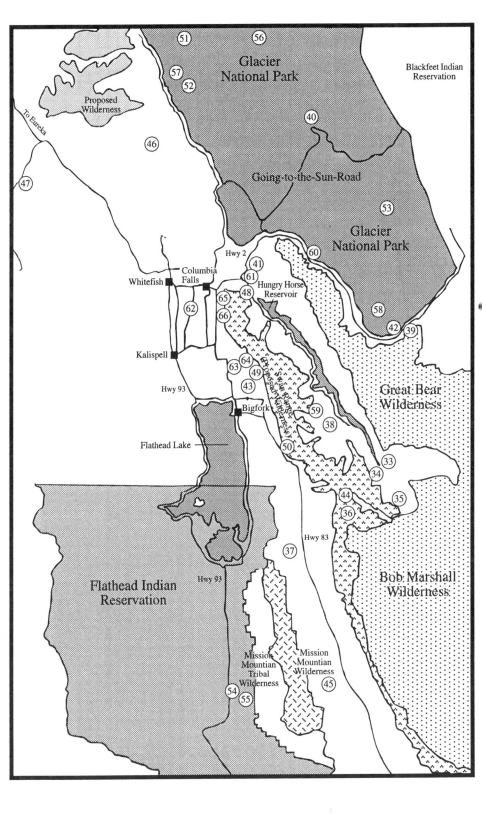

Richard Jackson

Angry bear.

Chapter 17

Family Saga

This is a family saga, the story of a mother, two daughters, a grandson, and a granddaughter. Theirs is a tale of pathos, humor, and tragedy. It's also one of vandalism verging on violence; and it's a story of exhaustive research and authoritative investigating. But most of all, it's a tale of survival. As evocative and intriguing as the story may be, however, its primary value is to raise a question: *Was the effort and expense of trying to rehabilitate problem bears worth both their vandalism, and their very real risk to humans who might have unwittingly encountered them?*

The bear had been hanging around for a month, coming usually in the dead of night to clean up left-over horse and dog food. She soon graduated to breaking and entering outbuildings in search of grain and horse pellets. Complaints were made.

The old Blankenship homestead is at the confluence of the Flathead's North and Middle Forks. North and east of the two rivers is a little-traveled corner of Glacier National Park, secure habitat at its very best for grizzlies. The entire surrounding land is home to one of the largest concentrations of the great bears in the lower 48. Northwest of Blankenship, the country is largely Flathead National Forest. To the south and southwest, along both sides of the river, are isolated rural homes and private woodlots.

The capture form was filled out by Louis M. Kis, Warden Captain for Region I, Montana Department of Fish, Wildlife & Parks. The document was brief. It listed the grizzly's sex as female, its reproductive status as no cubs, its condition as excellent, its age as 8-1/2.

The bear's offense was described as, "generally too close to homes and children."

There was a time, a few years before, when this bear would've been swiftly destroyed. But with a change in emphasis from grizzly removal to grizzly survival, reproductive females were considered doubly important; a decision was made to give the sow a second chance.

The warden captain also recorded the release: Distance moved 50 air miles, release personnel were listed as "Kis & Cross," release site was "N. Fork of Bunker Creek, end of road—Sub Alpine."

The document detailed drug dosage, number and color of ear tags, and type and frequency of radio collar installed. The date was September 27, 1985.

According to subsequent data gathered from radio telemetry, the female's rehabilitation seemed to go well. She moved south through some of the roughest country in the Bob Marshall Wilderness to the area around Big Salmon Lake, where, during the deep sleep of winter, she gave birth to twin female cubs. All through spring, summer, and autumn of 1986, the family group roamed the tough mountain terrain south and east of Swan Peak. But sometime during her next hibernation, the sow lost her collar. By spring of 1987 the family moved north of the Wilderness boundary, where all three were snared by trappers working as members of the new South Fork Grizzly Study team. Each bear was ear-tagged, radio-collared, and, as the initial animals trapped during the project, assigned numbers 1, 2, and 3.

A month later, the three grizzlies made their first raid on an unattended outfitter camp. By the following spring, the family moved into the Spotted Bear area, feeding on remnant grain from ranger-station and guest-ranch corrals. In early May, they'd trekked across the still snow-clad Swan Range and into the valley beyond. There the clan crossed Swan Highway 83, just north of the Goat Creek Youth Center. The story of the matriarch, Number 1, ends near Fatty Creek—a case of mistaken identity by a black-bear hunter from Florida.

The two sibling females, now two and a half years old and able to fend for themselves, returned to familiar territory. By late May, they'd drifted apart, and they eventually staked out claims to portions of their mother's former range.

Number 2, was now known as "Jessie" to children at the Swan Valley Elementary School, who "adopted" her in the course of their participation in the Brown Bear Resources educational program. Jessie selected the food-abundant low country around Spotted Bear, Meadow Creek, and Bunker Creek—a territory with considerable potential for conflict with humans. Number 3 chose to spend most of her time in the Swan Range's remote high country.

There was little to report about the siblings during the remainder of 1988, as the young females engaged in run-of-the-mill bear pursuits: digging roots and tubers in the marshlands and avalanche paths, grazing succulent grasses, scrounging carrion, and feeding on berries. They were three years old by 1989, and in mid-May, during the breeding season, Number 2 was observed near two male grizzlies. She was recaptured by the study team in June, fitted with another collar, and released. Oddly, she and her sister partnered up through much of October, then drifted apart forever.

Number 2 emerged from hibernation with one female and one male cub at her side. She headed straight for the food-rich riverbottoms around Spotted Bear Ranger Station and the three guest ranches nearby.

Cautious because of her tiny cubs—but perhaps also desperate because of them—she took up the activities learned from her mother, searching for food near humans, raiding garbage cans and stored grain. One such cache was a dumpster where remnants of deer and elk carcasses had been carelessly tossed after the previous hunting season and not yet hauled away in the spring.

As her offspring grew from cubs of the year to yearling bears, the family became ever more conditioned to humans and human foods. The yearlings were trapped, ear-tagged, radio-collared, and assigned numbers 32 and 33. Striking always at night, usually in the absence of forest rangers, camp tenders or lodge guests, the bears turned into more than mere nuisances.

An advisory letter to guest ranches and area outfitters dated September 24, 1992, makes their activities plain:

> Between September 14 and 17 a grizzly bear attempted to gain access to a feed storage trailer at the Meadow Creek Trailhead. The bear was unsuccessful in accessing the grain, but did damage the trailer. Shortly after this, around September 19 a grizzly bear entered a barn in the Spotted Bear area several times while stock was in an adjacent corral and people were sleeping nearby. Once in the barn the bear did find and eat some horse pellets."

The letter went on to emphasize the importance of securing human provisions and horse feed from bears and suggested that methods were being developed to minimize bear/human contacts.

A late-October release from Montana's Department of Fish, Wildlife & Parks provided a further update on activities of the family:

> A 2-1/2-year-old female grizzly is on her way to a zoo [in Oregon] after being recaptured near the Spotted Bear Ranch on October 14 by Montana Department of Fish, Wildlife and Parks Bear Warden Dave Wedum. The grizzly had been captured in the same area in late September after getting into a barn and eating livestock feed."

The report told how young Number 32 was first relocated to the Ear Mountain Wildlife Management Area northeast of Choteau. The zoo in Oregon must have seemed like an ideal solution to the problem after the juvenile bruin, traveling crosscountry from Ear Mountain through one of the wildest sections of the northern Rockies, nearly beat wildlife officers, driving their four-wheel-drive truck, back to Spotted Bear. Then the report revealed the fate of Number 33, the young male:

> . . .the female grizzly is the sibling of a young male trapped and destroyed earlier this year. Both bears

were involved in damage to camps, horse trailers and guest ranches in the Spotted Bear area. The mother of these bears is known to have a long history of habituation to human-use areas.

Habituation? Yes, indeed.

"There was a hunting camp about two miles up the Spotted Bear River," one of the Grizzly Study's team members explained. "They had horses and tents more or less like any hunting camp. But they started getting hit by a bear. So they put horse pellets out in the woods—pounds and pounds of horse feed—to keep the grizzly away from their camp."

When I stopped laughing, I asked, "You mean they tried to save themselves from being hassled by a grizzly bear by feeding it?"

The researcher nodded and drummed his fingers on the table. He wasn't smiling.

What each news release about the cubs failed to portray adequately was that their mother was still alive and well—and still out there. The reason no information was forthcoming about Number 2 was because she had lost her collar and no one had a clue to her whereabouts.

It seemed clear that mom was keeping a low profile. At least there were no remote camera photos of Jessie throughout the fall of '92, nor was she identified in any photos taken the following spring.

South Fork Grizzly Study trappers did capture Number 2 on May 30, 1993, but failed to identify her as the missing bear. She'd lost her ear tags, and because a lip tattoo had apparently faded away, the men did not recognize her as the lost Jessie. It was only later, while monitoring the newly trapped bear's movements, did they realize she followed the same patterns as that of Number 2.

Meanwhile, out in southwestern Oregon, Number 2's female offspring, Number 32—dubbed "Trouble" by her zoo handlers—made news in a daring break from confinement. According to a May 7, 1993, story in Kalispell's *The Daily Interlake*, picked up from an AP report:

> *Oregon officials were trying today to recapture an escaped grizzly bear that had been banished to a game farm there after it perfected its acrobatic and trap-dodging skills near Spotted Bear.*

The young grizzly confounded authorities by squeezing through a nine-by-thirty-inch hole that was seven feet off the ground. "We feel it is still in the locale," said Lieutenant Larry Belcher of the Oregon State Police.

Weeks elapsed without a trace of the escaped bruin. A joke made the rounds at Spotted Bear that the young female would soon be back, raiding camps and horse trailers in the area.

Finally, an Associated Press release out of Grants Pass, Oregon, datelined September 5, reported officials declaring the escaped grizzly as missing and probably dead. Those officials had egg on their faces the very next day as headlines blazed that a grizzly bear was killed by Oregon black-bear hunters who claimed she charged them.

"Trouble" had traveled over forty miles north across rugged mountain ranges to the South Umpqua River Valley. There, she'd reverted to form, breaking and entering unoccupied summer homes and barns, even ripping up a mobile home.

The hunters claimed they hadn't known they faced a grizzly bear until after the shooting stopped and the animal lay dead just a few feet from them.

Fate sometimes seems like a series of coincidences. It was in the Umpqua River Valley of southwestern Oregon where as a stripling, I faced my first black bear while gopher hunting with a single-shot .22. The "100 Valleys of the Umpqua" was where I went through an important personal rite of passage in respecting wildlife—on a day when I passed a threshold of compassion and maturity by refraining from stoning a cub to hear it whimper.

Even more odd is that one of my former Oregon hunting companions owns a ranch just a few miles from where Number 32 died. Willis Weaver was fishing the beaver ponds with me when we spotted a sow grizzly and her cubs—a grizzly whose unexpected behavior I described earlier in this book; the one that let herself be scared off by a scrawny black bear boar. Will sent me a clipping about Number 32's demise. He'd scribbled an accompanying note suggesting that I "keep my grizzly bears home."

While federal wildlife officials debated whether to prosecute the Oregon hunters for shooting an animal protected under the Endangered Species Act, another of the great bears made news back home. First, a grizzly was seen rocking a horse trailer in the Spotted Bear area, apparently in an attempt to reach horse pellets locked behind its doors. Then it was reported that a bear rocked a camper trailer near Spotted Bear while its owner quailed inside. And finally a bear adopted a most innovative method to gain entry—removing windows from unattended vehicles in order to pilfer food caches locked within.

Grizzly Study team leader Rick Mace at last realized they were dealing with their old nemesis when he matched the habits of a bear trapped earlier to the radio-location patterns of missing Number 2.

"It became almost like a cocaine addiction for this bear," Mace said. "The harder humans made it for Number 2 to find food, the harder she worked at getting to it. She seemed to go to all possible extremes."

No charges were filed against the Oregon hunters after Number 32's carcass was examined by a forensics laboratory and four bullet holes were found, all in the front. "Trouble" had indeed charged the hunters. Thus ended her role in the family saga.

And Number 2's vehicle rampages ended September 18, 1993, when she was snared for the last time and sent to a Texas zoo.

I picked up my notes and stored the tape recorder as the South Fork Grizzly Study team leader drummed his fingers again on the conference table. The man looked as if he had more to say.

"Something you'd like to add, Rick?"

"Nooo. No, I guess not." Then his eyes met mine. "Unless you'd want to ask if the results were worth the effort, to say nothing of the expense."

Rick's question haunted me, as it haunted him. Enormous effort and expense went into attempting to rehabilitate bear Number 1 and her offspring, as well as Number 2's offspring. Great efforts went into what Warden Captain Louis Kis's capture-and-release document titled "A Nuisance Grizzly Bear." During the experiment, the bears caused considerable damage to private property and posed substantial risk to human life. So it's appropriate for Rick Mace to ask the question: *Was the effort worth it?*

A knee-jerk reaction might be to say no. Number 1 was a nuisance grizzly with undesirable habits she passed on to Number 2, who then passed on those habits to Numbers 32 and 33. Attempts at rehabilitating all four bears failed. Each was ultimately removed from the system. Dollars have been expended on a grand experiment that fizzled.

Oh? But aren't we forgetting Number 3? Remember, the original female—grizzly Number 1—had two cubs, not one. Is Number 3 still out there? Though she lost her collar in May of 1991 and has never been recaptured, Rick Mace feels she is not only alive and well, but has cubs at her side. What makes him think so?

"Where she lives, we had a series of snares set out this spring. And our bait sets were getting hit by a very, very smart bear with a lot of history behind her—a brilliant bear!"

"Well, how do you know it's even a female?"

"There were cub tracks, too."

Number 3's habitat is not frequented by humans. And though she is her mother's daughter, a very smart bear, she has never been known to vandalize human camps, human food stocks, or human buildings. Yet without the effort made to rehabilitate Number 1, there would be no Number 3. Nor would there be offspring from this exemplary bear.

Too, what value should we apply to our own gain in knowledge and experience? Have we learned enough from this nuisance family saga to advance other efforts to rehabilitate similar bears?

So, how about it now? Were the results worth the effort? ■

Chapter 18

Another Perspective?

Doug Chadwick is everything I'm not. His hair is dark and curly; mine is mostly gone and what's there is shot with gray. His body is chiseled from granite; mine is less muscle than meat. He's handsome, debonair, articulate before crowds; I whine and stammer if I receive an invitation to a church social.

The guy exhibits the youth and vigor of a man twenty years my junior. But why not? He *is* twenty years my junior; a pup, still, with plenty of thump left in his tail. He holds a master's degree in biology; I never finished high school. He studied mountain goats in the high country at an age when I ogled girls at hamburger joints.

Oh, I may have a tad more outdoors experience because I've lived longer and for decades made my living as a guide. But his outdoors has been far more varied: the Himalayas, Borneo, Sonoran Desert, Arctic Wildlife Refuge, South Sea Islands, Serengeti, Denali, Baja.

He's a fine writer, often on overseas assignment for top publications utilizing both his writing talent and his training as a biologist. He has several extraordinarily fine books to his credit. With Doug Chadwick so often on assignment in foreign lands and me wrapped in my guiding business for decades, perhaps it's understandable that, although we lived only a few miles apart, there was little time to maintain a close friendship. But I've cherished our too-seldom chances to rap.

I'd just been charged by my first bear, and we were chatting, Doug and I. Politely, he waited for me to finish my tale before beginning his own. As well as I recall, this is that tale from fifteen years ago:

Chadwick was working on a mountain-goat study project deep in Glacier National Park. His research required him to travel to a remote portion of the Park, and he hiked a seldom traveled trail. It was a hot July day, with temperatures hovering in the nineties. Because he planned to be out for a week, his backpack weighed upwards of sixty pounds. Sweat ran down the small of his back, so he paused, slipped off his shirt and trousers, and continued up the trail wearing only hiking boots and a pair of polka-dot boxer shorts.

Naturally, he still toted the heavy backpack and the cumbersome .44 magnum revolver that Park biologists, in those days, were permitted to carry for protection against dangerous wildlife. The holstered magnum was belted around his middle.

Doug rounded a trail bend, head down, walking hard, breathing hard. A sow grizzly and two cubs fed on greening shoots near the trail. She charged!

Doug did what I had done when charged by a bear—waved his arms and shouted at the top of his voice. As happened with me, the grizzly broke off the charge just a few feet away, turned, and with neck hair still standing, walked stiffly away. Then, like my bear, she roared and wheeled to charge again. She broke off her second rush at little more than two arm-lengths' distance to walk huffily back up-trail, gather her youngsters underfoot, and disappear into the bush.

Time passed as the young man gulped great mouthfuls of air. With a start he remembered the heavy revolver hanging at his side—the .44 magnum with enough wallop to stop a charging grizzly bear in its tracks.

"You just can't imagine the rush of adrenaline that comes with a charging grizzly. I had to burn some of it off. So as soon as I was sure the bears were gone, I took off, walking up the trail as fast as I could, shouting the first thing that came to mind at the top of my voice."

"And what was that?"

"Nursery rhymes. Don't ask me why—I was hiking up this remote trail in the middle of Glacier Park as fast as I could, shouting nursery rhymes. And I rounded another trail bend, and you know what was there?"

"What?"

"Two guys standing in the middle of the trail, holding each other for support. Their eyes were as big as saucers and they looked like Sitka deer quivering to bolt."

Doug paused while I thumped the ground in glee. Then he continued:

"Well, they both took one look at me in boxer shorts and a belted six-gun, spouting nursery rhymes at the top of my voice, and they took off at a gallop back the way they'd come. I tried to catch them to explain what happened, but I never did see 'em again."

On another occasion, Doug and I had a chat when he had just returned from Nepal, where he'd been on assignment for *National Geographic*. We talked that day of the dangers inherent in traveling grizzly country, and his experiences and observations in Nepal. Those observations contained a lesson I'll never forget:

"Karen [his wife] and I floated the Indus River in skin kayaks. Even in Nepal, near its headwaters, the Indus is muddy. We'd drift around a river bend and see twelve-foot crocodiles slide from the clay bank into the river, then we'd float over the spot and see air bubbles rising to the surface and know he was down there somewhere. And we knew there was nothing between us and him except a skin kayak. It was eerie."

Doug paused to collect his thoughts as I shivered. "And you know what else they've got in that country?"

"What?"

"They've got five-ton elephants that can step on you and leave nothing but a grease spot. There are two-ton rhinos in the canebrakes that will charge at the slightest sound and gore you into pulp. They've got ten-foot snakes that, if they strike you, you've got about fifteen seconds left to live."

He paused and I muttered, "Go on."

"There are striped cats as big as our grizzly bears that blend with the scenery and move as silently as a shadow stealing across the forest." His voice trailed off, and he seemed to be deep in thought.

"And?" I prompted.

"And they've got little brown men—millions of 'em—running around in that jungle barefoot, wearing nothing but loincloths. And there's almost no elephants or rhinoceros or tigers left. The reason crocodiles slipped into the water at our approach was because they're being hunted and hounded by those men. And you can wander their jungle for years without running up against a cobra."

Silence fell between us as I absorbed the lesson and he relived memories. At last, Chadwick muttered, "So maybe we've got to put the grizzly bear in perspective." ∎

Chapter 19

The Grizzly Daughter
I Never Had

He was trapped. The smoothly professional biologist with the precise, polished, and admirably clear answers seemed at a loss.

"Rick, you say all but perhaps two females out of dozens in the study live shy, reclusive lives." I glanced at my notes. "Your precise words were 'She was boring.' You said, 'Number 5, in boringness, seems typical of all but a couple of females in the study.' But you also say Number 5 was somehow special to you. It doesn't make sense."

The South Fork Grizzly Study team leader hesitated before nodding. I pushed: "So let's try the question one more time. Why your affinity—your affection or whatever—for Number 5?"

The biologist studied his folded hands. When the answer came, the man's voice quivered:

"Have you ever walked into, say, a day-care center or a schoolroom and there's this little kid over in the corner? You don't know who he is, but he's got these sparkly blue eyes and you make visual contact. And something clicks inside."

Rick Mace paused and looked up with a sheepish grin. "She taught me about the big bears. It was through her that I chose to learn a lot about grizzlies." He took a deep breath. "She was the daughter—the grizzly daughter—I never had."

Bear Number 5 was trapped in 1987, just three weeks into the study. She was snared by Mace himself on a small mountain, completely surrounded by roads and human activities—and, as it turned out, surrounded by other grizzly bears.

Weighed, aged, and fitted with a radio collar, Number 5 was released and monitored thereafter. With over 320 location fixes on the shy female throughout the study's first six years, she became the most closely monitored of the fifty-odd bears thus far trapped and collared. Biologists knew the exact dimensions of her home range, her feeding habits, hibernation sites, security spots. They knew the elevation levels she utilized during each season of the year and how she avoided human presence. And they knew how other bears encroached with impunity upon her scant but vital range.

It was evident early on that Number 5 faced stiff competition for survival. Clearcut logging patchworked her home range. Haul roads and skid trails crisscross the mountain's drainages and wind up its slopes. During summer, huckleberry pickers comb roadside and hill. During fall, valleys echo with whistling challenges from bull elk, and ridgetops sparkle with orange-clad humans. The sounds of gunshots are not at all alien to creatures inhabiting her tiny domain.

Number 5 —"The grizzly daughter I never had"— a year after her first capture. Note collar and ear tags. Taken with FWP remote camera.

To compound her problem, a key portion of the reclusive bear's home range turned out to be the Swan Mountains' single most important boudoir for mating grizzly bears. Perhaps more ominous, the home ranges of other big bruins overlapped hers, and they included aggressive bears not inclined to be tolerant of a retiring female scratching for survival.

Scrutinizing monitored locations during the six study years demonstrates the shy bear's squeeze: just fourteen percent of her time was spent below five thousand feet where vegetation is more lush and food usually more plentiful; forty-eight percent was spent between five thousand and six thousand feet, and thirty-eight percent was spent at elevations over six thousand. But during her last three years, time spent amid the more food-abundant lower levels declined dramatically—to eleven percent below five thousand and thirty-nine percent between five thousand and six thousand. During her last three years, Number 5 spent half her foraging time *above* six thousand feet.

Seven years old and of breeding age when first snared, Number 5 was distinctive by her lack of cubs. Neither did she emerge from her den with cubs in the spring of 1988. That's why researchers were jubilant when, in the spring of 1989, Number 5 showed up with a single cub snuggling hard against her leg. The shy bear's rotten luck held, however, and her growing cub disappeared in mid-October.

Came the dawn of the '90s and Number 5 still lived a solitary life, largely relegated to the upper third of a single mountain. It wasn't until the spring of 1991 that the shy eleven-year-old female again emerged from the den with nurslings—this time not one but two cubs. Only one of those twins made it until fall. That single cub emerged with its mother as a yearling in the spring of 1992, however. And finally, her one successful cub, now a capable two-year-old, was turned loose to fend for itself as autumn leaves turned to gold.

As Number 5 entered her '92 den, she at last seemed on track—a mature 13-year-old with maternal experience. Perhaps the worst was behind the timid female and her future would be long and fruitful.

The spring and summer of 1993 were among the wettest on record, even into the fall. As a consequence, aerial reconnaissance was spotty for bear researchers. And for Number 5, there's a tragic three-week gap from September 17 until her collar was retrieved on October 13, when the reclusive female's movements went unrecorded. When researchers reached the site of what they hoped was a slipped collar, they found only scattered remains. A report by investigators stated that "numerous species had been feeding on the carcass, including grizzly bear, black bear, mountain lion, and coyote."

Rick Mace's grizzly daughter was no more.

It's ironic that in life Number 5 provided so much information, but in death, none. So scant were the remains that not even cause of death is known. The investigative report said, "It appeared as though a grizzly bear had buried the carcass." But whether the shy bear was actually killed by another grizzly cannot be determined. Could her death be human-related? Possibly, but:

"The carcass was approximately 300 meters from a double-gated, permanently closed tertiary road and cutting unit. I observed no evidence of recent human travel." There were no horse prints, no boot tracks in the mud, no dirt-bike marks.

It may be appropriate, however, to recall the lengthy lapse between the last recorded monitoring and the discovery of Number 5's remains. That lapse included an entire week of track-washing rains.

Is it possible the shy bear died from stress? The man who was closest to the bear thinks so:

"Knowing where she lived, the relationship she had with other bears surrounding her, the level of human activities—roads, logging, hunting, berry pickers, all within her home range—suggested she was going to have a stressful life."

I asked about her marginal ability to raise cubs. The study leader shrugged. "Here's a shy bear that's trying to make it, maybe with a couple of cubs. And the only real spring opportunity she has is to take them where five or six males and a bunch of other female bears are going to be coming in. Or her other choice is down where there's a lot of open roads, hunting activity, and a lot of humans running around. She could very easily have sat up on that mountain and said, 'Which way do I go?'"

The man paused, then added, "Or maybe she was just a poor mother."

There's little doubt that grizzly bear Number 5 offered a dramatically different portrait than have others in these profiles of South Fork Grizzly Study bears. Charisma? Compared to most everybody's hands-down favorite—the big, clever, ghost-like Dairy Queen Bear—Number 5 wasn't even in the same league. Neither did she elicit the grudging admiration for shrewd intelligence and vengeful daring of the snare-springing Mud Lake Bear. Nor did she achieve the renown of the camp raiding family group that included the bear nicknamed "Trouble." The mere fact that Number 5, the longest-running bear in the study — until she died — never achieved a high enough profile to earn a nickname says something.

But is the life of grizzly bear Number 5 an aberration or the norm? Shy and retiring, studiously—perhaps desperately—avoiding contact with both humans and other grizzlies, beset by pressures of human development and possibly too-dense bear populations (though researchers aren't yet ready to accept that suggestion), Number 5 survived for over thirteen years. That fact might be a tribute to a timid but courageous sow dwelling on the margin.

One wonders if there's more to be learned from her than from more charismatic bears. How much can be understood about

Rick Mace's "grizzly daughter I never had" (left) and her one single offspring raised to maturity. Biologists consider it possible this young female consumed her dead mother. Taken with FWP remote camera.

wild bear behavior from food-conditioned garbage raiders; from a huge boar who attacks man's traps with vindictive glee; from big, bumbling "Digger," the Dairy Queen Bear? Isn't it much more to the point to discover how a reticent, low-on-the-pecking-order sow survives against deplorable odds? Might it not be more important to discover root causes and effects leading to her stress, and possibly to her demise?

Grizzly Number 5 was distinctly different from the other big carnivores I've described. But so do most of the other bears profiled in this book differ from the slavering, blood-dripping monsters standing over scantily-clad maidens that pepper many books about bears. That's because the bears presented here are the real bears; others are aberrations. Monster maiden-slavering grizzlies no more represent the ursid world than Jack the Ripper represented genteel British society.

Individually, the bears in this book can tell us little. Collectively, they tell us much. If we're lucky, they—and others— will provide enough information so that we can make course corrections that can aid in retaining a sustainable population of the big bears. That's what the South Fork Grizzly Study is all about, and why it's contributing enormously to our rich—and very much American—quality of life.

Number 5 is gone now, and from her we'll learn no more. Or will we? In all her years, Number 5 successfully raised only one cub. That cub, officially listed as Number 17, took over her mother's home range. Number 17 is also radio-collared and monitored. Early location fixes on Number 17 seem to indicate the young bear's territorial aspirations might be more extensive than her mother's; twenty percent of her monitored locations are below five thousand feet, just ten percent above six thousand.

Does this mean Number 5's daughter is more aggressive than her mother? Is it possible the grizzly bear who fed on the remains of Number 5 was her own daughter? Or—even more unthinkable—is it possible the daughter killed her mother?

What's more important, will the daughter be more successful at propagating her species? Or will she even survive as long as her mother? A great many questions are still to be answered. It's a loss to us all that Number 5 failed just one time in her timid, retiring quest for survival. It's our tragedy that we don't know why. ■

Chapter 20

The Grizzly's Strange Life Cycle

It was March 22nd. The sun had long ago begun its swing back to the north. Amid the northern Rockies, daylight, for the first time since September, equalled the hours of darkness.

Down in the valleys, only remnant snowbanks remained. But atop distant mountains, ten-foot drifts still blocked ridgetop trails and twenty-foot cornices hung perilously from lee-side cliff faces. Yet even up there, warming winds puffed fitfully and a steady drip, drip, presaged spring.

On a north-and-east-facing slope as steep as the roof of a Swiss chalet there stood a copse of gnarled whitebark pine. One particular expanse of snow at the base of a pine lifted and wobbled and convulsed, and finally erupted as a shiny black snout thrust free, followed seconds later by a shaggy furred head as large as a beach ball.

The head lolled to one side. A minute, two, ten, twenty. Then more snow flew as shoulders and torso burst onto the white land. Soon a gargantuan grizzly bear lay beside the exit hole, panting, still lethargic after the winter's sleep.

The pungent odor from the hole was overpowering—the result of four months and five days of close confinement. Shadows stole across the silent, snowclad forest as the giant sprawled at his den entrance, occasionally lifting his massive head to gaze into the darkening forest, nose testing wind currents. At last he struggled to his feet and staggered seventy-five yards to the spreading limbs of a half-grown spruce. He crawled beneath and within seconds was fast asleep.

Daylight drove the great beast to his feet and, with his metabolism accelerating, he bee-lined down the slope and into a glacial cirque where a tiny snowmelt rivulet was also emerging from its winter's sleep.

His thirst quenched, the mighty beast again lifted his nose to the breeze, then plodded across the bottom of the cirque's headwall toward the far ridge and the gentle basin beyond. By then the sun blazed down, softening the snow's surface until the five-hundred-pound bruin broke through with every other stride.

A sudden crack came from above. The bear paused for a second, then exploded into a rolling, floundering gallop as a collapsing snow cornice plunged onto the nearly perpendicular slope of unstable snow, triggering an avalanche.

The cascade swiftly gathered momentum, funneling first into a chute, then fanning out below, ripping and carrying ten- and twenty-foot trees, thousand-pound boulders, and huge blocks of snow along its front. The bounding, stumbling grizzly plunged into a copse of large spruce trees with just seconds to spare. In the safety of the thicket, he stopped and turned to watch as the giant snowslide roared past.

Eight hours later the bear was still in the same place, sprawled on his belly, with nose and muzzle stretching across forepaws. Moonbeams filtered through the towering forest to sparkle in his fur. A deep chill settled across the land, but the bear, still in winter pelage, seemed not to notice. At last, the animal raised his snout to downwind currents, then came easily to his feet. He stretched and again tested the wind before plodding on his way, across snow frozen enough to support his weight.

The bruin crossed a spur ridge, striking a man-trail. Though the path was still buried beneath ten feet of snow, it was clear of logs and trees and brush and followed the land's contours to provide the best travel route between two points. At a switchback, another bear slept, still buried beneath a snowfield two hundred yards to the east, in a den filtered by the roots of a mammoth whitebark pine. Unaware that another of his kind was denned beneath the pine, the big boar turned at the switchback, following the path used many times.

He crossed the mountain rampart's main spine at three a.m. and was into the foothills by daylight, seventeen miles from where he'd begun his evening stroll. He paused, virtually invisible in shadow at the edge of a new logging unit, to sort out the discrepancy between memory and reality. Machines roared beyond a low ridge, so he turned aside for a more circuitous route around the smell of crushed forest and churned soil.

Soon he encountered a barbed-wire fence and cleared it in one mighty bound, landing cat-footed beyond. He skirted the tumbled-down old shack that hadn't changed since he followed his mother along this ancient bear path as a cub. And, twenty minutes later, moving steadily, the animal passed two old and leafless apple trees where he sometimes fed in the fall. Shortly thereafter, he circled out beyond sight and sound of the farmhouse and woodshed and barn, to emerge on the forest road, following it to a swamp. There he sought out a low ridge where he lay all day sniffing wind currents and keeping a vigil on "his" marsh.

Just after dusk, the grizzly moved into the wet forest at the swamp's upper end. Within minutes, he'd dug and gulped a half-dozen skunk cabbages—the first food he'd had in a hundred and thirty-one days, thirteen hours, and fifty-six minutes.

Eighteen days, six hours, and eleven minutes after the boar pushed snow from his den, a similar awakening occurred at the center of the snowfield spreading two hundred yards from the switchback on Alpine Trail Number Seven, near the head of Wheeler Creek. This animal was a female, a much smaller bear and, though terribly soiled, she was almost blond. She, too, lay atop the snow, panting and resting, trying to focus her velvet eyes, still drugged from almost five and a half months of hibernation.

The day was overcast, and rain peppered down. The sow's eyes cleared within minutes, and she lumbered to her feet and staggered into the basin bottom. The rivulet that weeks earlier had furnished water to the great boar was now a roaring cascade.

After quenching her thirst, the female plunged into the torrent to emerge on the far side, muddy water streaming from her coat. Within minutes she sniffed the first bare soil along a south-facing slope, not far from her winter's den. She stopped in mid-stride, lifting her nose to test air currents. She sniffed, sniffed again, then climbed the ridge above to sniff yet again.

An hour later, the sow stood screened by a patch of stunted alpine firs, studying the avalanche's terminal debris. Her nose told her a godsend lay within—almost too good to be true! Still, though it took an additional hour to circle the avalanche out-wash, the sow did so, satisfying herself that she was the first carni-vore to scent the treasure. Only then did she approach the debris and begin digging.

In no more than two minutes, she uncovered a leg, then another two, until her mighty forepaws sent ice blocks and bro-ken saplings spinning so she could grasp the aromatic dead moun-tain goat by the head, wrenching it from its grave. Not bothering to seek out a more comfortable dining area, the sow sprawled across ice blocks and began feeding. It was the first meal she'd had in one hundred and sixty-five days.

Male grizzly bears do not, as a rule, den as long as females. The male I described at the beginning of this chapter entered his den on November 17, 1989, and exited on March 22, 1990. The female entered her den on October 27, 1989, and emerged on April 9, 1990.

Females tend to remain in their dens longer because food is scarce in early spring. Nutritious vegetation is in short supply until most tubers and berries mature, beginning in July. Sows, especially those with cubs, are under considerable stress just to survive until food becomes abundant.

The sow described in this chapter was lucky to discover the goat carcass killed in the same avalanche that almost trapped the big male. Unless another, larger bear happened along to take the carcass from her (always a possibility), the sow would gorge for a week. The feast would provide a tremendous protein and caloric boost lasting clear into spring.

The male, of course, was not so lucky. But he was an aggressive animal, not at all afraid to enter humans' domain. Though not his first choice, in the past he'd raided a dairy farmer's livestock boneyard and helped himself to an occasional dumpster full of tasty garbage. In addition, he had staked out as his own one of the most food-productive forested marshes along the entire mountain front.

Scientists are fascinated by the bears' hibernation process, and they are currently focusing on the metabolic slowdown of the bruins' physical systems. The mysteries of the process (not considered true hibernation by hair-splitters among physiologists) may even hold revelations of practical use to humans. NASA, for instance, desperately wants to know why bears do not experience any reduction of bone mass during long periods of inactivity—one of the biggest problems associated with humans during space travel.

Another difference between male and female grizzly habits is that a sow is apt to utilize a home range somewhere around one-fifth the size of that of most boars. Because males tend to be more aggressive, occupy larger home ranges, and have shorter denning periods, they're more likely to come into conflict with humans. They're also more pugnacious toward each other. As a result, males live, on the average, but half as long as females.

It was in early May that war broke out over the rich, food-productive marsh the silvertipped male grizzly considered his own. The trouble began when a larger, older boar, down from the high country for his first visit, blundered into the swamp. Had the newcomer been content to eat his fill and move on, nothing would have happened. But no! The immigrant marked trees at each end and down one side, reaching to full height and scratching to the ground, until the sap ran. Then the intruder stood and rubbed the long guard hair of his back into the scent, marking *this* swamp as *his*.

The battle was titanic. After all, it was over food, not some silly female during mating time. Hair and blood flew and rocks were dislodged and saplings and brush were bent and broken. Their roaring was deafening and their endurance fantastic. But the struggle proved inconclusive. It was also futile. The newcomer, ignorant about man and his ways, died soon afterward in a confrontation with a frightened human who carried a 12-gauge shotgun loaded with double-ought buck.

The male with the prior swamp claim knew nothing of his rival's fate; he'd already packed up and crossed the mountains, looking for pliant females. Eventually he met an unusually sleek, blond female with doe-soft eyes who backed all the way across a forest glade to reach him. Theirs was a big bear hug. And just to demonstrate that he wasn't the type to kiss and run, the big male hung around for a couple more days, discouraging other suitors from making advances on the sleek female. Then he was gone.

The paths of the boar and sow crossed infrequently during the summer and fall. The big male, pursuing a feeding plan that sometimes took him thirty miles across rugged mountains in a single night, alternated between the rich berry lands of the western foothills and the populated valleys, while the shy female fed in peace atop her isolated mountain retreat.

The male crossed her home range in mid-July to check out huckleberries along Hungry Horse Reservoir, then crossed back again when he remembered that August serviceberries should be ripening around Swan Lake. Later in August, the shy female abandoned a lush, high-country huckleberry patch to the big male, then crept back to feed on his leavings after he remembered ripening apples at isolated homesteads along Foothills Road.

Despite her isolation, the timid female dwelt that year amid abundance. The high-country huckleberry crop was rich and frosts were late, with sweet, delectable berries still hanging in isolated pockets as late as the first week of October.

It was October 25 when they met for the last time that season. The sow fed industriously on a hillside's last mountain-ash berries when the male chanced to stand on the other side of the bush. Her surprise was complete. She spun around and dashed down the hill like a runaway bulldozer through menzesia brush and across wind-thrown pines. Not pausing at the basin bottom, she rushed up the opposite hillside onto her own isolated mountain.

Along the way, she startled two deer and a spike elk and left a white-faced elk hunter who'd been stalking the spike. The trembling hunter, as it happened, had heard the sow crashing through the underbrush and readied himself to take the bull elk of his dreams. Instead, a barreling grizzly that looked "bigger'n a house" nearly ran him down before he could throw off his rifle's safety, leaving the poor man so shaken that hours later he slopped more whiskey than he drank.

The male, characteristically, dropped casually to all fours as the sow rushed off, finished the mountain-ash berries, and sauntered over the ridge to the south, wandering toward the country where he'd previously denned. This time he chose a steep west-facing, sixty-degree slope amid a tangle of tag alder and alpine firs where he hung around for several days until he decided the time and place were just right. Then he started digging furiously, dirt and stones flying between his hind legs, down the mountainside.

Meanwhile, the sow recovered from her frightening encounters with the short-tempered male and the orange-clad human. She, too, chose her den site carefully, digging it on an east slope, beneath the roots of a huge spruce tree, then lining it with beargrass and boughs ripped from nearby spruce and fir saplings. The view from her "porch" was fabulous—southeast to the mountains of the Bob Marshall Wilderness, east to the peaks of the Great Bear Wilderness, and north to Glacier National Park's Livingston Range. She spent more time, however, staring into her den than out at her view.

Both dens were remarkably cramped for the size of the animals excavating them. The entry hole into the sow's den was no larger than the steering wheel on a pickup truck, and the boar's was only a little larger. Neither sleeping chamber was long enough to accommodate a stretched-out scientist, or high enough for a short man to sit erect.

Bears—even autumn-fat grizzlies wearing their winter coats—look much larger than they are, however, and such dens are adequate. Besides, cramped dens are nature's way of using even the lowered body temperatures of hibernating bears as a heat source, especially when covered by upwards of ten feet of accumulated snow.

There are several requirements for a den. More often than not, bears choose sites on north slopes, usually at a level above six thousand feet. At a location of that sort, snow will seldom melt until spring, and accumulated snow is good insulation, as well as effective camouflage. In the den, even a powerful grizzly is torpid and listless, sometimes taking hours to fully awaken. A hibernating grizzly is, therefore, vulnerable to lesser creatures. That's why bears dig their dens early, leave for a period, then return to enter amid the first blowing, drifting snow that will cover their tracks into hibernation.

Speculation is that steep slopes—up to sixty-five or seventy degrees—are chosen because thrown-out dirt, rocks, and debris are removed by gravity during the excavation process. Too, the soil of steep mountainsides is usually dry and more likely to shed moisture during spring's snowmelt. There's even some speculation that spring avalanches may clear overburdening snow packs from some den sites sooner than the snow would thin by simple melting.

As it was an unusually warm and dry fall, the female did not enter her den until November 15, during a six-inch snowfall. The male chanced upon a dead cow elk in a logging clearcut and hung around until he'd cleaned up its flesh. A pair of hunters walked up the clearcut's logging road until they'd struck the boar's monstrous tracks in a snow skiff. The hunters paused only a moment, talking loudly. Then they turned and retraced their way back to camp, glancing fearfully over their shoulders as they went. The male entered his den on November 22.

The female, as it turned out, did not spend the winter alone. In late January, twin cubs—male and female—were born. The birth process among bears is unusual. The phenomenon is known as delayed implantation.

When the sow mated, two eggs were fertilized by the male's sperm, and they began to develop into tiny embryos. But almost immediately their development ceased and they remained free-floating—not attaching themselves to the uterine wall and therefore not continuing to develop, as in most mammals. As a consequence, bear embryos remain dormant for months, in a state of suspended animation. It is a marvel of evolutionary adaptation. Here's why:

Spring is ideal for mating; the weather is usually good, food will soon become abundant, and the bears are wandering around looking for it—a perfect time to find a mate. But summer through early or even mid-autumn is not a good time for a female bear to be developing and nourishing one, two, or possibly three embryos. Instead, she needs all the nourishment for her own body, to build up fat reserves for winter. Her problem is solved by delayed implantation, which takes the problem out of summer pregnancy.

In late fall, if she has fed well and is in good condition, the tiny, undeveloped embryos drift to the uterine wall and become attached to it—implanted. Development can then resume, and it does—very quickly. That way, their birth is timed for midwinter, in the warmth and concealment of the den. And by then, the

Avalanche chutes can sometimes provide "bonus" food for bears through other animals trapped and killed during a snowslide and exposed, in time, as summer arrives.

Tom Ulrich photo

dozing mother has begun producing plenty of rich milk for them. They suckle and sleep and grow (and their growth is prodigious) until the time comes to emerge from the den.

Fertilization of the sow's eggs, of course, took place in a tiny forest glade in late May. The sow was receptive, and she was in comparatively good physical condition, principally because of the mountain-goat carrion discovered early in the spring. Though her normal home range was extremely limited in size and productivity, the season produced an excellent huckleberry crop that hung on clear through an unseasonably warm, dry fall. The sow entered her den in the peak of condition, her weight at three hundred and forty-eight pounds, an all-time high for her.

The cubs, when born, weighed only four ounces each—no larger than juice glasses. That they quickly found their way from their mother's birth channel to her mammary glands is both mystery and fact. By April 15, when they emerged from the den alongside their mother, both were as large as footballs. In two months, they would match the weight of a cocker spaniel and have the disposition of a pit bull.

Their mother, however, would continue to lose weight for two months, finally bottoming out at one hundred and eighty-four pounds—almost exactly half her weight upon den entry. Hers was full-time work—digging roots and feeding on grasses during every waking moment, avoiding other bears, avoiding humans. Finally, in mid-July, berries began to ripen.

Come winter, the cubs, if they survived, would den with their mother as yearlings. And they would remain under her watchful eye throughout the next season, denning with her as two-year-olds.

Upon emergence in their third spring, however, evil times will befall the cubs as their mother, growing increasingly irritable, unceremoniously boots them out to fend for theirselves while nature prepares her for another mating process.

Neither of these two cubs survived to reach that process, however. The male drowned while crossing a spring-swollen creek in mid-May of his second year, and the female was killed and eaten by a mean-tempered boar who surprised her in the middle of a berry patch when she was eight months old and had strayed a few yards from her mother for the first time.

Life is harsh in the bear world. ■

Chapter 21

The Giefer Griz

The moon was full but fitful, sneaking only occasional winks through scudding clouds. Even when shafts of light took a swift swipe across the land, they barely reached into the forest depths where the grizzly moved as stealthily as a house cat approaching a weed-patch mouse.

The bear paused to test the night air with his nostrils, then drifted into a leafy alder copse where he stood motionless for several minutes while studying the dim outline of the cabin and its woodshed beyond. Even to *Homo sapiens'* relatively insensitive nose, the foul odor was pungent. To the great bear, the smell of rotted meat was most pleasant—what one might call "bearable."

Again the bruin moved. This time moonbeams stole through clouds to shower the animal's rippling silver fur with a thousand points of light as he slipped boldly through the old cabin's tiny clearing. He paused one last time in the shadow of a bushy spruce to again survey the target.

The rotted deer carcass lay in a pile of jumbled, decaying logs left from long-ago days when the homesteader first wielded his axe. The carcass would be easy to take: simply move to the opening, reach in, and snake it out; then carry it a safe distance for a leisurely meal. Nothing could be simpler, and he was hungry. He took a step forward. Moonlight filtered to kiss his massive head as he swung to peer behind, at the cabin. Another step.

The bruin stopped abruptly and sprawled to his belly, laying his dish-faced head atop his forepaws. There the bear lay for two hours with only his surprisingly tiny black eyes moving. The rotted deer carcass lay but four feet away. Just a few inches from the razor claws of the grizzly's forefeet, the snare cable's loop lay covered with leaves and forest duff, ready to snap shut at the first rustle of the rotting meat.

One other thing moved in the clearing that night—a tiny electronic pulse in the collar band around the bear's neck.

The man snapped the radio receiver to off and laid the antenna in the pickup box. He grinned at his companion. "He's down. That makes two hours and he hasn't moved. We've got the Giefer Griz at last!"

High-fiving each other, the two game wardens leaped into the pickup with the Montana Department of Fish, Wildlife & Parks logo on the door, and sped away. The logo had a grizzly head pictured in its center.

"I don't believe this," the first warden said, minutes later.

"What'd he do? Just lay there and look at it?" the second trapper mused.

The bait and snare were just as they'd been left by the trappers. The only sign a bear had ever been in the vicinity was a patch of flattened grass as big as the bed of a black angus cow—and it only inches from their cable snare.

The veteran warden grinned. "No way out of it—you got to hand it to him. He's one son-of-a-bitch of a bear."

The receiver picked up no radio signals from nearby, so the wardens returned to the high point they'd occupied earlier and tried again. Still nothing. "He's out of range," the elder warden said. "He's already out of range. We'll have to start all over again."

Three nights later, the big grizzly again eyed the secluded cabin from the darkened forest. A soft rain fell. Ignoring the pungent aroma wafting from the deer carcass, the bear walked directly to the vacant cabin and smashed the door from its hinges.

The Giefer (pronounced "guy-fir") Grizzly first came to the attention of Montana Fish & Game wardens in the spring of 1975 when he developed a propensity to break and enter summer homes in the Giefer Creek area along U.S. 2, near the Continental Divide summit at Marias Pass.

There was nothing particularly notable about the animal that wardens captured in a baited culvert trap set near the ravaged Giefer Creek cabin. He wasn't unusually large for a ten-year old male; there were no detectable injuries, and he appeared to be in good health. Neither did he act especially aggressive.

A year or two before, the bear's pilfering ways would have consigned him to the ash heap of history. But grizzly bears' recent listing as "threatened" under the Endangered Species Act provided a second chance for the bear. He was moved a hundred and thirty road miles to the Flathead's South Fork and dropped off near the edge of the Bob Marshall Wilderness.

Nothing is known of the Giefer Grizzly until the following spring, when he again showed up at the doorstep of summer homes along Giefer Creek. As before, the bear wasn't constrained to mere doorstep observation. He was trapped again, this time with a cable snare before a baited cubby set. Again he was paroled, this time to the Flathead's North Fork. One of the terms of this second reprieve was that the annoying bear was fitted with a radio-transmitting collar.

It was the last time marveling researchers, frustrated wardens, blood-eyed home owners, and wannabe bear huggers dripping with charity would get a clear look at the animal who revised standards for demolishing rural cabins. Before he was through, the Giefer Griz punched out windows and doors in more than a hundred clandestine entries into remote North Fork cabins. Some he penetrated as many as four times despite beefed-up doors and shuttered windows. No matter the double-locks and dead-bolts. No matter that barbed wire twisted in strands as thick as a child's wrist crisscrossed windows to hold him out. No matter that thirty-penny spikes was driven through planks and anchored atop porch floors and entry steps to deter him. The bruin simply ripped out a new opening.

Yet no one saw him. Some said they did. Some even said they got off a shot at the marauder. Some said they'd killed him. Or they knew positively of someone who'd killed this infamous *Ursus arctos horribilis*. Then another cabin would be opened like a canned ham, and speculation would burst anew.

Newspapers got into the act, feeding the rumor mills with editorials about the bear's demise, suggesting it was a good thing, too, and that the Powers-That-Be should never again release "problem" bears into civilized society.

And the Giefer Griz would strike again.

The truth is, the bear was never loosed into civilization to begin with; he was first dropped into the Flathead's remote South Fork, then released for his second chance amid the wild Tuchuck drainage, near Canada and the summit of the Whitefish Range.

But the bear must have tracked the Fish & Game truck to easier pickings because, before the week was out, he'd struck his first cabin and before another week was out he'd left busted doors, strewn furniture, and broken glass in a dozen more.

Before the month was out, the Giefer Grizzly was a legend in a land of legendary ursids. And before winter hibernation, the bruin was listed as "Public Enemy Number One" in area newspapers. Jokes were made about the Governor declaring the North Fork a disaster area, qualifying it for emergency relief from Washington, D.C.

Federal relief was already on hand in the form of professional government hunters, called in with the express purpose of applying capital punishment to a single bear. Kill bears they certainly did. But not the right bear. Not the Giefer bear. While hunters pursued him in the northern portion of his range, he practiced rural rehab in the south end portion. When they moved south, he moved north. There were times when he seemed to be working both ends the same night.

Odds are good that the Giefer grizzly was credited with more breakings and enterings than he actually accomplished—sort of the way Jesse James was held responsible for a train robbery in Arizona Territory and a New Hampshire bank holdup during the same week.

On the other hand, Jesse *did* travel to Northfield, Minnesota, and the Giefer Griz did roam at will up and down the North Fork while wardens and professional hunters and biologists circled in light planes and pickup trucks and talked back and forth on their two-way radios.

Unlike Jesse, the Giefer Griz had a sanctuary of sorts across the North Fork of The Flathead river in Glacier Park. If he kept his nose clean while in the Park, he could thumb it at trappers and hunters and wardens and maybe even biologists. But Glacier was not where the cabins were. And cabins were like a narcotic to the footloose bear. There was this thing about Canada, too. Dance across some imaginary line, and pickup trucks and professional hunters stopped as if the same road the bear had just ambled along fell off the end of the earth.

All in all, it was great sport. Despite white hunters and red-faced wardens and black-bearded biologists, despite steel-jawed traps and cable snares and enticing road-killed deer, despite the latest in electronic communications and media attention that reached to *Reader's Digest*, despite newspaper editorials and drunken wakes celebrating his supposed demise, the great bear shuffled blithely on from cabin to cabin.

Then came his lucky break, or—as some say—his canny insistence on a level playing field. Just as the chase narrowed, the Giefer Griz left his collar lying amid the wreckage of his umptillionth cabin. Without a radio beacon around the bear's neck to prove them wrong, the rumor mills were free to embellish their wildest dreams:

A logger ran over the Giefer Griz with his pickup truck. No, a rancher shot it inside a hay barn. No, the government boys quietly handled the creature's demise so as to suffer no further embarrassment. No, he's on his way back to the Middle Fork. No he's in Northfield, Minnesota, or New Hampshire or Arizona Territory.

Same bear, another cabin. And another.

Some second-home owners gave up and left their cabin doors smashed open, their windows broken. They removed all foodstuffs to their first homes in California or Helena or Puget Sound and resigned themselves to abandoning the field to the victor.

It was not so easy for those whose cabins weren't their second home but their first, their only home. To them, their single refuge lay in turning their cabins into occupied fortresses. There was little visiting between neighbors and trips to town were put off until there was no other way. And after a rapid transit to a supermarket, they raged upon returning to trashed cabins.

Finally, in November, relief came with hibernation. Most of the winter was spent reinforcing their buildings or planning a counterattack come spring.

With spring came yet another report on the demise of the Giefer Griz. There are those among us without isolated cabins in the rural North Fork who had become skeptical of the Giefer's death—it'd happened so many times. But this time it was true.

The bear who had learned to avoid traps with the uncanny verve of Willie Sutton sidestepping First National's burglar alarms, and who had never—ever—ransacked an occupied cabin, had not recognized the peril of a distant hunter's magnum rifle.

To the north, some Canadian provinces permit a spring grizzly-bear season. British Columbia is one. It is not known where the Giefer Grizzly took his winter sleep, but he grazed greening shoots along British Columbia's remote Wigwam River on April 27, 1977. He was killed from one hundred and fifty yards by a Pennsylvania hunter guided by a Cranbrook, B.C., outfitter.

The Giefer's career was like that of a brilliant shooting star blazing across the sky briefly, then fading to nothing in the atmosphere or crashing ungainly to earth. Though the bear bore press scrutiny for two of his twelve years, he really occupied newspaper headlines for just one season. But what a season!

Rick Mace, the veteran bear biologist who heads Montana Fish, Wildlife & Parks South Fork Grizzly Study, was a pink-faced youth right out of college when he was assigned, along with other trappers working with Chuck Jonkel's Border Grizzly Project, to snare the Giefer bear. It's Rick's opinion that he has never come up against a more intelligent bear.

"He was incredibly smart. The way he avoided our best sets, the way he stayed clear of cabins when people were around. . ."

"And you feel he was smarter than your Mud Lake Bear?"

"Oh, yeah. Much smarter."

"The Mud Lake Bear was pretty sharp."

The research biologist nodded. "But a bear can be smart about some things and not others. The Giefer Griz knew about people and traps, but he didn't know about guns and hunting. The Mud Lake Bear? Who knows? Maybe he's still out there, but I doubt it."

"How about the Dairy Queen Bear? He's still out there."

"Yeah, Digger's out there. And you've got to give him credit, although nobody's trying to catch him like they did the Giefer Grizzly." The man's eyes took on a faraway look. "Talk about cagey!"

Now, typing these words into my computer screen, I'm still awed. But the Giefer Griz has been dead these many years. And I remember wondering, when he died, if there was any deterrent or aversive conditioning for bears that didn't have lead in it. Did anyone have the answer?

Back then, in 1977, the silence was deafening. ∎

Looking down upon Bear Creek Ranch from near where photographer Charles Gibbs was killed when he encroached too closely on the space of a grizzly sow with cubs. Giefer Creek cuts into the photo from the middle left. Both the Giefer Grizzly and the Lindbergh Lake Bear first attracted attention in this area.

Chapter 22

Magnum Substitute

A steady in-shore breeze brought lowering clouds and a modest chop to the water. A kayak perched upon the sand spit, its occupants off to the side photographing Admiralty Island brown bears fishing for salmon. One bruin swung a monster head to peer their way, then gazed back into the water as if pondering a sensitive philosophical question. The bear wheeled and waded from the water, ambling toward the two men. The kayakers huddled together, eyeing their beached craft, turning as one to measure the yardage to distant trees. The bear, still dripping water, continued to stalk their way, closing to thirty yards. It was a scene with disaster written all over.

John Hyde, an Alaska Fish & Game Department Specialist, had just topped the sand spit. He recognized the animal as one with a reputation for bullying and frightening humans in order to rifle their possessions for edibles. Hyde drew the canister hanging in a belt holster and hurried forward. In his own words:

"I stepped up and tried to bluff her away. The sow closed to within eight feet. The wind was in our faces, so I tried to turn her downwind. . . . She continued to circle us with ears laid back, all the while chomping her teeth and salivating. . . . I had always been able to bluff her away before. Suddenly she pounded both front paws into the sand and unexpectedly lunged at the man on my left, her claws missing him by less than thirty-six inches. . . . I fired the canister full force into her face. She reared up, turned one hundred and eighty degrees, and took off running. About two hundred yards later, she stopped, turned to look at us, and then ambled off to her favorite bed. The man next to me first proclaimed his relief that I had shown up when I did, then asked, 'What is that stuff?'"

In April, 1988, that "stuff" was a relatively new development in aggressive-animal deterrent known as "Counter Assault." It was ranger Hyde's first experience with its use. And though he was at first skeptical, the incident and subsequent others served to make him an ardent advocate of capsaicin (pronounced "cap-sigh-sin") spray as a defensive weapon for folks working or playing in bear country.

"The second encounter," says Hyde, "occurred with the same animal two days later. Since Counter Assault had previously proven effective, I was now more confident in its ability to repel bears. This second application was used at a greater distance and prevented any further approach. This time the can was fired when the sow was about fifty feet away. The repellent didn't reach the bear but instead hung in a cloud, between both parties. She [the bear] encountered the cloud, at which time she sniffed, wrinkled her nose and walked away."

A third potential attack three days later, according to Hyde, was prevented by merely raising the can and threatening to discharge. The sow merely "turned her head away and backed off."

Capsaicin is a bitter chemical compound (C H NO) derived from cayenne pepper. According to Carrie Hunt, who methodically tested an array of proposed bear deterrents during a stint with the University of Montana's Border Grizzly Project, the compound "causes pain to the nerve endings of the eyes and nose. The spray temporarily robs them of their senses and causes pain, but there is no long-lasting effect."

Hunt, using captive "problem" bears trapped from Confederated Salish and Kootenai Tribal lands and Glacier and Yellowstone National Parks, initially discovered that the only deterrent to have any significant effect was a commercial dog-repellent spray containing capsaicin. Dog repellents, however, appeared too weak for use on bears, so Hunt encouraged entrepreneur Bill Pounds to create a significantly stronger capsaicin formula delivered in a more powerful aerosol stream. Here's an excerpt from a report on subsequent tests:

"During 77 tests, bears were sprayed while charging or aggressively approaching a human who was on the other side of a barred door or fence. Responses by all bears were remarkably similar. When sprayed, all bears (100%) were repelled. Most responded by immediately turning and running away; during a few tests bears quickly backed away. After an initial retreat of several meters bears usually stopped and pawed at their faces before continuing to move away. At no time were any aggressive responses noted. . . . Capsaicin affected bear behavior in subsequent tests, reducing the frequency of immediate charges and the overall tendency to charge."

But what about wild bears? Might not there be a difference between the reaction of free-ranging bears and that of caged bears that stood no chance of reaching the object of their rage? Though attempts were made to deter free-ranging garbage-dump bears with capsaicin, tests were limited and therefore inconclusive. Researchers could only await reports from the field.

The first came swiftly (July, 1984) from Yellowstone National Park, where Doug Dunbar, a research biologist with the Interagency Grizzly Bear Study Team was charged and knocked to the ground by Number 84, a huge male that Dunbar and partner Jim Hayden had tracked through radio telemetry.

Dunbar sent two bursts of capsaicin at the bear as it closed to twenty feet, but the grizzly burst through the spray cone, knocking the researcher to the ground and straddling one very terrified man. Dunbar sprayed the bear full in the face. As quickly as the attack began, it was over. The bear whirled and ran, pausing to paw at his eyes and wipe his face on the ground. Dunbar suffered only scratches and one minor puncture wound.

One testimonial does not a testament make, however. So capsaicin-spray producer Pounds was jubilant when he received a letter dated April 15, 1987, from writer and researcher Terry Domico, who was gathering information on Asian Black Bears on Honshu Island in Japan. Domico wrote:

"As our research team approached the den entrance a large (485 lb/220 Kg) male bear suddenly exploded from the entrance in an attack. The team dropped everything and scattered. But the bear had singled out one of Maita's [study team leader] student assistants. Trying to escape, the young man broke through the snow crust and the bear closed in on him. That is when I hit the bear with a blast of spray. Allowing the man to scamper away, the bear immediately turned on me. I hit him again with another blast of spray. The bear wheeled and ran, down the hill, and out of sight. We were shaken, but unharmed. . . . Maita's first words to me were, 'I must have that spray!'"

In the years since those initial reports, the preponderance of favorable evidence has become overwhelming as more and more bear-country travelers arm themselves with one of several different types of aerosol bear sprays now on the market.

Glacier National Park administrators recently released an analysis of within-the-Park human/grizzly incidents involving pepper spray. Here are some excerpts:

1986 *(Grizzly) Self Defense. Began spraying at 18 ft. Bear cont. to 10 ft. Sow appeared to attempt to avoid spray & circle to right. Aimed at her for a "crucial couple of seconds" before can emptied. Bear woofed a couple of times. All bears disappeared.*

1993 *(Grizzly) Self Defense. A charge deferred by spray. Sprayed direct hit on face & head. It retreated.*

- *(Grizzly) Self Defense. Charge. Sprayed by person other than injury victim. Bear retreated & not seen again.*

1994 *(Grizzly) Self Defense. Person turned & ran. Did not note bear's response.*

- *(Grizzly) Self Defense. Ranger was charged. Sprayed at 10 ft. Ranger did a half trot down trail. Bear paralleling & moving into the cone of spray. After 4-5 seconds bear broke off & retreated. Most of can used & most found its mark giving bear a "good dose".*

1995 *(Grizzly) Self Defense. Sprayed directly into bear's face at 3 ft. range, while bear attacking another person. Emptied whole can. Bear's face had wet appearance. Bear was growling. It stopped mauling & ran away.*

Though the evidence seems so overwhelming, biologists—the men who feel the pulse of wild, free-roaming bears—still express doubts. Chuck Jonkel, Border Grizzly Project Leader and the man who instituted experiments with aversive conditioning, is quoted as saying pepper spray is not a total answer to an aggressive grizzly bear. What pepper spray does, according to Jonkel, is "it merely messes them up long enough so you can get the hell out of the area."

Nevertheless, Jonkel gave his endorsement to the product when he wrote: "In all phases of our testing and aversive conditioning programs, the capsicum product, variously packaged as Animal Repel, Counter Attack, and now Counter Assault . . . has given us the best results."

Jonkel wrote of the products' effectiveness in his Border Grizzly Study's aversive-conditioning research: "We have tested both commercial and concocted products; we have tested them in the field, in the laboratory, and in garbage dumps. The conditioned bears were released back into the wild to determine if a lasting aversion to people resulted from the repeated treatments in lab. So far as we have been able to determine, only two bears caused additional problems after conditioning. . . ."

Other biologists, however, stress that few wild animals are as notoriously unpredictable as grizzly bears. "Who can say a bear would not have broken off an attack without being hit with pepper spray?" asked one Montana biologist.

Even Bill Pounds, manufacturer of the capsaicin-based Counter Assault, isn't one hundred percent positive why his product is so effective in deterring aggressive grizzlies:

"It's possible the cloud of spray itself changes the bear's mind-set. I mean he's in an attack mode, with only a selected target on his mind. Suddenly there's this big orange cloud puffing up in front of him and he has to channel his mind to cope with a new development. I'm just saying that kind of factor may be instrumental in deterring a bear from attack mode."

Pounds may have something—there was an incident recorded in Glacier where a hiker deflected a grizzly's charge by suddenly popping open an umbrella.

Still, some experienced bear-country travelers are reluctant to carry canisters of pepper spray, feeling the product may provide a false sense of security that encourages a hiker to be less alert in bear territory. Your best tool for defense against aggressive bears, these experts say, is to look for signs of bears, provide plenty of warning by making copious noise, and be especially watchful where visibility is impaired.

Rick Mace, the venerable South Fork Grizzly Study team leader, is one biologist who feels that canister pepper spray might be overrated. He believes in the individualism of the bears, and thinks what works with one might not work with another. Mace is also quick to point out that variable conditions such as wind or rain or rage of the bear might have something to do with the pepper spray's effectiveness.

Mace, who began with Jonkel's Border Grizzly Project in the late 70's, mentioned bear conditioning and used a livestock-killing bear as an example. He said the "problem" bear was brought into their aversive-conditioning experiments. "We used dead cattle and sheep and sprayed that bear every time he approached a carcass until he wouldn't even look at one. We threw everything at that bear for a month, then took him up the Swan and dumped him off. So what happens? He goes right out and kills a bunch of chickens."

When I stopped laughing, Rick continued: "And Jonkel says, 'Well, we never threw chickens at him.'"

Mace told that story at a meeting between field biologists and entrepreneur Pounds. My purpose for being there was to get a sense of the effectiveness of capsaicin sprays and an idea of where future developments in deterrents and aversive conditioning might be headed. I got an earful. The first thing I learned was there is considerable difference between the meanings of "deterrent" and "aversive conditioning."

Consensus between biologists and the manufacturer seemed to be that aversive conditioning of free-ranging bears was a management technique applied to change an animal's mind set. An example might be demonstrating to the bruin that he should not rob a beehive or apple orchard, invade a livestock pen or summer cabin, look for food in garbage cans or unattended backpacks or campers' tents.

Aversive conditioning works best before a bear becomes conditioned to rewards for breaking human rules. "And that's the difficult part," says Tim Manley, FW&P Region I Grizzly Bear Management Specialist. "I get a call that a bear is hanging around Many Lakes. But by the time I get there, the bear has moved to Mountain Brook, then Echo Lake. It's hard to find an opportunity to practice aversive conditioning on a bear if you never see the animal."

Deterrent, on the other hand, means stopping a bear from an action he's currently engaged in—an attack, for instance. "Deterrent is necessary when there's a rage factor involved," says Bill Pounds. "You've got to change the behavior instantly."

Dan Carney, biologist for the Blackfeet Tribe sees potential value in capsaicin spray as an aversive conditioner if an adequate system can be developed to deliver the spray "a couple hundred feet."

That, as it turns out, may be the best analysis of difference between deterrence and aversive conditioning: If a bear is close and coming after you, a deterrent is needed—fast! If he's at a distance, trying to make up his mind whether to pursue an aggressive course, he might be conditioned by an unpleasant experience to distance himself from humans. But are such long distance-delivery systems available?

No. Cracker shells fired through a shotgun make a loud noise and can be delivered accurately to some distance. But they've proven largely ineffective in changing bear habits. Experiments with pepper-spray delivery via shotgun shells have been made, but the quantity of capsaicin delivered in such tiny containers is insufficient to deter bears.

So it comes down to the type of system Carney feels he needs—one that delivers a grenade-size pepper-spray container designed to release on impact. Pounds says the problem is that aerosol sprays are designed to release best when the canister is held in upright position. but his organization is working on that problem right now and he promised Carney he'd have something for the biologist to use soon.

"Why do you need a delivery system to reach out a hundred feet?" research biologist Mace asked the Blackfeet management biologist.

The unflappable Carney replied, "I have cases [of human/grizzly confrontation] where I've done everything I can do to change the habits of people. These are folks who live near the mountains and want to see the bears survive. And they're already doing everything they can to avoid problems. They haul their garbage out regularly and leave no food unattended to encourage the bears. But when a grizzly starts hanging around under their yard lights of an evening, they don't like it."

Carney stared at me, at Mace, at Pounds and others in the room. I thought he'd finished, but then he added, "I've either got to find a way to condition that bear to avoid humans or I must destroy it."

In the silence that followed, I polled the biologists, asking how many carried pepper spray while in the field. Every single one, including Rick Mace, said they did.

"That says it all," I mused. "How can anyone ask for a better endorsement?"

Glacier Park furnishes capsaicin spray canisters to their field personnel. They also provide guidelines for its use:

- *Wind speed and direction may affect spray pattern.*

- *Wet, rainy weather and/or wet bear fur may influence the effectiveness.*

- *Extreme cold or heat may reduce the effectiveness of the aerosol propellent.*

- *The recommended shelf life for most product lines is three (3) years.*

- *Most product lines have an effective maximum range of 15 to 30 feet. Timing of the spray discharge can influence the outcome.*

- *Pepper spray is delivered in a high volume, high velocity cone pattern. It does not require great accuracy, but the facial area of the bear is the target of choice.*

- *Accessibility of the pepper spray during the attack is important. You may not have much reaction time.*

- *The quantity of spray available and the quantity delivered during the spraying incident may influence effec-*

tiveness. Most product lines contain from 4 to 15 ounces of spray.

- *Familiarity with the product design and capabilities is important. Practice firing of bear spray can prove to be invaluable in actual use.*

I re-read Glacier's guidelines, especially noting that use of pepper spray does not require great accuracy. Pounds says his product is developed to provide a cone of spray before a bear's face.

"If it's delivered properly, the animal should run into a deterrent cloud. That's why," he says, "it's important for the spray to stay atomized, to hang in the air, rather than settle to the ground. You need the spray in his face, not on his feet."

So arm yourself with a canister of pepper spray, practice using it until you're smooth in handling and efficient in delivery, and you'll never have to worry about a grizzly again, right?

Well, not exactly. There's an addendum about brains. The spray is no substitute for common-sense avoidance tactics while traveling or camping in bear country. Consider pepper spray as sort of an insurance policy. Insurance is great when you need it, but I remember my daddy telling me I'd be better off in the long run if I pay for insurance yet never need to collect on it.

In short, there are no guarantees that every bear will be deterred. Consider this latest, hot-off-the-press information from a recent study abstract, *Field Use Of Capsaicin Sprays As A Bear Deterrent*, by Stephen Herrero and Andrew Higgins of the Environmental Science Program, University of Calgary, Alberta, Canada:

"Sixty-six cases of field use of capsaicin sprays between 1984-1994 were studied. Regarding aggressive brown/grizzly bear incidents associated with sudden encounters, in 94% (15/16) of the cases, the spray had the effect of stopping the behavior that the bear was displaying immediately prior to being sprayed. In 88% (14/16) of the cases, the bear left the area after being sprayed. In six cases, the bear continued to act aggressively; in three of these cases the bear attacked the person spraying. In one of these three cases, further spraying caused the bear to stop and leave. Of the three encounters that resulted in injury to the sprayer, two involved a mother with cub(s) and the other involved a single bear."

The other cases involved garbage-raiding grizzlies (100% effective)and black bears (less effective than with grizzlies).

So, do you still want to put all your marbles in the pepper-spray sack?

Entrepreneur Pounds says his capsaicin spray is merely a stopgap until the next generation of deterrents can be developed. The man mentioned ultra-sound systems that may have the capability of knocking a bear down; and he mentioned high voltage electrical charges that also might produce eerie popping and snapping sounds.

Aerosol may not be the perfect answer, but what's most needed is what capsaicin spray offers—a deterrent or aversive conditioner that doesn't include lead missiles in calibers such as .357 or .44 or 30.06. Before pepper sprays, serious human/bear encounters usually led to injury or death of one or the other (or both). The case of John Petranyi succinctly illustrates:

Petranyi, an experienced outdoorsman from Wisconsin, knowledgeable about bears, hiked alone near Glacier's closed and boarded Granite Park Chalet on October 3, 1992. What exactly happened will never be known, but Buck Wilde from Ketchum, Idaho, discovered Petranyi's mangled and partially consumed body.

Evidence on the scene led investigators to believe Petranyi died in a surprise encounter with a grizzly sow and two cubs. Seven days after his death, what were thought to be the guilty bears were located by helicopter and shot by rangers on the ground.

It's possible John Petranyi and the three grizzlies would have died even if the man had been armed with pepper spray. But it is also possible they wouldn't.

Remember the case of Mary Pat Mahoney? Remember how the bears took her from her tent during early morning hours while the girl cowered in her sleeping bag? Remember how two bears had been in that same campground just four days before? How they'd chased two fishermen into Fishercap Lake on the same day they visited the campground? How bears had chased Iceberg Lake hikers into trees three times within the previous month and a half?

I can draw no conclusion other than the strong probability that Mary Pat—and perhaps the bears, too—would have survived if capsaicin spray had been available in 1976.

There's no question about it, I feel safer hiking in grizzly country with a canister of pepper spray hanging from my belt. But I'll still plan on waltzing with the same watchful, careful tactics that brought me to the dance for the last thirty, forty years. And so should you. ■

Richard Jackson

Chapter 23

Three Bears, Three Profiles

There are Houdini bears and Einstein bears, Ma Barker bears and Rasputin bears; bears with short fuses and others with infinite patience. Some rustle cattle, knock off beehives, or pilfer apples. Some make the front pages; others are only mentioned in obituaries. Most of the great beasts go through life avoiding us annoying bipeds when possible. Most lead exemplary (by our anthropomorphic standards), disciplined existences, only to stumble once in a situation for which ursine elementary had not prepared them. The Rottweiler Bear was a classic example.

Number 144 must have been a smart animal. That the big silvertip had already weathered ten berry seasons and dug ten dens under the roots of north-slope whitebark pines when trappers first snared him was proof enough of the bear's canniness— free-roaming male grizzlies don't often reach advanced maturity for a variety of reasons. But to other bears, Number 144 must have been one mean Jack the Ripper and Jeffrey Dahmer, rolled into a single nasty-tempered, territorial tyrant.

He ate his first bear—a black—just a few days after biologists aged, weighed, lip-tattooed, ear-tagged, and radio-collared him. A mere month later, the yet-to-be-named Rottweiler Bear cannibalized his second bruin in an argument over the summer's first ripening berries.

The second bear consumed by Number 144 was an aging grizzly sow, well into her third decade. She, too, had been trapped and collared. Thus, by monitoring signals from both bears, researchers knew they were in close proximity to each other. When the sow's transmitter disclosed no movement for a couple of days, the men moved in to find only scattered remains of the emaciated female.

For the remainder of that hot, dry summer of '88, while forest fires raged in Yellowstone and throughout the West, Number 144 led researchers into the Swan Range high country, feeding on roots and berries and shoots of greening alpine grasses. Finally fall came and the big male denned at sixty-four hundred feet on the north slope of a mountain off the southeast corner of the popular Jewel Basin Hiking Area.

Aerial trackers again picked up the big male's radio signal at the end of May, 1989, in the Swan Mountains' central grizzly-breeding boudoir. There's some mystery as to Number 144's previous whereabouts that spring, but interest in that puzzle was overshadowed by the work of monitoring dozens of other collared grizzlies. Neither is it known if the big bear's amorous instincts improved his disposition toward ursine females. I asked Rick Mace, study-team leader, if the Rottweiler Bear was known to have killed and eaten bears other than the two listed earlier.

"To be honest, Roland," Mace said, "we aren't even sure if he killed either of those first two."

"But," I said, "you know he ate them!"

"Yes. But the black may have been wounded during spring black-bear hunting season and got away to die. Or it may have died for other reasons. Same with the little old sow grizzly. Her time may have come, and Number 144 just happened to be there at the right time."

"So, did the Rottweiler Bear ever feed on another bear, to your knowledge?"

Mace shook his head. "But he could have. I mean, we're touching base with him by air perhaps once, twice a week. We can't know everything he fed on during most of that time."

Again Number 144 ranged the Swan's high country throughout the summer and fall of '89, finally denning higher on the same mountain he had chosen the previous year.

This time, researchers monitored the den more closely, hoping to track Number 144 upon emergence. They struck paydirt on

March 21, tracking the bruin across the Swan Range down into Deer Creek, reaching the Flathead Valley floor on April Fool's Day. By mid-April, the bear had wandered ten miles north, past farms near Mud Lake and resort homes surrounding Echo Lake, to the upper-end subdevelopment in the Many Lakes area.

Number 144 stayed in that area for two weeks. School children walked to bus stops and commuters motored to jobs in Kalispell and Bigfork with not one person aware a big male grizzly was in the vicinity. Then the bruin's biological clock began ticking toward May's breeding season, and he headed for the grizzly heartland where both sexes concentrate for reproduction.

In thickets east of Mud Lake, the big, tough, 13-year-old, bear-nasty Rottweiler bruin bumped into a comer, a second big, mean—but younger—male grizzly, the Mud Lake Bear described in Chapter 15. How the fight began, no one knows. Nor, really, how it ended. But blood and handfuls of bear hair were scattered amid ripped-up bushes and churned ground. The Mud Lake Bear's collar had been ripped off, the Rottweiler Bear's ear tag torn out. And inexplicably, a dead terrier dog was sprawled nearby and an incomprehensible arrow was stuck in the ground. Bloody though the battle must have been, both bears survived—for a while.

Whatever ursine programming had compelled the fray, it interrupted the Rottweiler Bear's return across the Swan's crest to seek a mate. Searching for food, the bear made his first—and only—mistake: he preyed on dog food.

It happened that the dog-food pan was inside a twenty-by-thirty-three-foot pen occupied by dogs bred for a savage willingness to engage bears.

Leo Turner, the dogs' owner, was mystified over the rapid disappearance of his animals' rations. It seems the disabled Vietnam veteran was in the habit of keeping the pan full so his dogs could eat any time they wished. But for the last two mornings, the oversized pan's polished bottom had glittered. Turner decided to pay closer attention. The man heard a noise sometime after eleven p.m. Upon investigation, he discovered a huge grizzly crouched over the dog dish, while his rottweiler bear dogs cowered miserably in a corner, trying desperately to blend with the wire mesh fence. Turner said the bear charged. He fired.

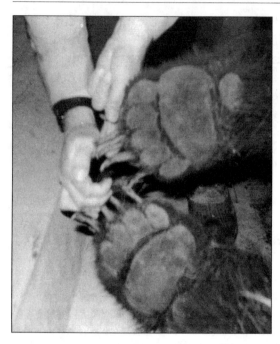

The only passable photo of the Rottweiler Bear, taken posthumously. It's value lies in comparing the size of the bear's front feet with the man's hands holding them.

FWP remote camera photo

1. Candy—Number 45—in a FWP remote camera photo sequence. Here she discovers the bait at trap station #207. Note the bear's relatively poor condition, considering the July 21 photo date. Smoke still lingers from the trapper's warning fire.

FWP remote camera photo

2. Candy leaves her mark on a tree. Most biologists believe this action to be "territorial"— she's clearly marking this bait site as belonging exclusively within her domain.

FWP remote camera photo

3. Spooked, probably by the remote camera's motion sensor-triggered shutter, Candy dashes away.

The Rottweiler Bear had made his one mistake. There would be no second chance.

Could it be that nothing in the bear's experience had prepared him for facing an angry, or frightened, dog owner armed with a shotgun? Or had this big male grizzly, accustomed to running unchallenged through bear country, underestimated the Mud Lake Bear's strength and ferocity? Perhaps beaten in the struggle between titans, he had lost his normal caginess for a brief but fatal period.

Whatever had caused his downfall, the Rottweiler Bear was nicknamed posthumously.

The bear named Boots was first captured on October 18, 1978, by a then youthful Rick Mace, working as a trapper for Chuck Jonkel's Border Grizzly Project. She proved to be eight years old, weighed three hundred pounds, and measured forty-two inches around the chest. Her front claws measured a smidgen less than two inches long, and her overall length was sixty-three inches. The mature female was assigned Number 297 and for no documented reason was nicknamed "Big Boots," later condensed to just "Boots."

Monitoring was sometimes unreliable during the Border Grizzly Project. Thus, little is known of her life and travels during the 1980's. She was snared for the second time on June 5, 1990, by Montana's South Fork Grizzly Study trappers. It's interesting to compare data between October, 1978, and June, 1990. Her 1990 age was, of course, nineteen. But the matriarch's weight was down from three hundred pounds to a hundred and eighty-five, though her overall length remained sixty-three inches.

"Why the weight loss?" I asked the first biologist I could buttonhole.

He eyed me as if I was unusually dense. "One is spring weight, Roland, the other fall. I can assure you she weighed at least three hundred by the time she went to bed in 1990."

The elderly female was assigned Number 45, and she was collared. Candy-stripe ribbons was placed in her ears for visual identification. The striped ribbon apparently led to a third nickname for the matriarch: "Candy."

It's intriguing to note the description in the report under "special markings"—"White claws and fangs." And she must be beautiful—"Blonde saddle, *heavy* silvertipping on head, shoulders, sides & rump."

Candy's second trapping was not without mishap, as biologists erred in the drug dosage used. From their report:

> *Thought it was #149 since his signal was right there &*
> *heard from the airplane. So dosed the bear for his*
> *weight 350 pounds.*

It's not clear when they discovered their error, but presumably they identified the animal correctly after she was tranquilized and could be safely approached and handled.

> *#149 was right at the site so we stayed in the pickup*
> *watching her [Number 45—Candy] until she got up.*
> *We were afraid #149 may harm her. She couldn't use*
> *her head until about 9:15 p.m. Then at 9:30 she got*
> *up and charged us in the truck & chased us. We got*
> *stuck & she walked around the truck. She started to*
> *move off & we tried to turn around & she charged*
> *again. Finally she left when we kept still.*

So Number 45, alias 297, alias Big Boots, alias Boots, alias Candy, is not exactly a shrinking violet. What would future monitoring disclose?

Rick Mace says, "Number 45 lives up there on top of the Swan Range, minding her own business and shying away from people. She's twenty-five years old now and still bearing cubs, usually two, every few years."

Good bear? Bad bear? Nope. Just bear.

It's unlikely that any bruin since the Giefer Grizzly has earned as much ink as did the Lindbergh Lake Bear. Initially accused unjustly, trapped, and relocated arbitrarily, the young sow tried to cope with what must have seemed a world in flux. What was especially newsworthy, however, was the way she did it.

Never part of the South Fork Study (or any other official grizzly research), the Lindbergh Lake Sow, like the Giefer Grizzly before her, was a "problem" bear. Also like the Giefer Griz, the Lindbergh Lake Sow fell afoul of authorities around Giefer Creek, which flows from the crest of the Rockies near Marias Pass and U.S. Highway 2. Here are excerpts from Tim Manley's initial 1992 report:

5/29 . . . *grizzly problem at Bill Beck's [Bear Creek Guest Ranch]. Was having Warden Wedum investigate and set trap. Dave Wedum called in evening. Reportedly an adult female with cubs. A colt being raised as orphan had been killed about 2 a.m. this date in corrals near buildings. Had set trap & disposed of remaining colt carcass.*

5/30 7:30 p.m. *Wedum called. Had adult bear in trap.*

5/31 8:15 a.m. *Wedum called. About 350 pound female in trap. No cubs. Not lactating. Called Tom Wittinger [U.S. Forest Service officer] re: relocation. 5:15 p.m. Wittinger called back w/ ok on relocation to Beaver Creek (Swan) site. Ok with District Ranger.*

6/1 *Brought to R1 [Fish, Wildlife & Parks] Hd. Five to 7 year old female. Appears to be in oestrus. No sign of prior lactation & nursing. Filled transmitter and ear tags. Released in Swan site in p.m.*

Tim Manley, Fish, Wildlife & Parks Region I Grizzly Management Specialist, assigned Number 11 to the mature sow.

Initially, whether she rated "nuisance" status seemed questionable to him. It took a little over a year for her to remove all doubt.

From the outset, Number 11 demonstrated disconcertingly little fear of humans. Drifting from her release site on National Forest land to the shores of scenic Lindbergh Lake, the bear was frequently seen by residents of summer homes in the vicinity.

Lindbergh Lake, named for the famous aviator who was first to fly solo across the Atlantic Ocean, is a little-known summer-cottage retreat for a growing number of humans seeking privacy. Of late, many of those summer cottages are turning into year-round retirement homes. The arrival of the Lindbergh Lake grizzly proved a mixed blessing to residents of the sylvan region.

Though not aggressive toward humans, neither did the bruin exhibit fear of her two-legged neighbors, virtually ignoring them. But this very aloofness gave rise to fears amid a few home owners.

"The fact she is not obviously fearful of hanging around where there are people is a concern to us," Manley told a newspaper reporter.

Then the bear disappeared, and her radio signal vanished with her. Both residents and wildlife managers breathed a sigh of relief. But Number 11 showed up again during the spring of '93, and a wary watch again began.

The Lindbergh Lake Bear turned into a clover lover. Clover, of course, is a prime ingredient of lawn seed, so Number 11 became a frequenter of summer-home lawns. Fish, Wildlife & Parks received complaints from frightened home owners. Although there was no direct interaction between humans and bear, the final straw came when the sow charged two whitetail bucks standing regally on the lawn of a home belonging to Carroll and Dawn Mann.

It was a savage attack by a powerful killing machine. The charge was so swift that neither buck would have had time to move. Each was knocked from its feet with a single brute blow. Both were Styrofoam archery targets.

The Manns were especially shocked since the fake deer had occupied their yard for a couple of months prior to the surprise attack. Dawn Mann had previously shouted and thrown a rock at the bear as it fed on lawn clover, but the bear seemed no more nonplussed by the rock than she appeared to be upon discovery that her great deer ambush would yield no meat.

Although Mann was amused at the bear's attack on the fake deer, he was also concerned. He claimed his wife was "petrified."

"It's so bad right now," he was quoted as saying, "my wife is afraid to cut the grass." So Management Specialist Tim Manley set a trap. His report read:

> Local residents were very concerned that this bear showed no fear of people. She knocked down two deer decoys in front yard and obtained improperly stored garbage. Informed local residents to properly store garbage and pet food in enclosed buildings. Told residents to scare bear away instead of taking photos.

Number 11 was captured and released on the same day Manley's report was filed—August 18, 1993. This time, release was in the Unawah drainage. Unawah Creek is surrounded entirely by National Forests, with no private land in the vicinity. In addition, it's just across the a mountain summit from her original home range near Marias Pass.

There's a stretch of uneventful time between the summer of 1993 and the summer of 1995. But when the Lindbergh Lake bear next surfaced, she'd graduated into advanced devilment in the Flathead Valley's Many Lakes region, abutting the Swan Range's west side. Unlike the brief will-o'-the-wisp presence of the big males (the Rottweiler Bear and Mud Lake Bear), which few residents suspected, the Lindbergh Lake Sow, accompanied by yearling cubs, moved in to stay.

Not content merely to raid valley apple orchards, as did the Dairy Queen Bear—and as a young male was doing in the very same suburban range occupied by Number 11 and her two cubs—the Lindbergh Lake Sow specialized in grazing lawn grass and raiding bird feeders, pet food, and garbage cans, raising the ire of country dwellers wherever she surfaced.

The problem, as Manley discovered when his telephone began ringing from its hook, was that Number 11 had adopted new tactics which eluded the efforts of those responding to her depradations. Striking Pratt Lake one day and Morning Brook the next, she and her cubs might disappear for two days, then resurface on Krause Creek, only to return to Many Lakes the following evening.

Finally, after a month-long effort, the dogged Management Specialist, along with retired warden Dave Wedum, trapped the sow and her cubs near Foothills Road. With clearance already obtained, they transported the family intact to the Logan Pass area of Glacier National Park. The date was October 15, 1995.

Glacier's spokeswoman, Amy Vanderbilt, pointed out that the bears had no history of trouble with humans, and had been trapped and relocated only as a "pre-emptive, preventive measure." It was hoped, with winter weather in the high country well on its way, that the family would quickly settle into a den. Never in the history of human/bear relations had one bear received so many chances.

The end came just a month to the day after relocation to Glacier. It had taken the bear and her cubs but a week to make their way back to their home range near Marias Pass. Had she then been content to remain in the upper Middle Fork, all might have gone well. But she did not. Instead, the family headed for electric lights and civilization. There, she ransacked garbage cans, even breaking into outbuildings for food.

When Kirk Giroux spotted overturned garbage cans, he rushed from his Coram home with rifle in hand. Giroux said Number 11 was "on the charge" when he fired his Winchester .308 from fifteen feet, striking the animal in the neck. Death was instantaneous.

"It could have been a man in a gorilla suit," Giroux told reporters, "and I would have shot the thing. It scared the hell out of me."

Fish, Wildlife & Parks employees were waiting to ambush the bears at a nearby dump when Giroux called to report the incident. FWP spokesman John Fraley said officials had already decided to destroy the bears as a last resort if they could not be hazed from the area. The Lindbergh Lake Bear had exhausted the last of her nine lives.

Her cubs, unfortunately, were guilty by association. Deemed incorrigible by reason of habits learned from their mother, the two cubs were trapped and sent to a Fish, Wildlife & Parks detention center near Bozeman to await transfer to a willing zoo somewhere in the world. A November 14, 1995, press release advised:

> *Officials have tried, so far unsuccessfully, to find a zoo or research facility to take the bears. . . . If no zoo or facility is found for the two cubs, they will be euthanized by lethal injection.*

Joseph Brady, a physical-fitness trainer who lives in Kalispell, wrote a poignant commentary on the future of the Lindbergh Lake Sow's offspring:

> *After getting my van worked on in Ronan, I decided to spend the rest of the day at the Bison Range looking for buffalo, elk and other animals. I pulled up to the highway and saw what looked to be a pickup truck pulling a bear trap, so I pulled up behind the rig and saw the face of one of the orphaned grizzly cubs looking back at me. I stayed close and watched, and I got sadder as each mile went by. The bear that stayed to the back had his nose up against the wire door, with one paw hooked in the wire. He would look at me and then move from side to side hoping there still might be a chance to be free. You could see it in his eyes. To see a bear in the wild roaming free is one of nature's greatest gifts. I didn't know it at the time, but their mother lay dead in the back of the pickup truck.*
>
> *My heart was breaking as I looked on knowing their freedom was going to be taken away forever. . . .* ■

Chapter 24

The Lessons We've Learned

The bear never looked up as the pickup truck skidded to a halt, shifted to reverse, and backed until the men inside had a clear view.

"My God!" one exclaimed. "It *is* a grizzly!"

"What's he feeding on? Looks like a black angus—no! It's a moose."

The driver switched off the ignition key.

The bear ripped off a long strip of meat, pointed its nose to the sky, and swallowed with a gulp. Switching its attention to the truck, the animal stared for a few moments, then turned to amble from swamp into forest.

"Wow! Wasn't that a sight?"

"Even with the ear tags."

A Montana game warden, alerted by the two men, staked out the site until the bear returned. He noted the ear-tag color and relayed the information by radio to Wayne Kasworm, a U.S. Fish & Wildlife Service biologist engaged in Cabinet Mountains grizzly-bear research. By the color, Kasworm identified the animal as a four-year-old sow captured in British Columbia in the summer of 1994, then released into the Cabinet Mountains in an attempt to shore up the isolated range's dwindling grizzly population. The bear had been fitted with a radio collar, but had lost the device a few weeks after release. Without a transmitter collar in place, Kasworm had no way to track the sow into hibernation, or follow subsequent movement.

Discovery of the bear fifty miles from her release site was a godsend to the researcher, who'd had the misfortune to have two other transplanted bears also slip their collars. Kasworm hurried to the moose carcass towing a trailer-mounted culvert trap baited with rotting deer carcasses. The young grizzly sow was nabbed within twenty minutes of the biologist's arrival.

Kasworm fitted her with a new radio collar and hauled her back to the Cabinets where she was liberated into the general area of her original release.

Not so fortunate was a grizzly found swirling in a deep pool below Hungry Horse Dam on the Flathead's South Fork. The partially decomposed bear, discovered by fisheries biologists snorkeling the river, bore ear tags and a radio collar. It proved to be a six-year-old male, captured and fitted with telemetry as a yearling. After two years, the bear's radio collar had failed and biologists lost track of his movements.

Initial necropsy on the carcass disclosed broken ribs on both sides, one of which was reported to have pierced the heart. There were no bullet holes. There was water in the animal's lungs, indicating possible drowning. But the inference was uncertain because the carcass had been in the river for perhaps three months.

The remains were shipped to Montana Fish, Wildlife & Parks forensic biologist Keith Aune in Bozeman. Aune's analysis showed the real cause of death to be severe injuries from a radio collar that had grown too tight around the bear's neck. Evidently, the bear must have grown weak or dizzy and lost its balance in the rocks above the river pool, plunging to injury and ultimate death, perhaps by drowning. But the real culprit was slow and agonizing strangulation by the radio collar as the animal matured.

Collars are designed so that a portion of the material will eventually deteriorate until it simply falls off. The intention is to avoid the very thing that happened to the unfortunate boar. "It's a good system," said regional wildlife manager Harvey Nyberg, "but this time it failed."

The discovery exacerbated the debate between opponents and proponents of research tracking by means of radio collaring.

Trappers themselves agonize over each installation. *Is this too tight? Or too loose? Will the collar fall off the first time the bear scratches an ear on a tree root?*

There's a tremendous investment in each collared bear. Such work is labor-intensive, and there's considerable equipment expense: vehicles, portable two-way radios, cameras, snares, and the transmitter collars themselves. Once the animal has been trapped and collared, the work has just begun; now comes tracking, data processing, and, ultimately, analysis. Airplane overflights are expensive. So is ground tracking. So are computers and their programs, plus the training of those involved with data entry.

Too tight? Or too loose? Collars are slipped by bears all too frequently, considering the effort involved in placement. Three of Kasworm's four transplanted Cabinet Mountains bears slipped their collars. And lost collars are mentioned elsewhere in this book.

But aside from cost, application of proper techniques, and risks to animal and scientists, the question most often asked about trapping and collaring is of obvious importance: Does trapping and handling of grizzly bears lead to familiarity with, and resentment of, all humans?

Scientists asked the question of themselves. And in an effort to draw definitive conclusions, an analysis was made of subsequent activities of eighty-one northwest Montana grizzly bears captured and released for various field studies between the years 1975 and 1985. The data revealed that thirteen bears (16 percent) wound up in conflict with humans. Of those thirteen, eleven were engaged in livestock depradations, one was destroyed by a landowner as it loitered near his residence, and one was killed in defense of human life. Eighty-four percent of those research bears did not come into subsequent conflict with humans.

Comparisons were made with other known problem bears, extrapolating to population estimates based on research. The conclusion? According to long-time bear researcher Rick Mace:

"There is no indication that capturing and handling of grizzly bears leads to an artificially high level of human conflict."

Despite these findings, there is continuing concern about the effects of handling. A yet-unproven research alternative to radio tracking is DNA testing, which is viewed as having promise, although there are questions about its efficacy. Proponents explain that scat samples scooped from trails, or individual hairs retrieved from brush or tree limb can be matched to individual bears. Not only can individual animals be identified, but their ancestry can be traced through DNA analysis to provide information on overall genetic health of specific bear populations. Given enough manpower for collections over an adequate time period, proponents promise an accurate population picture of bears occupying any particular area.

The inadequacy of such a program, according to detractors, is that DNA analysis of scat samples taken from points A, B, and C will not disclose where the animal wandered and what he did in the interim. DNA analysis can yield valuable but limited data; it cannot provide a real picture of the bears—where and when they feed, sleep, breed, and fight. And it's that very picture which is becoming so important to public education—and acceptance.

Another rub to DNA testing, according to detractors and proponents alike, is that long-term DNA analysis is expensive— even more so than trapping and tracking through radio telemetry. There are, however, indications that market dynamics within our free-enterprise system will bring the cost of DNA analysis down, given time.

On the distant horizon might be less obtrusive radio transmitters designed to last a bear's lifetime, perhaps inserted beneath the hide. Such an unobtrusive mechanism still requires capture and handling. And the debate continues to rage over benefits as opposed to disadvantages.

The essential issue beneath the surface of the collaring debate is whether any research affecting free movement of wild animals is appropriate. How can we consider animals wild and free if their life is interrupted by intrusions of scientists? Harassment, so goes the argument, can come from student researchers jotting every movement of grizzly bears foraging for cutworm moths on a talus slope.

But without research, how would we know bears foraged for cutworm moths on talus slopes? Without research, how could we learn what adjustments we must make to insure survival of *Ursus arctos horribilis* into the twenty-first century?

Or is survival of the grizzly of any importance?

One essential aspect of grizzly bear physiology uncovered through research is that sub-populations of the species differ, adjusting in some degree to their environment. Bears along the Rocky Mountain Front average a little larger because, Montana FWP management specialist Mike Madel believes, the area supplies plenty of spring carrion's high protein. Over the mountains to the west, bears may be developing a capacity to survive amid rapidly expanding human habitation in the animals' spring and fall ranges.

Survival of grizzly bears, it was traditionally held, can only be accomplished through retention of vast wild places where individual animals can roam far from human development or intrusion. The consequences of recent bear/human interaction seem to disprove that axiom. Perhaps grizzly bears and humans can co-exist.

As our understanding of the great bears advances, so does our ability to refine management procedures benefitting the animals. As scientific knowledge of the grizzly advances, so, does public education. With education comes public understanding, and then public commitment also advances.

There are bound to be jolting bumps along the road to understanding and commitment, however, such as the tampered radio collar found immersed in Hay Creek, some forty miles up the Flathead's North Fork. The collar had been worn by a five-year-old sow, part of a U.S. Fish & Wildlife Service study monitoring travel corridors. Enforcement wardens for Montana's Fish, Wildlife & Parks believe the bear was poached. The news release concerning the incident included a plea for the public's active help in the campaign against poachers:

> *Anyone with information about this incident should call FWP's poacher number, 1-800-TIP-MONT. Those wishing to remain anonymous may do so.*

That big gaps still exist in the public's understanding of grizzlies can be seen in a story that appeared in area newspapers on September 7, 1995:

Neil Batterson raises wolves in a pen near the foot of Broken Leg Mountain. He keeps a barrel of meat scraps for the wolves in the back of his pickup truck.

Batterson heard a noise around midnight and, thinking it was a dog trying to get at the meat, rushed from his house carrying a broom. The man was at the tailgate of his pickup before he realized he was dealing with a grizzly bear. A *big grizzly bear*! "I was only ten feet from the bear before I realized what was on the other end of my broom!"

Beating a hasty retreat to his house, Batterson dialed 911 and then fired warning shots into the air with a .22-caliber revolver. The bear ambled into the darkness. Montana FWP bear biologists, responding to the call for help, confirmed that it had been a grizzly bear in the bed of the pickup truck.

Batterson told a reporter he'd lived in the area for eleven years, and he'd seen only one black bear and no prior signs of a grizzly. It's difficult to understand how he could have been unaware that grizzlies frequented the country where he lived, even if he'd not seen them. The foothill area below Broken Leg Mountain is, and has always been, favored spring range for Swan Range grizzlies. Bear sightings and encounters, described in news reports, were common between Mud Lake on the north and Swan Lake on the south, extending clear out to Ferndale and the Swan Hills to the west. It seems obvious that a thirty-two-gallon barrel full of meat, squatting in the open bed of a pickup truck, is an invitation to certain disaster. That both Batterson and the bear survived unscathed seems more of a testament to the bruin's prudence than to the man's.

Education and enforcement are keys to grizzly survival into the twenty-first century. Education, unfortunately, won't directly prevent poaching, though it can lead eventually to peer censure with a possible long-term effect. In the short term, however, only apprehension and punishment deter poachers. Fortunately, apprehension grows more sure and punishment more severe as society ups the ante relative to retaining wildlife for posterity.

More frustrating are holes in the educational process. With the flood-tide of research, and the media rushing to meet insatiable public interest in the great bears, it's always bewildering to discover there are people who simply do not know the most elementary sanitation rules for preventing conflict with grizzlies. But with a constant influx of newcomers arriving, perhaps from distant metropolises, a constant flow of cautionary information is crucial and the potential for conflict continues.

"I'm for the grizzly bear," is a refrain often heard from a rural resident who's had his garbage can tipped over by a hungry bruin, "but,"—there's always a "but"—"I think they should stick to their place."

How do you get through to him that he's constructed his dwelling in the *bear's* place? That he's storing molasses-flavored horse pellets in an open bin where the bear once stripped ripe service berries? That the concrete pad where garbage cans now perch was formerly a tiny glade where the bear dug for lomatium bulbs in the spring? How do you get across to the newcomer that by trying to change this habitat to conform to the one he fled, he risks destroying the very thing that attracted him here in the first place?

The answer—the only possible answer—is education. One excellent example is a brochure called "Living With Grizzlies," produced by Montana's Department of Fish, Wildlife & Parks and the Flathead National Forest. The brochure provides tips on hiking, hunting, fishing, and camping in bear country. It makes suggestions about options to pursue in a sudden encounter with a grizzly, and it offers a list of precautions homeowners might take to reduce the risk of conflicts. Some of those precautions are:

> *Garbage should be stored where bears can neither smell or gain access to it, either in a bearproof container or inside a building that bears can't get into. Use outside garbage cans for non-food items only. Haul garbage to an approved disposal site as often as possible.*
>
> *Fruit trees attract bears, especially when wild foods are scarce. Electric fencing is the most effective way to*

*keep bears out of orchards. Pick all ripe fruit from trees
and from the ground as soon as possible. Do not leave
fruit on the trees through the fall.*

*Livestock food and pet food should be stored in bear-
proof containers, preferably inside a sturdy building
that bears can't get inside. Cut down on spillage of oats
and pellets by feeding from buckets or other containers,
and don't leave leftover livestock food out overnight.*

Besides ideas on how to store pet food, there's advice on
supervising children at play, as well as tips on raising sheep, raising bees, and the use of bird feeders in bear country. This section
concludes with a piece of common-sense wisdom:

*If you find that bears have gotten into your garbage or
livestock feed, remove the attractant immediately.
Repeated use of a site by bears is much harder to stop
than a single instance. Bears will move on if no attractants are present. Bears that associate food with
humans and the places where humans live can become
dangerous. These bears usually have to be trapped and
relocated, or killed. Use common sense; it's in every-
one's best interest.*

Government is learning, too. In some cases, collection-site
garbage dumpsters now have heavy metal doors that open and
close hydraulically, denying access to raiding bears. As replace-
ment collection systems are needed, bearproof dumpsters are
ordered at considerable added expense.

Where government is slow to act, privately funded organizations have stepped in. Brown Bear Resources has helped with
dumpster purchases, and the Great Bear Foundation helps in
compensating ranchers for cattle and sheep killed by grizzly bears.
(Funding remains a problem, however; the Great Bear
Foundation's compensation efforts were three years in arrears, as
of October 29, 1995.)

Meanwhile, a plethora of state and federal agencies share
responsibility for management of the grizzly bear. The animal's
status as threatened under the Endangered Species Act provides

leverage for abundant management actions, some leading to public anger and even ridicule. National Forest road closures to protect bear habitat rankle a lot of people, but are supported by a strong cadre of the public and especially by people who regarded past forest management as biased in favor of road construction.

There was no discernible public support, however, for a set of proposed rules covering National Forest camping, issued by the Region I U.S. Forest Service, on July 30, 1993. In fact, howls of protest were heard from hikers, horsebackers, hunters, and auto campers. The proposed regulations mandated that no camps be left unattended even for day hikes; that food must be stored in bearproof containers or suspended at least ten feet in the air and four feet out from the support tree or structure; that game carcasses must be likewise suspended; and that big-game entrails must be removed at least 200 yards from any National Forest System trail. The proposed new regulations raised a storm of controversy.

What is a "bearproof" container?

Have you ever tried to hang an elk ten feet above the ground or drag the entrails hundreds of yards?

If a couple of guys pack in on their own, how can they arrange for one of them always to be at their camp? Impossible.

Down in Yellowstone, one Park spokesperson suggested that people should abstain from having sex while in grizzly country because the odor might attract grizzly bears. A woman, speaking in an open meeting, sarcastically asked if it'd be all right to have sex as long as it occurred ten feet in the air and four feet out from the trunk of a tree?

Editorialists had a field day. Organizations representing recreationists mobilized. Congressional representatives saw an opportunity to make points in their constituents' behalf. The Forest Service backpedaled. A second draft was issued, but it still contained many of the first draft's objectionable elements.

Though "bearproof" was changed to read "bear-resistant," such packboxes would cost several hundred dollars each. And it simply isn't practical to demand that food be suspended in alpine country where trees seldom grow ten feet tall. I wrote in one of my newspaper columns:

I've camped in lots of places in these northern Rockies where there are no trees as tall as ten feet. Besides, one would have to rig a pole or ropes between dual trees. That pole or rope would have to be at least 15 feet high in order to swing elk hindquarters ten feet from the ground. Not in all my years of outfitting in the middle of the Bob did I have a meat pole so high. (Incidentally, the gable peak of my home is 15 feet high). Compliance is simply not possible. That's not to say I won't or do not wish to comply, but that I can't."

Glacier Park backcountry regulations, it's pointed out, require suspension of food. But structures for suspension are furnished within the Park, and the available camps are carefully regulated with regard to numbers and sites. No such facilities are available on U.S. Forest Service lands, nor are backcountry campers inundating National Forests and wildernesses to necessitate costly permit systems. The final regulations issued by the U.S. Forest Service deleted much of the most onerous rules and at last passed public muster, although some visitors were still disgruntled.

Disingenuous tactics are sometimes used, not only by management agencies, but even by institutions supposedly engaged in research. An example was a survey conducted by the University of Montana's Department of Recreation and Tourism at the popular Jewel Basin Hiking Area trailhead near the crest of the Swan Range. The survey's purpose, according to information handed out at the trailhead, was to analyze "ways to communicate with backcountry visitors to adopt appropriate behavior to minimize confrontation with grizzly bears." A graduate student handed each of us a six-by-eight-inch bright orange card and instructed we read the message on it before beginning our hike. The card warned:

Hiking and camping in grizzly country can be dangerous. Brett Simmons will never be able to describe exactly how dangerous it is. He was killed by a grizzly bear while sleeping in his tent. The grizzly then dragged him over 50 feet from his campsite. . . ."

"Is this some kind of rotten joke?" I asked.

The following Monday I called the resource forester for the Hungry Horse Ranger District where the trailhead is located. Fred Flint, who is supposed to know about these things, said the study was being conducted in order to develop improved strategies for giving out messages to the public.

"How about Brett Simmons?" I asked. "I'm not aware of any grizzly attack *ever* occurring in Jewel Basin. The card sounded like it happened, though."

Fred didn't know who Brett Simmons was, either, and to the best of his recollection, there had never been a bear encounter leading to human injury in Jewel Basin.

I told him we found the card's opening statement offensive—designed to shock and frighten. "Fred, we actually saw other hikers frightened out of taking their planned hikes."

Fred said the inflammatory opening had been "watered down three times" before his district allowed the study to begin. Then he added, "There are people in this outfit who think we shouldn't be in the business of trying to scare people."

To find out more about the Jewel Basin survey, I phoned Dr. Stephen McCool, head of the university department in charge of the project. I asked about Brett Simmons.

As it turned out, there was no Brett Simmons. However, the professor assured me, the terrifying attack so vividly described on the orange card was patterned after an incident that occurred near West Yellowstone.

So Brett Simmons wasn't even a real person. A real grizzly bear had never attacked a real Brett Simmons or dragged a real Brett Simmons from his camp. And the incident that never really happened never happened in Jewel Basin.

The following weekend found our party of four back at Jewel Basin's Camp Misery trailhead. While there, I mentioned to the graduate student who had distributed the cards the week before that we thought the fictitious scare story offensive. "And to find out it was watered down three times!"

She said that wasn't true—the fear message wasn't watered down three times. "Not *three* times," she said again.

Hiking companion Marilyn Chestnut summed up our reaction best when she said, "It's a funny way to develop better methods of communicating with people—by lying to them."

So what's the message about research and management? That some is good and some bad. But most important, it's that neither will succeed in saving the grizzly without winning public support. Unfortunately, that's an elementary truth not factored into college biology 101. And that major educational flaw handicaps the biologists, who turn out to be human, too, just like you and me. ■

Hiking in Jewel Basin.

Chapter 25

Asinine Acts and Ursine Facts

The Endangered Species Act—crucial though it may be to the survival of many forms of plants and animals—has proven to be no end-all to some kinds of wildlife. In fact, it may even cause, rather than solve, problems. As a result of federal intervention in wildlife management, for example, the grizzly bear is becoming a hot topic in the everlasting issue of states' rights.

Chris Servheen is a man embroiled in the controversy. Servheen is Grizzly Bear Recovery Coordinator for the U.S. Fish & Wildlife Service. As Recovery Coordinator, one might assume his primary objective would be to increase the great bears' numbers until grizzlies could be delisted from their present threatened status under the Act. Delisting would return management of the animals to the states of Montana and Wyoming, and residents of those states are eager to assume the responsibility taken from them by the federal government.

Some conservationists are alarmed, however, by what they perceive as Dr. Servheen's dispatch in facilitating a "paper" recovery that cannot be authenticated in the field. Using the word "dispatch" to describe how the recovery coordinator does what he was hired to do seems unfair, however, when one considers that the man has been at his present job for more than fifteen years. All the same, Montanans from governor to grain grower, believe they've been betrayed by Servheen and the U.S. Fish & Wildlife Service. They charge that Servheen and his agency established recovery targets to allow state resumption of management, then changed the ground rules just when Montana was on the threshold of meeting those targets.

California may have a grizzly on its state flag, but Montanans' affinity for the great bear extends beyond lip service. It was 1982—the same year the USFWS brought out its first Grizzly Bear Recovery Program plan—when Montana schoolchildren, in an exercise in how state government works, elected the grizzly bear as Montana's State Animal. Over fifty-five thousand students, representing four hundred and twenty-five schools, nominated seventy-four animals. The grizzly won over runner-up elk by a landslide two-to-one margin. Characteristics of the grizzly—his massive size, muscular strength, and a certain poetic beauty—were said to be those of Montana. And the great bear's historical significance, particularly in connection with Lewis and Clark, also influenced the voting.

The schoolchildren's choice was ratified in a 1983 bill presented for the Montana Legislature's approval. More than a thousand schoolkids attended hearings at the State Capitol. Governor Ted Schwinden, wearing a cap with the emblem of a grizzly embroidered on it, signed the legislation into law on April 7, 1983.

Such affinity for the great bear is not just a recent development. Geographic place names memorializing the grizzly are abundant in the Treasure State. I've visited Brownie Basin and Grizzly Gulch and climbed Silvertip Mountain. Around the state are entire ranges named the Beartooth Mountains, Bearpaw Mountains, and Bruin Peaks. There are myriad Bear Creeks and Bear Gulches. There are Bear Springs, and a Beartrap, and Bear Skull Creek. There's a Curly Bear Peak in Glacier National Park and a Bear Prairie and a Spotted Bear Mountain in the Bob Marshall Wilderness. And I could list quite a few more.

So it cut deep into the hearts of Treasure State people when the federal government took control of the way Montana's great bears were managed. State wildlife officials were outraged. They had two primary reasons:

The first was the ancient states' rights argument. Each state, so Montana says, holds its wildlife in common for all its citizens. The authority for state control over wildlife within its borders does not enjoy a Constitutional mandate, however, but stems from public revulsion with European tradition that wildlife belonged to the King who, in turn, bestowed the right to take "royal" game animals upon privileged retainers, wealthy landowners, and members of his court.

The concept of state control was first breached with laws concerning migratory waterfowl, then with ocean fisheries. Chaos had reigned when each state went its own management way without considering its effect upon sister states that also provided homes to migratory species. Therefore the precedent for subordinating state management of some forms of wildlife had long been established when Public Law 97-304, the Endangered Species Act, was signed into law by President Richard Nixon in 1973.

The second reason Montana regarded loss of management authority as a tragedy involved depradation control. Simply stated, Montana utilized the hunting of grizzlies as a measure for controlling problem bears. Prevailing wisdom within the state's Department of Fish, Wildlife & Parks held that occasional bears become conditioned to human food sources, thus developing into threats to life and property. The menace was reduced, according to that school of thought, whenever an animal threatened a hunter equipped with a high-powered rifle during hunting season.

Some research scientists agreed that carefully engineered, limited hunting of nuisance grizzlies could be instrumental in winning support for the great bears among folks dwelling in grizzly habitat. But support for hunting grizzlies drew, at best, tepid support from the environmental community. And when the state's Fish, Wildlife & Parks proposed a spring grizzly season as a control measure for bears moving from wilderness mountains into prairie communities along the East Front, litigation resulted. The state lost. And lost, too, was Montana's opportunity to manage their bears.

The decision by a federal judge in Washington, D.C., halting any further hunting of Montana grizzlies, added rancor to a debate over the worth of the Endangered Species Act.

One particular irony was that, when the court ruling came down, Montana permitted only fourteen grizzly mortalities during one year—by any means. Only six of those fourteen grizzly mortalities could be females. In other words, if two marauding female bears were removed from the system, two more died in collision with train or automobile, another was destroyed during an attack on a human, and another was inadvertently killed during research trapping, Montana's grizzly season was closed for that year, though it might not have yet opened.

The argument over hunting was not entirely an "us-versus-them" fight between Montana natives on one side and "tree huggers" and outside interlopers on the other. Even a few resident hunters wondered whether the state could justify the intentional killing of any innocent grizzlies? They asked this pointed question: "Since most bears are taken by hunting over gut piles [entrails left from the legal take of elk or deer], or by spotting a grizzly at a distance and stalking it to within shooting range, what makes you think the bears that are shot are the same ones raiding a camp kitchen tent in the middle of the night? Or the one breaking into isolated cabins?"

I relayed that question to Arnold Dood, Montana Department of Fish, Wildlife & Parks Endangered Species Coordinator. Dood said, "You can't look at it [the legal taking of a grizzly] in terms of individual bears. But overall, the take is going to eliminate rogue bears. You have to think in terms of the species, Roland. And we'll stand on our assertion that hunting is a viable—even necessary—means for controlling rogue bears."

Still, Montana lost that argument to environmental activists and a distant federal judge. Treasure Staters did not, however, put all their eggs in that one basket. They had a plan. Montana's Fish, Wildlife & Parks had grudgingly accepted the U.S. Fish & Wildlife Service's first (1982) Grizzly Bear Recovery Plan (authored by Don Brown, retired Director of Montana's Fish & Game Department, on contract to the Fish & Wildlife Service) and moved to meet its requirements to justify delisting the bears. Since they did not have sufficient data to satisfy the guidelines for delisting, FW&P made two significant decisions that have had a tremendous impact on citizen understanding and acceptance of our ursine neighbors.

The first was a decision to implement an intensive and comprehensive study of a strategic grizzly population—one that had been both subjected to hunting pressure and impacted by human development of its habitat. Thus the South Fork Grizzly Study was born.

The second landmark decision was to move beyond research into actual management by having specialists respond to problem situations between grizzlies and humans. The result of that decision was to assign Mike Madel, Tim Manley, and Kevin Frey as grizzly-bear management specialists in key regions. Their responsibilities are to educate the public about bears, and to respond to conflicts between bears and people. They've been very effective at reducing mortality among bears, as well as the threat of injury to humans, and assisting in controlling bear-caused property damage.

Both the study program and the management effort entail enormous commitment of financial and human resources by a state determined to win back authority to manage its native wildlife.

The South Fork Grizzly Study was projected to have a life of ten years, at a cost of some $800,000. Actually, most of the research was completed in nine years, but the study's expenses exceeded a million. The educational and management work of Madel, Manley and Frey has been so spectacularly successful, that no end is in sight. The cost? Presently $200,000 per year! The combined cost for both programs? A cool two mil. With that kind of investment in human and financial resources, state officials were confident they could meet all the fed's recovery objectives and again be allowed to manage their bears. Were they?

No.

Convinced that the grizzly bear was still in decline, conservationists attacked Servheen's second draft revision of the recovery plan on two principal points. According to the Alliance for the Wild Rockies, an activist group, the original Fish and Wildlife Service recovery plan was fatally flawed in that it did not allow for adequate protection of habitat beyond that presently occupied by the great bears. Mike Bader, Executive Director of the Alliance, asks, "How can you recover a species if you only provide protection for habitat occupied by an animal that is already threatened with extinction?" The second critical point raised was that most research and management money presently allocated to the big bears, in reality, stems from federal sources, including the funding of both the South Fork Study and Montana's effective grizzly management specialist program—a misleading assumption relative to the three management specialists, as further research disclosed. Here's the breakdown:

Mike Madel says he receives no federal dollars and, according to the Rocky Mountain Front grizzly bear management specialist, never has. Instead, Mike's work is funded entirely with sportsmens' license dollars.

Private dollars fund one-third of Tim Manley's grizzly management work in northwest Montana. The other two-thirds are split between federal dollars and state sources.

Kevin Frey spends only half his time on grizzly management. Private dollars fund two thirds of his budget, the remaining third is derived equally from state and federal sources.

Yet the assumption that Montana does not fund grizzly bear management continues to thrive.

U.S. Fish & Wildlife Service response to criticism of the initial recovery plan was to develop a new plan with new objectives and targets. And Montana's investments in time and money to meet the old guidelines had apparently gone for nothing, angering state officials. There was a sense of betrayal. "How can you meet targets," Region Four Administrator Mike Aderhold asked, "when those targets are continually shifting?"

Aderhold's question turned out to be academic since conservation activists were dissatisfied with Chris Servheen's new recovery plan and sued to prevent delisting of the grizzly bear based on the new guidelines. Again, they won. This time, however, it may have been a Pyrrhic victory, as Montana administrators pushed for legislation to modify the Endangered Species Act itself. Glenn Erickson, Wildlife Management Bureau Chief, said state personnel participated in drafting legislation for the proposed changes.

I asked what his department hoped to achieve.

"The state would like to see the Endangered Species Act modified," Erickson said, "so we can implement programs to recover the species, using guidelines established by the U.S. Fish & Wildlife Service, without the fear of those guidelines being altered halfway through the process."

What Erickson's statement implies is that the Endangered Species Act actually prevents Montana from implementing programs to recover the bear. How? Here's one way:

Region Four Supervisor Aderhold says Mike Madel told him there are three or four bears along the East Front he considers "ticking time bombs." Yet the Bear Management Specialist is powerless to do anything about them, prevented by federal rules governing state management of grizzlies. "Guys like Madel and Tim Manley are out there dealing with these bears, Roland," Aderhold said. "They're the ones who actually smell the bears' breath. Yet they're made to feel impotent. Are they supposed to wait until those bears kill someone?"

Keith Hammer, an articulate environmental activist representing the Swan View Coalition, has studied the Endangered Species Act extensively, and he says the Act allows wildlife managers like Madel to file applications for the disposal of marauding bears. I asked Madel if he had applied.

He had not. But it's not hard to read between the lines. Born to the outdoors, Mike Madel is an expert with few peers. He is not, however, nearly so effective at shuffling papers as he is in the field. Though he's too polite to say so, I suspect he regards the application process for handling problem bears as cumbersome, ridiculously lengthy, and time-consuming for a field man who's already spread too thin.

Erickson says states have three alternatives to regain control of threatened or endangered wildlife: "They can follow guidelines developed by the U.S. Fish & Wildlife Service for delisting the animals; they can attempt to modify the Endangered Species Act; or they can sue the federal government. We've tried following the guidelines and have been totally frustrated. Litigation can be very expensive and drag on for years with an uncertain outcome. To us, the better alternative is to try for modification of the enabling act."

But many conservation activists fear state management of grizzly bears. And the fear isn't primarily about inadequate commitment of financial resources, or even whether the state would permit limited hunting. What worries them most is whether politics would interfere with management at the state level.

"How can anyone question Montana's bear management versus that of the federal government?" asks Arnold Dood in exasperation. "Tell me, name the layer of government that has most negatively impacted grizzlies? It's the feds, that's who. It's logging and roads, and back at the turn of the century, it was government trappers thinking of grizzlies as vermin and exterminating them in the name of predator control."

Dood asked if I knew that back in 1917 the state's Fish and Game Commission had proposed protection for the grizzly bear. I hadn't known about that.

Arnold sent me a copy of a proposal entitled "Protecting the Bear," included in the Commission's report for the years 1917-1918. The second paragraph struck me as particularly significant:

> Montana is probably the home of as many, if not more bears than any state in the Union, and to date they may be hunted, trapped and murdered during every month of the year. They are only protected by their habits of annual hibernation and if, by chance, their dens are discovered during this period, they are dispatched while in a helpless condition.

The Commission's purpose, of course, was to make the grizzly bear a game animal for sport purposes, but this proposal represented the first effort by a governmental agency—a state agency—to protect Montana grizzlies. The proposal ended with this plea:

> . . .Then why not protect this truly game animal against the unfair, cruel treatment he has received from trappers and pot hunters for years?

Grizzly bears were classified as game animals in 1923. Even before that, in 1921, hunting bears with dogs was prohibited in Montana. So was the practice of baiting—luring or enticing game animals to food sources for the purpose of shooting. Montana's first grizzly-bear research was undertaken through a survey by Bob Cooney in 1941. There were additional surveys in 1953, '54, and '57. Then came Chuck Jonkel's Border Grizzly Project Study, initiated in 1974, and a significant East Front Grizzly Study by Allen

Schallenberger in 1976, and a follow-up, more focused state study by Keith Aune in 1980.

The Treasure State's legislature weighed in, declaring that "the policy of the state of Montana is to protect, conserve, and manage grizzly bears as a rare species of Montana wildlife." Under the Endangered Species Act, however, Montanans no longer have the option of managing the great beasts. The Governor, in a personal letter says:

> . . .It was Montanans who saved the grizzly bear from extinction. Yet now, it is the federal government who manages grizzly bears in Montana . . .
>
> Bear populations are stable or growing in the Yellowstone, Glacier Park, and Bob Marshall/Rocky Mountain Front areas, and a new population exists in the Cabinet Mountains.
>
> . . .My longstanding and firm belief is that we have a stewardship responsibility to our native wildlife. . . ."
>
> Finally, Montana has grizzly bears and I strongly advocate that Montanans manage Montana wildlife. I support making the Endangered Species Act more flexible and that we should move to delist species when possible. Montanans deserve the chance to control our own future and this place we call home. I firmly believe that if we are to have grizzly bears in the future, control must be local, flexible, and guided by common-sense management.
>
> —Marc Racicot, Governor

So, with the highest level of administrative support, Montana's Department of Fish, Wildlife & Parks is joining the effort to modify the Endangered Species Act. Keith Hammer believes that's insane.

"Montana's own documents state if that bear is off the Endangered Species list . . . they have no authority whatsoever to stop the Forest Service, or the BLM [federal agencies] or another state agency from trashing grizzly-bear habitat." He emphatically added that "there would be no legal way for the conservation community, or any other sector out there that wants to be involved in the process, to force federal or state agencies to manage grizzly-bear habitat to benefit bears."

Questions about the level of state funding for grizzly bears also concern Hammer, and his concerns are echoed by many conservationists, biologists, and even some agency managers, After all, Montana has been using federal funds, available because of the Endangered Species Act.

Chuck Jonkel, who trained most of the current crop of senior bear biologists and, along with the Craighead brothers, pioneered grizzly research in the northern Rockies, says, "That's why I split with the state so fiercely, because all they'll spend is other people's money. They won't spend state money on bears."

The lack of commitment, according to Jonkel, ". . .goes back to the University. Bear management still isn't taught in the University [of Montana]. Bears aren't in the textbooks. Bears are damned seldom even thesis topics. . . . So [the graduates] get to be regional managers and they think spending money on bears is silly. We've still got that disease real bad in Montana. And it's even worse in Wyoming."

While Keith Hammer believes a commitment from the state to fund bear research and management is essential, he worries about the state's powerlessness if the bear is delisted. "It's a matter of funding and authority. They will have neither in sufficient quantity to take care of bear habitat. The day the Endangered Species Act is gone, the state Fish & Game will have absolutely no recourse to tell the Flathead National Forest that they have to have a road density standard to protect grizzly-bear habitat."

The question is—can grizzlies wait for humans, who profess to care about the great bruins, to agree on how best to save them? ■

Chapter 26

The Essence of Absence

"Pierre the Elder" raised his massive head to gaze up at the circling Cessna 185, then dropped it back to rest upon his forepaws. Scattered trees prevented graduate student Nancy Kehoe and her cautious pilot from spotting the animal carcass, but little else could attract one of the great bears in midwinter, keeping him from denning.

Pierre's behavior seemed to be another piece of evidence that a few grizzlies were developing new techniques for survival in this isolated locale, perhaps staying out all winter, driving mountain lions and possibly wolves from their deer, elk, and moose kills. It was December 24, 1994, Christmas Eve, a time of year when all grizzlies are snuggly denned—or so it was supposed.

Nancy Kehoe did not fly again that winter. And by the spring of 1995, her job as research biologist with Chris Servheen's U.S. Fish & Wildlife Service linkage-zone study in the Flathead's North Fork ended with the refusal by Montana's Department of Fish, Wildlife & Parks and Glacier National Park to extend trapping and monitoring permits.

Pierre the Elder was first captured by Tom Radandt and Tim Thier, USFWS linkage-zone trappers, on September 17, 1993. He was snared on the west side of the Flathead River's North Fork, four miles south of the Canadian Border. Pierre was assigned number 834. At nineteen, Pierre was old for a male grizzly. His weight was estimated at four hundred pounds. He was fitted with a radio collar and released.

Number 834's next location was recorded ten days later amid dense forest on a hillside above Bowman Lake, some sixteen air miles from where he was captured. The bruin hung around the area for a couple of weeks, then moved onto the North Fork Valley floor where, near a marsh, he was recaptured and released.

He drifted back to Bowman Lake, then was visually recorded on October 25 wandering through the rapidly revegetating lands burned during the 1988 Red Bench fire.

A long period of inclement weather in the winter of '93 prevented Nancy Kehoe from flying her survey until January 20, 1994. Radio signals indicated that Number 834 was denned at surprisingly low elevation northeast of Bowman Lake. He was still denned on April 11. While still asleep, Pierre the Elder was selected as part of Brown Bear Resources "Adopt A Bear" educational program for schoolchildren.

Some time between April 11 and April 19, Pierre emerged from his den, bee-lining for the North Fork Valley bottom, north of Polebridge. The elderly bear was located twice more during the spring, then disappeared until a June 9 search flight discovered him on the far side of extremely rugged mountain country twenty miles to the east, near Canada.

Pierre remained near the crest of Glacier's Rockies for almost two months, outside the focus of the linkage zone study. That's why it was a surprise when the bear was next monitored, on August 16, in the Tuchuck area of the Flathead National Forest, thirty-five miles west of his previous location. Unfortunately, there is no information about how, where, or through which linkage zone the bruin moved en route from Glacier Park to the Whitefish Range.

Number 834 was next located on August 27 right along the Canadian Border, near Mount Hefty. Apparently, the bear found the area's huckleberries much to his liking, for he continued to work between Hefty and Review Mountain for more than a month.

On September 27, Pierre was located east of Quartz Lake in Glacier Park, forty miles southeast of the Tuchuck country.

In early October, Number 834 worked his way down to the North Fork Valley, ranging along Glacier Park's bottomlands, moving slowly northward.

All other study bears were denned by November 19, 1994, but Pierre was spotted ambling along a snow-covered trail in the Kintla Lake region of Glacier Park. Then came the Christmas Eve overflight when Nancy and her pilot, Dave Hoerner, spied Pierre lying amid the trampled snow, with no apparent intention of denning.

Chris Servheen is Grizzly Bear Recovery Coordinator for the U.S. Fish & Wildlife Service, so the buck stops at his desk when someone questions the present status and future health of the species *Ursus arctos horribilis*. His job performance, one could politely say, is not without its critics. Environmental activists are especially harsh, as many of them believe Servheen is hell-bent on removing the grizzly bear from the endangered list even if he must structure research data to fit preconceived targets. They even question his competency.

Servheen graduated from the ranks, working on Jonkel's Border Grizzly Project back in the 1970s, and writing his doctoral thesis on Mission Mountains' grizzly bears. Yet many of his peers seem only lukewarm in their judgement of his performance. He was hired as Grizzly Bear Recovery Coordinator by the U.S. Fish & Wildlife Service in 1981. His duties are defined as "Coordinating all grizzly-bear research and management in Washington, Idaho, Montana, and Wyoming." He also coordinates a few research programs with Canada.

The most severe criticism of current grizzly recovery efforts is a failure to address continuing fragmentation of habitat and the subsequent isolation of grizzly sub-populations. Eventually, conservationists believe, this could lead to species failure through genetic limitation. The U.S. Fish & Wildlife Service's Grizzly Bear Recovery Coordinator is aware of the potential problem and has advocated protection of linkage zones—travel routes between occupied habitats.

The basic problem in addressing corridor needs is the lack of definitive research—documentation of existing routes. Yet without exception, wildlife must cross valleys to travel between mountain ranges, inevitably encountering homesteads, farms, ranches, and summer dwellings located along most valley floors.

There may be no better classroom for defining corridor components than in the glacier-sculpted Swan River Valley, lying between the sprawling Bob Marshall Wilderness and the Mission Mountains. Having written his doctoral thesis on Mission Mountain grizzlies, Servheen knows a bunch about the sub-population in danger of being cut off by Swan Valley development from the enormous gene pool of Glacier Park and the Bob Marshall Wilderness. The isolated Mission Mountain Range enjoys the highest possible protection from development; the eastern slope lies within the Congressionally designated Mission Mountains Wilderness, while to the west lies yet another, equally large Wilderness designated by the Confederated Salish and Kootenai Tribes of the Flathead Indian Reservation. But, Servheen says, "The juxtaposition of wilderness and development is pretty amazing when one stands atop the peaks and looks down on the checkerboard of roads, ranches, subdivisions, and timber plots below."

In winter, while asleep in their high-elevation dens, the bears are safe. But come spring, the animals move quickly from the snowy high country into lower valleys to feed on greening grasses, dig for roots, and search for the carrion of winter-killed wildlife.

According to Servheen, "The bears can't keep up with the level of change or the pace of change in their habitat. The places they went as young bears are filled with houses, and their ability to understand the change is limited."

Servheen estimates there are no more than ten to fifteen grizzlies left in the Missions. The population is being decimated in two primary ways: conflict with humans and human development amid critical travel corridors.

The Grizzly Recovery Coordinator tells of one home owner who shot an adult female grizzly as she fed on garbage piled outside his home. "He stuck a shotgun out the window and killed her. Bears cannot survive that kind of minefield. And with so few adult females, this one particular loss was immense."

Because of his prior work with Mission Mountains grizzly bears, Dr. Servheen originally intended to research bear movement through Swan Valley corridors from the Bob Marshall Wilderness into the Mission Mountains. But by the time a critical corridor study was readied, the Mission grizzly population appeared too low for effective trapping and monitoring. So Servheen proposed a corridor study of the North Fork of the Flathead.

The North Fork offered advantages to research not found in the Swan, such as a plethora of bears and a Congressionally designated Wild & Scenic River Corridor along the river's entire length, providing at least some restraints on development. As a consequence, North Fork bears may be less pressured and thus more natural in their travels through the valley.

Initiating a study is never a simple task. In order to trap bears on lands managed by other federal and state agencies, it was necessary for the Fish & Wildlife Service to obtain permits from the U.S. Forest Service, Glacier National Park, and Montana's Department of Fish, Wildlife & Parks. As expected, each agency reviewed Servheen's proposal before approval. Complaints were initially raised over scientific methodology to be employed in Servheen's proposed five-year study, but the underlying sticker appeared to be a perception of the man's precipitate decision to embark on yet another study without due process and consultation with other involved and concerned agencies to identify and prioritize research needs. Still, permits (to be renewed annually) were granted and the study began.

Tom Parker is a rangy, rawboned young man in his early thirties. He's a hunter's hunter, a houndsman, an outfitter and guide. Parker and his dogs were retained for a study of timber wolves and mountain lions in the North Fork of the Flathead. A team led by renowned lion authority Maurice Hornocker was researching interactions between the species.

Wolves began repopulating the Flathead's North Fork during the 1970s, wandering down from Canada. Their sudden appearance was considered almost mystical by conservation biologists, and they were dubbed the Magic Pack. Ultimately, the Magic Pack split into two Glacier Park packs, and some animals migrated throughout much of western Montana to establish other packs.

Though wolves migrating outside the North Fork are known to have killed domestic livestock, that charge has never been leveled against either of the resident Magic Packs. True, opportunity to prey on domestic stock is limited in the North Fork, but the real reason North Fork wolves have never preyed on domestic animals is a relative abundance of ungulates, primarily whitetail deer, but also mule deer, elk, and moose.

A question of the relationship of wolves to ungulates arose, necessitating telemetry research on whitetail deer, as well as wolves. Then Dr. Hornocker became intrigued with mountain lion/wolf competition for the same food sources, and the research was expanded. Biologist Jaime Jonkel, son of renowned bear researcher Chuck Jonkel, signed on as a team leader. Tom Parker and his hounds were retained for capture purposes. During the bitter winter of 1992-93, Jaime and Tom discovered their research into lion/wolf competition included a third competitor. Tom says: "It was in early February when we approached the upper end of Kintla Lake on snow-covered ice and found bear tracks in the snow. We were surprised a bear might be out this time of year; even more so when we reached the cabin and found where he had lain up against the outside logs."

Jonkel and Parker snowshoed sixteen miles from the North Fork Road to attempt treeing and radio-collaring of mountain lions preying on deer and elk herds along remote Starvation Ridge, north of Kintla and Upper Kintla Lakes. Despite its name, Starvation Ridge is prime winter range for deer and elk, and therefore, attracts wolves and mountain lions.

Parker continues: "As we began searching for mountain-lion activity as far as Upper Kintla Lake, we found grizzly tracks of various ages; some of them you could barely read in the snow. Some bear tracks and bear trails could have been a month old, because you don't get a lot of snow there and all of the tracks seem to stay somewhat preserved. And many of the lion and wolf kills we found in that area had been scavenged by a grizzly bear."

Because of research constraints imposed by Glacier Park management, the cat researchers were not allowed to release their dogs in pursuit of mountain lions if grizzly bears or wolves were active in the immediate surroundings. Tom said, "There was so much fresh grizzly activity nearby we finally had to vacate that area."

Initially they believed it was a single bear, but the next winter [the winter of '93-94] tracking conditions were better, and they realized there were probably two bears.

One bear during the winter of 1992-93, two bears during the winter of 1993-94. Was Pierre the Elder the bruin who pioneered wintertime opportunism among Kintla Lake grizzlies?

No. Nancy Kehoe tracked him to his winter den near Bowman Lake in January, 1994. Having already denned, Pierre was not one of the two grizzlies working the Starvation Ridge country that winter. Perhaps it could have been Pierre the year before, but if he'd learned a terrific new approach to survival, why wouldn't the cagey old bear employ it the following winter?

Remember, however, that Nancy and her pilot Dave Hoerner spotted him on Starvation Ridge on Christmas Eve, during the winter of 1994-95. Is it possible *three* bears have learned to winter on Starvation Ridge lion and wolf kills?

Kehoe and Hoerner witnessed a once-in-a-lifetime sight on October 25, 1993—a pack of seventeen wolves in pursuit of a grizzly sow and her cub. The chase took place along a meadow edge while the plane circled overhead. Kehoe told reporters, "The wolves were biting at the bear as she moved along. Some of them looked like they were getting in some good bites."

The wolves managed to separate the sow from her cub, whereupon five wolves attacked the cub while the rest fought a delaying action against the sow. But the mother bruin re-entered the fray, leaping a log and scattering wolves right and left. The chase began anew, finally entering the forest where Kehoe and Hoerner believe the cub darted up a tree.

Alberta biologist Stephen Herrero, in his book *Bear Attacks*, writes that wolves will occasionally kill a grizzly cub. But the incident reported by Kehoe and Hoerner is the first documented case of wolves attacking grizzly bears in the Lower 48 since wolves began re-colonizing Montana.

Wolves do not make a habit of seeking out choice grizzly cuts for dinner. On the contrary, researchers continue to document cases where the big bruins just as readily confiscate the fresh kills of wolves as they do from mountain lions.

Chris Serrheen's linkage-zone study required annual approval. Grudging renewal was extended for a second year for the project, but was doomed when in year three, both Montana's Fish, Wildlife & Parks and Glacier National Park declined to re-issue trapping permits. Dan Vincent, Supervisor for Region 1, Montana Department of Fish, Wildlife & Parks, wrote:

> The need to assess linkage zones in the North Fork is not a research priority. . . .
>
> The biggest problem with this objective is the lack of a biological basis to assume that North Fork bears use or require linkage zones. Marking bears in the river bottoms will only prove the obvious: bears captured in or near the linkage zones use the linkage zones.

Vincent continued with a complaint about the U.S. Fish & Wildlife Service's priority process—a complaint that I heard often:

> We feel it is most important to determine the highest priority work activities in the ecosystem and then work together to develop the best projects to accomplish these objectives.
>
> Until that initial process is complete, we feel it would be inappropriate to proceed with this project.

Still hoping he could salvage his linkage-zone study in order to address criticism from the environmental community, the embattled Dr. Servheen agreed that a multi-agency group to prioritize research is a good idea. But when Glacier National Park decided to join Montana in refusing to grant further permits for the project, the Recovery Coordinator threw in the towel.

Kate Kendall is with the U.S. Biological Survey in Glacier. She is responsible for advising management on research decisions affecting the Park. I talked with Kate at some length about the decision not to grant the U.S. Fish & Wildlife Service another linkage-zone research permit.

"That research request was the most shallow, incomplete proposal I've ever seen," she said. "We told them it would not work two years ago—that it would not provide useful information."

She said Dr. Servheen changed objectives several times. "He was supposed to gather population data, and we said the study was too short to do that. So he dropped population numbers from his proposal. He was supposed to identify narrow corridors essential to bears. Don't make me laugh! What kind of detailed information about linkage-zone corridors can you get by flying only once a week? And then in the middle of the day? Roland, both the study and the proposal are technically insupportable."

And Kendall reiterated Dan Vincent's primary concern: "We used to set research targets collectively. Now Chris goes out and establishes his projects alone, without prioritizing with other agencies."

I also asked about the flow of information about the great bears to the public. She replied in an exasperated tone, "What information has reached the public after two years of Servheen studies?"

Which led me to wonder what information about Glacier Park bears has reached the public after eighty years of Park research?

I think Chris Servheen is sincere in believing linkage zones to be the key for addressing the problem of fragmented bear populations, but I have to admit the study appears flawed, even to a layman.

For example, when Pierre the Elder left Kootenai Peak in Glacier to travel forty miles across the North Fork Valley to the Flathead National Forest, or when he finally left that area for Quartz Lake in Glacier, there is no information whatever on his travel route because, as Kate Kendall says, Servheen's study was so flawed in design it could not obtain that information.

But it's hard to believe Chris Servheen is flawed in *everything*, as some of his detractors seem to believe. He was instrumental in persuading large timber companies, state and federal agencies, and Swan Valley landowners to join in a conservation agreement restricting developmental activities on low-elevation tracts during peak bear-use seasons. The agreement is designed to give grizzlies safe access to feeding grounds and to aid them in passing safely between the Mission Range and the Bob Marshall Wilderness.

The Recovery Coordinator also hopes a few Bob Marshall bears will use the protected linkage zones to cross in reverse, from the Bob Marshall into the Missions. "This is all about numbers,"

FWP Photo

Unmarked bear still out on November 3, 1992. He—if it is a "he"—appears to be following prior bear tracks in the snow. FWP remote camera photo.

he said. "The bears are getting killed, and there simply aren't enough reproducing females to make up the difference."

Perhaps the most notable thing about the Swan Valley agreement lies in the word "agreement"—it is just that. Private landowners held public meetings to hammer out clauses constraining activities on private lands, and timber companies carefully scrutinized their document before signing. The Swan Valley agreement finally represents a victory for the long-suffering Grizzly Bear Recovery Coordinator. The guy finally orchestrated a victory for the bear.

Plum Creek Timber Company was last to sign the Swan Valley Grizzly Bear Conservation Agreement. Just days afterward, a conservation group, Friends of the Wild Swan, notified the U.S. Fish & Wildlife Service of intent to sue over the agreement. The environmental group's litigation threat followed Plum Creek's announcement that it is examining twenty-five hundred acres in the Swan for potential real-estate development.

Environmentalists pointed out that rural housing can use up grizzly habitat, as well as increase conflicts between bears and people when bruins are lured to garbage, dog food, or bird feeders.

If it wasn't for bad luck, Chris Servheen would have no luck at all. ■

Richard Jackson

Chapter 27

They Called The Bear Brother

Triple Divide Peak is the only place in the entire world where melt water from a single snowbank flows into three oceans. It's not a particularly prominent landmark amid an array of stunning peaks in northwestern Montana's Glacier National Park, but droplets melting from that single peak's snowpack flow west to the Pacific, east to the Atlantic, and north to the Arctic Ocean.

Jane and I accompanied three other geriatric couples to the summit of Triple Divide Pass. It's a beautiful hike from road's end at the Cut Bank Ranger Station to the pass, a round trip of about fifteen miles. As we trudged the last mile to the pass, we could see an azure gem of a lake nestled far below amid a glacial cirque. My map lists the enchanting tarn as Medicine Grizzly Lake.

"How did it get the name?" Jane asked.

The answer lay in a book, *The Old North Trail*, by Walter McClintock, first published in 1910. One of McClintock's stories was entitled "The Medicine Grizzly of Cutbank Canyon." The story began with a battle between a Blackfeet war party returning from Kootenai country and a band of Gros Ventre raiders:

> *The Blackfeet opened fire and killed all except their [Gros Ventre] leader. He stood his ground until his ammunition gave out, when he took refuge in the underbrush.*

Our people clipped the branches off all around him with their bullets, but could not hit him. Finally they made a charge, but the Gros Ventre chief fought savagely with his knife, roaring all the time like a grizzly bear at bay and calling to the Blackfeet "Come on, I am not afraid. My name is A-koch-kit-ope and my medicine is powerful." When day broke, our people were uneasy, thinking the Gros Ventre chief might have supernatural power. They told him he was free to go, but they would scalp the others. A-koch-kit-ope replied, "No, they are my brothers and I will not leave them." Feeling thirsty, he walked to the river and drank, daring any of the Blackfeet to stand forth for a hand-to-hand conflict. When our people finally killed him, they discovered that the grizzly bear was his medicine. He had a grizzly claw tied in his front hair. The Blackfeet were so afraid that some of his power might escape, that they built a fire and burned A-koch-kit-ope's body. If a spark or coal flew out, they carefully threw it back into the fire, to prevent the possible escape of any of his power. They scalped the other dead Gros Ventres and had a scalp dance around the fire.

According to the legend, the Gros Ventre chief's spirit escaped, took the form of a huge grizzly bear, and followed the Blackfeet who had slain him. The legend has it that the bear charged into the Blackfeet as they were pitching camp, killing some while others fled in terror. When amicable relations were later restored between the two tribes, the Blackfeet learned that A-koch-kit-ope was a great Gros Ventre medicine man who had predicted he could not be killed unless all his followers were first slain in battle.

And for years thereafter, a huge grizzly bedeviled any Blackfeet camped in the canyon, killing dogs, stampeding horses, stealing food, and frightening Indians into flight. None dared try to kill the giant medicine grizzly of Cut Bank Canyon.

Two native American peoples have reservations where grizzly bears roam. The great bears have considerable cultural and religious significance for both—the Blackfeet and, on the other side of the Continental Divide, the Kootenai-Salish peoples of the Flathead Reservation. Both are implementing programs designed to aid bear recovery. When it comes to topographic features of their respective lands, similarities end—where the high plains collide against the Rocky Mountain Front for the Blackfeet; whereas the Salish and Kootenai occupy a big, lush, mountain valley.

For centuries, the Mission Mountains rising between the narrower valley of the north-flowing Swan River and the much larger plain of the south-flowing Flathead River has been a particular stronghold for the grizzly bears. But in more recent years, Mission bruins have been in rapid decline.

Problems first arose with settlement along the western foothills—ranches and farms and, finally, subdevelopment. Bears died while raiding chicken coops and sheep paddocks, or for the sheer bad luck to be caught grazing the same pasture as range cattle. As much as a decade ago, the Flathead Tribal Council became so alarmed about the decline of Mission grizzlies that high alpine

Medicine Grizzly Lake from trail to Triple Divide Pass.

portions of their reservation were closed to non-tribal entry during periods of bear concentrations. Still the decline continued.

Development was slow in coming to the east-side-of-the-Mission's Swan Valley. But now that it's arrived, biologists consider the cumulative effects of clearcut logging, second-home development, road construction, and additional humans to be hemorrhaging upon Mission Range grizzly survival. All encroach upon vital corridors necessary for bear interchange between the Missions and the vast Bob Marshall Wilderness complex abutting the Swan Valley to the east. In short, development seems destined to isolate the entire Mission Mountains' bear population.

Though current field research may be a case of too little too late, biologists are racing to identify core corridors and essential escape cover. Perhaps the most significant development in the effort to maintain linkage zones between the Missions and the Bob Marshall's mountains to the east is an agreement in principle between the U.S. Fish & Wildlife Service and the three largest landholders in the Swan Valley—the U.S. Forest Service, Montana Department of State Lands, and Plum Creek Lumber Company (Railroad Trust Lands). The agreement provides for corridor retention, security habitat, limits to roads allowed to remain open, and restrictions on timing of activities that may affect bears during their spring and fall seasons of use.

Whether this tourniquet will stifle the ebb of grizzly vitality in time to save the Mission's free-roaming grizzlies is anyone's guess.

Grizzly-bear dynamics differ on Blackfeet lands, across the Continental Divide north and east of the Flathead Reserve. With their reservation abutting Glacier National Park's eastern boundary, Blackfeet grizzlies are also Park grizzlies. The Blackfeet, like the Salish-Kootenai Tribes, employ their own biologist. Though grizzly bears are but one facet of tribal wildlife, the great bears' survival is of paramount interest to cultural groups within the Blackfeet. The most ardent and religiously attached to the great bear will not talk to a non-tribal member about grizzlies—not even to biologists responsible for developing techniques for ursine survival.

The Blackfeet have a deep respect tinged with awe—and perhaps fear—toward the great bears. Most Tribal members would not think of killing a grizzly under virtually any circumstance. If a bear competes with them for a berry patch, they'll go elsewhere. Still, though cultural attachments to the bears run deep, there are many levels of fervor. A few Tribal members would feel no remorse if grizzlies vanished from their landscape.

What's even more confusing about the Blackfeet approach to all things, grizzly or otherwise, is that their governing council usually changes membership with each election, providing little continuity in philosophy or policy. Overall, however, tribal policy supports retention of the great bears for cultural reasons.

It's not easy for someone from my background to understand the depth American Indians feel for the natural world. In fact, it's not easy even to penetrate that belief, let alone understand. It was during the attempt that I talked with Fred Matt, Coordinator for Wildlands Recreation on the Flathead Reservation. Fred is a wind-and-sunburned outdoorsman with a wealth of experience who believes it is only through education that society can grasp the course changes necessary to conserve essential resources into futurity. My eyes fixed on a panoramic photograph above Fred's head. It depicted a down-jacketed man leaning against a huge rock face, staring upward. He wore sunglasses, carried a half-inch climbing rope around his body, and held an ice axe in his left hand. He also packed a .44 magnum revolver slung beneath his arm. The photo was of Fred Matt clinging perilously to the nearly perpendicular Garden Wall, a remarkable glacier-sculpted arete in the Mission Mountains. No doubt about it, Mr. Matt has all the right outdoorsman's credentials. I leaned forward as the soft-spoken man explained some of his people's attitudes and decisions:

"Indian people have this fear that every time they expose elements of their culture outside their own people, it will be used in a way not intended. But we have more opportunity to do the right thing for grizzly bears than you do. Our process is more streamlined. It doesn't take an act of Congress to get something done. For instance, we can enact change on a weekly basis simply by a motion in the Tribal Council—like we've done by closing the hunting of grizzly bears [on the Reservation]."

He nodded when I asked if that strength might not also be a weakness. But Matt was confident that the Tribes' long-term commitment to preserving grizzlies would endure. And the fact that the man had served on the Tribal Council lent a credibility to his optimism regarding commitment.

The wildlands coordinator mentioned the Mission Mountains Tribal Wilderness as an example of that commitment. "We've even gone beyond the Endangered Species Act to try and preserve the bear. We've set aside a ten-thousand-acre area known to be frequented by grizzly bears within the Tribal Wilderness. We close that place down July 15 to October 1 and don't allow anybody into the area, including our own staff and our own people."

Fred said they have two other roadless enclaves set aside on their Reservation as "Primitive Areas" for the exclusive use of tribal members. Grizzly bears, of course, benefit by using those sanctuaries.

I cut in to say, "Fred, I've heard that at one time, the Mission Mountains was home to the highest concentration of grizzly bears in all the Lower 48 states. Can that be true?"

"I don't doubt it."

"And now?

"And now?" He sighed, "Now there's a small population of grizzly bears just teetering every day on the brink of extinction because of the encroachment of many different elements."

"Why? With your Tribes' commitment to preserving the grizzly, how did we get to this point? And how will you save the animals?"

"The most reasonable thing to me in protecting those bears is to own the land. In our unfortunate circumstance, we don't own all the land."

The Flathead Reserve totals just short of one and a third million acres, but forty percent of the reservation lands are not owned by the Tribes. Twenty-two thousand acres belong to the federal government, managed by the U.S. Fish & Wildlife Service (National Bison Range and waterfowl-producing wetlands refuges); forty thousand are owned by the State of Montana (school trust lands) and a whopping four hundred and seventy-one thousand acres passed into non-tribal hands via a 1910 Presidential Proclamation declaring certain reservation lands as "surplus" and open to homesteading by American citizens.

Since 1970, the Confederated Tribes have aggressively pursued a policy to repurchase those non-tribal holdings through willing-seller agreements. That repurchase policy has resulted in the Tribes' acquisition, within the last twenty-five years, of an additional one hundred and fifteen thousand acres. If funds remain available, the day will probably come when their reserve is again in Tribal hands. But will grizzly bears still dwell in the Missions?

I asked Fred why he thinks his people have a higher regard for the grizzly than do Americans in general.

"Indian people believe all these little elements are important; the animals, the trees, the air, the water."

"So do environmentalists," I replied.

"But you haven't taken that last step."

"What step? What is the last step?"

Matt struggled with the answer. "It's sort of hard to explain—the difference is in the spirituality of it. Talk to some of our elders and the significance of the bear. . . ." The man's voice trailed off, and then he tried again to put the difference into words: "They called the bear 'brother.' The Indian people believed these animals carried messages to the Creator."

It's true. When people of most American Indian tribes spoke of the grizzly bear, they did so in veiled terms, sometimes employing words like "spirit" and "power." According to David Rockwell in his book *Giving Voice To Bear*, the Kootenai people "considered the grizzly bear to be the most powerful of the spirit guardians." And the Blackfeet, famous for their great warriors, considered the grizzly a proper "guardian for their best fighters."

Few—if any—environmentalists with whom I'm acquainted view the great bears spiritually. Instead, grizzlies are symbols of wildness, of a healthy ecosystem. They believe that if the bears were to disappear, it would be a clear indication that our environment was on a slippery slope to destruction. It's to avoid that doom that environmental activists employ tactics their Indian allies would hesitate to use—legal skirmishes, passive resistance, media campaigns. But religion? No. Unlike Indian peoples, environmentalists do not incorporate grizzlies in ritual. They do not invoke the bear to heal or bring abundance or protect them from real or imagined enemies. As important as the bear is to conservation-minded people across America, *Ursus arctos horribilis* is sacred only to the American Indian.

Tony Incashola, Director of the Salish Culture Committee, is keeper of the flame. Mr. Incashola's voice is soft and cultured, his hair a distinguished iron-grey. One needs but little imagination to visualize the man squatting before a council fire advising discipline and determination tempered with patience and pragmatism.

I sensed that the man did not entirely trust me. After all, I'd done nothing to win his trust, allowing insufficient interview time and acknowledging insufficient understanding. I recalled Fred Matt's statement that his people have a fear every time they expose elements of their culture to others—they risk betrayal. I snapped back to the present as the Director told me in his melodious voice that grizzly bears are no more important to his people than other animals—or than humans, for that matter.

"We feel that *all* living creatures are our cultural equals. We do not feel dominant."

I asked what effect the bear's spirituality might have on management on the reservation.

"Quite a bit, I'd hope."

"How?"

He smiled; deep wrinkles crisscrossed his forehead and creviced mouth corners. "Language is the most important element in preserving any culture."

I scribbled as he mentioned the tragic loss of a sow and three cubs, killed illegally by a non-tribal member. I glanced up. "Mr. Incashola, haven't Mission Mountains grizzlies also been killed by tribal members?"

"Unfortunately, we have members of the Tribes who have not had the advantage of being properly raised in a home where our culture is taught."

Sometimes even the best intentions and most devoted efforts can't save wild creatures from being tragically victimized. Take the bear tribal biologists call the Allentown Sow. Properly, the story is about a mother and her three male cubs, and it begins in early May, of 1994, when the sow and her cubs of the year first appeared at a ranch snuggling hard against the west face of the Missions Mountains, in the Post Creek area. Tribal biologists who later traced the family's movement reported that residents said they caused no problem, but these residents thought them vulnerable because they were "out during the day."

They also reported that ranchers "kind of took care of them [the bears], trying to chase them off the county roads when they got too close."

Biologists received an official report of a grizzly sighting in the State Wildlife Management area just east of Allentown on May 24, 1994. From their log: "Observed a grizzly sow for only a few seconds before she apparently bedded down in some cattails."

These excerpts from Tribal Wildlife Program specialists' daily log provide insight into what biologists routinely do to earn their pay:

May 25 - Bears stayed in the area. . . . Cubs were small . . . cubs of the year.

May 26 - Bears still in area, continued to monitor.

May 27 - Hauled a dead horse out of the area to keep from attracting the sow to a local ranch.

May 28 - Bears moved closer to [U.S.] Highway 93 late in the morning. The number of people stopping to look at her increased, but she soon bedded down in a shelterbelt about 1/8 mile from the highway.

On the evening of the 28th she again began to feed over toward Highway 93. Onlookers escalated quickly and soon became a highway safety hazard. . . . Called in Tribal Police and the [Montana State] Highway Patrol to take care of traffic on the highway and try to get people moving along. Wardens and biologists began to haze the bears away from the highway.

May 29 - The bears again became active in the early evening. They were hazed back towards the center of the section every time they ventured out toward the perimeter until it became dark.

May 30 - Bears moved east into Marsh Creek.

May 31 to June 9 - Continued to monitor area. No activity noted.

June 10 - A local resident was walking along Marsh Creek Road when the female stood up in the long grass near the edge of the road. The bear apparently made a false charge at the man. He left the area and the female did not follow.

June 14 - A rancher running an operation in the section just south of the Allentown section called and reported that the female was coming into his alfalfa field at night and digging up his field. The rancher was given some cracker shells and screamers to chase the bears off.

June 18 - Investigated a call that the female grizzly had returned to the Allentown area. We told some fishermen that the area was closed. . . .

June 25 - Grizzly returned to section behind Allentown and were getting within 150 yards of Highway 93 again. I hazed the bears out of section again.

June 26 - Local rancher south of Allentown section ran the sow and three cubs out of his pasture. . . .

June 27 - Bears observed along Post Creek. Monitored her until she went into the creek bottom to bed down. Talked to the rancher that works that section of land along Post Creek and he told me he did not mind bears being there.

July 2 - Bears again in section of land 1 mile south of Allentown. Rancher wanted them off his land. . . . Talked to folks living just south of where bears had been feeding and they told me they enjoyed having her around. Said she wasn't bothering anything.

July 13 - Call from a resident living 5 miles southeast of Allentown. Reported seeing a sow grizzly and 3 cubs and a single grizzly on his property. Said he did not mind them being there. He just wanted to report it.

Late July - Dam workers surprised female with 3 cubs while working in area near McDonald Lake Dam.

Aug 8 - Call about bear at a farm operation just west of Milly's Woods. Farmer was observing grizzly sow outside his back window during daytime.

Aug 9 - Call from warden about grizzly sow and 3 cubs and a single grizzly bear in farmer's field west of Milly's Woods.

Aug 10 - Visited with farmer about grizzly in his fields. Farmer has had bear around his house coming in to feed from an apple tree growing 10 feet away from house.

Aug 23 - Call from a residence just north of Milly's Woods. Last night had 2 cubs in yard feeding on fruit, but no sow. Watched them for 20 minutes or so. When they left they traveled 1/2 mile south into Milly's Woods. Cubs returned in morning and were feeding on fruit from trees in yard, but still no sow. . . .

The sow died on or before August 23. Her body has never been recovered.

Investigating officers, working from anonymous tips, did find the decaying remains of another grizzly in a pasture corner of land belonging to Robert Crump, a dairy farmer. Under questioning, Crump admitted shooting and wounding a second grizzly.

Robert Crump was arraigned in U.S. District Court in Missoula, Montana on November 10, 1994. He entered a guilty plea to two counts of knowingly killing a threatened species in violation of the Endangered Species Act. He was sentenced to a total fine of $1,500 and three years' probation.

Robert Crump perhaps should have been charged with removing five bears from the wild, because even as his arraignment took place, the unfortunate saga of the Allentown Sow's three cubs was being played out. One would die and two would spend the remainder of their lives in captivity.

The first cub was captured via tranquilizer dart on September 15, three weeks after his mother disappeared. But it took another three weeks before his two siblings were brought in to a holding pen. The log's last two entries read:

Jan 17 - Picked up bear cubs from holding facility in Kalispell. Bears had denned in a culvert trap that we had attached to the side of the holding pen, so it was just a matter of closing the trap door and loading the trap into a pickup. Drove to Choteau in the afternoon.

Jan 18 - The bears were driven to the trailhead in the trap. They were then drugged, fitted with external radio collars, and snowmobiled to the [previously prepared] den site. The cubs were brought up to the den in tarps and put in. Boughs and snow were placed to cover the entrance. The relocation to the den went off without a hitch.

I must tell you I've presented only excerpts from the biologists' logs. For instance, there's nothing about the frustratingly humorous chase of the three cubs: how wardens and biologists surrounded them in a willow thicket during one capture attempt, only to discover to their dismay, that they'd also included a big male grizzly in the roundup. The male burst through the thicket right at one of the cubs' would-be captors, bowling him over and roughing the man up as he sped by.

Excerpts don't do justice to the number of farmers, ranchers, and homeowners who told the biologists they were rooting for the bears. Excerpts don't adequately portray the show-stopping grizzlies—bears that brought sightseers from as far away as Kalispell and Missoula, lining up along U.S. Highway 93 in numbers to rival tourists at Glacier's Logan Pass at high noon on a sunny Fourth of July weekend.

Neither do excerpts give anything but a fleeting glimpse of the extent of human effort, time, and money spent to give those Mission Mountains grizzlies a chance for survival in spite of a deck stacked so overwhelmingly against them.

The cubs? In the spring, they emerged from the den site along the Rocky Mountain Front. One was soon killed by an adult male grizzly. The other two, without sufficient time to be prepared by their mother for spring survival, grew increasingly emaciated. Management Specialist Mike Madel finally trapped them in order to save their lives.

The two survivors' home now is the Bronx Zoo, in New York. ■

Chapter 28

What Makes Dominant Grizzlies Playful?

Rick Mace does not believe dominant male grizzlies are necessarily the biggest, toughest, most aggressive bears on the block. After more than twenty years of hands-on grizzly research, Mace says, "Age has a lot to do with it. Yes, and size. But a male grizzly doesn't get to be big and old by going around looking for trouble."

"What then makes a bear dominant?"

"I'm not sure what you mean by the word dominant."

"Okay," I replied. "Let's say there's an attractive sow in heat and she's between two big males. And say both are the same size and age. Which one will get her?"

The man's eyes crinkled like I'd just slipped during a soft-shoe routine. "The point is, they'll both get her. It's just a question of which one gets her first and which second. Every one of our females that comes into heat runs up with most every one of our big males."

I suppose I looked incredulous because the biologist added, "One male might spend three days with a gal in Wheeler, then he's all the way down to Bunker chasing another. And somebody else comes in. These females are catching it from everybody."

"So you don't know what male genes are going into the cubs?"

The researcher shook his head. "To me, the dominant male is the one who checks out all the females before the breeding season even starts. Three weeks before the breeding season starts, these big males will be roaming every female's home range, making sure who's where, who's got cubs, who's ready and who's not. That's so he'll know exactly where to go. He's got all his cards laid out before the females actually come into heat. To me, those are the dominant ones—the ones who know where all these females are, and make sure they get to every one of them."

"As opposed to?"

"As opposed to a smaller, younger bear that's sort of—duh—walking around and—oops!—here's a sow with a funny gleam in her eye. If he runs into one, he runs into one. But these guys [dominant bears] have got it down. It's like computerized—two days here, two days in Wheeler, two days in Bunker. They're programmed weeks before the female even comes into heat, so there's no waste of time. [They're saying] 'I got twenty-eight days to breed with as many as I can.' You'd be busy, too! And it'd behoove you to know where every one of them is."

When I stopped laughing, his smile had vanished.

"To me, Roland, that's dominance. But who wins in a fight? I don't know."

"A grizzly is mature at six, right?"

Mace nodded. "An older bear might be a better puncher is all. He might have the right moves."

"But that can be offset by a more aggressive younger bear?"

The researcher nodded at what he must have thought an immature question. He replied in measured tones, underscoring his not-well-known-point:

"But the way to be an old grizzly bear is not to fight. Sure, there might be a lot of posturing and he might rough it up a little. But being dominant in the bear world is being alive."

Being alive in the bear world. . . .

There was a time, millenniums ago, when we humans were challenged to stay alive in a world dominated by great cave bears. *Homo sapien* evolutionary advancement was rapid, however, until today, living means much more than mere survival: Concordes to Paris, wetlands drained for shopping-mall parking lots, "ranchette" subdevelopments amid key wildlife ranges. And as a result, to Ursus of all shapes and sizes, staying alive means far more than merely maintaining social graces in encounters with others of their kind.

But for me there's another aspect to being alive in the bear world. I cannot imagine how I could live in a world without grizzly bears. Absent the great beasts and there's no wild in wilderness; what's left is a blemish on a mountain, a blister on God's creation. I can express it no better than this fine passage from John Murray's *The Great Bear*:

> *"Those who have packed far up into grizzly country . . . know that the presence of even one grizzly on the land elevates the mountains, deepens the canyons, chills the winds, brightens the stars, darkens the forests, and quickens the pulse of all who enter it."*

I touched my wife's arm. She paused in midstride. The lady's head swung as she panned the meadow below, knowing something was there. Then, still standing on one leg like a stork, she turned to me and silently mouthed, "What?"

I mouthed, "Bear." Then I held a forefinger across my lips before pointing.

A clump of trees blocked her view, so she tiptoed to the side, focusing first on her feet, then beyond the forest edge. She gasped!

He was monstrous, a classic silvertip, grazing out in the peat-moss meadow. Jane glanced my way, eyes shining as they did on our wedding night. She later said my grin was so big it looked as if my ears would topple in.

We stood on a raised bench amid scattered spruce and pines. The grizzly was a good two hundred yards distant and perhaps fifty feet below. Behind us, the forest dwindled to an open bunch-grass prairie, spotted with gnarled old pines, limbs almost to the ground. Our position could hardly have been more secure. I slipped 10-power binoculars from my daypack.

Early morning sun highlighted rich silver guard hair along his back, rippling and shimmering almost mystically as he grazed through the meadow's emerald carpet. I wet a finger and raised it, testing air currents. Good! A slow drift in our face.

The bear took in mouthfuls of greening shoots, not clipping them as does a horse, but as an opportunist at work—seizing and tearing blades from whatever clumps chanced into his mouth, ripping and chewing and swallowing and head swinging like a scythe. I passed the glasses to Jane.

"He's magnificent!" she murmured.

Yes, indeed.

This Glacier Park meadow was a glacial "kettle" during the last ice age. The kettle turned swamp, turned peat bog, turned finally to grass-filled meadow. We'd visited the place many times in the past and had never chanced to see more than an occasional whitetail deer. But there was always evidence that both elk and bear frequented the lush spot and I'd told Jane it was a matter of time. "Someday we'll top out here and spot a grizzly or a herd of elk."

"Well, you were right," she whispered as she returned the binoculars.

The bear appeared remarkably fat for the third week of May—still spring amid the northern Rockies. When he grazed away, his hinder waddled like a cartoon rendition of a fat fry cook in a pancake house.

We stood rooted, passing the glasses back and forth like teenagers at a pop concert, whispering in hushed tones about this once-in-a-lifetime godsend.

"The sun shining through his coat. . . . It's . . . it's stunning!"

The bear grazed in an arc, now shuffling and feeding in our direction.

"He looks like an overweight sumo wrestler."

"There must be a million diamonds shimmering in his hair."

"Look at those shoulder muscles flex as he moves. You ever see such power?"

"Awesome."

The beast grazed to a hundred and fifty yards. Jane leaned over and whispered, "How close will you let him come?"

I grinned and passed the binocs. She raised an eyebrow as she took them, lifting the glasses to peer at the majestic creature. Soon the lady was so entranced she did not notice that he grazed to less than a hundred yards and neared the strip of trees where we stood.

I tested the wind again; still drifting from bear to admirers. He could not know we watched. Jane leaned to whisper, "He's walking into the brush."

The bear disappeared into a belt of willows that had taken over the entire southern end of the meadow. "Hmm. I don't like this."

The grizzly was out of sight, though I saw willow tips wriggle a time or two. A Canada jay called from across the meadow, then another. Everything fell quiet. Jane stared first at me, then where the bear had been, then shifted to where she feared he would burst from the fringe of forest, heading our way in a rolling gallop. At last she looked longingly back the way we'd come.

"Another few seconds," I whispered. "If we don't spot him soon, we'll move away."

Her voice overlaid mine: "There he is!"

The silvertip stepped from the willows about where he'd entered them, as if emerging into a hallway from a boarding-house bathroom, striding purposefully to the same spot where we'd first seen him. He took up grazing where he'd left off.

I handed Jane the glasses. "You reckon he came back to the smorgasbord table for a second helping?"

No longer fearful that the bear was upon us, my wife again became absorbed. She shifted left for a better view while studying the big bruin—and stepped on a dry limb. It snapped. I wheeled, glaring. She covered her mouth and reddened. As if on cue, both of us turned back to the meadow. The bear appeared not to hear.

I glanced at my watch. We'd been here an hour. Now the bruin, still grazing, moved farther away toward the forest across the meadow. A single pine tree stood aloof in the meadow; though it was only a two-needle lodgepole pine, the tree was big and gnarled and barren of limbs for its first ten feet.

The bear stopped to stare in the direction of the tree. "He sees something," Jane murmured. Then the monster walked stiffly to the pine, sniffed it, and ambled on.

"I thought he was going to rake it with his claws," I said.

As if overhearing, the grizzly wheeled and walked back to the tree, stood on hind legs, and raked its sides with claws as long as sixteen-penny nails. Then he dropped to all fours, turned hinder to the tree, and backed to rub his butt for several long minutes. The bruin reared to stand full length with his back against the tree. Then he began sliding up and down. Scratching? Leaving a scent mark?

Jane had the binoculars, and I wondered if her gasp of delight carried across the meadow. "My turn," I said, reaching for the glasses. She ignored me so I snatched them just as the grizzly dropped to all fours and ambled off into the forest.

"What now?" my wife asked after we'd sprawled in the grass and watched for the bear's return for a good fifteen minutes.

"What now?" I murmured. "I don't know what you plan to do, but I want to see that tree."

She smiled and clambered to her feet. "Good! You first."

Ours was not the first bear who'd rubbed this ancient tree. We'd seen such rub trees many times before. But this was the first time we'd watched a bear rub-in-progress.

"Will another bear come along and mark this tree, too?" Jane asked.

"Likely," I murmured, "but from what we just saw of this old boy, he'll be able to protect his turf."

"Do you think he heard us?"

I shrugged. "He may have heard the limb snap, but I'm not sure a big male grizzly needs to pay any attention to occasional limbs popping in his domain."

"Then why did he leave?"

I chuckled. "He may have eaten his fill and wandered off to find a compliant female. Or it may be his bedtime. Or he may have a sixth sense that told him to move on—that something wasn't quite right at this meadow."

"Could he . . . could he be watching us right now?"

"He could. Or he could have known we were there from the outset. And simply didn't care. . . ."

The Boulder Pass griz didn't care.

We'd paddled canoes from the campground at the lower end of Kintla Lake, then hiked five miles to a campsite at the head of

Upper Kintla. From there, on day two, we planned to hike to Boulder Pass and return to camp, then hike and paddle back to the roadhead the following day.

Canoing down Kintla Lake.

Boulder Pass, near the Canadian Line, is one of the more remote sections of Glacier and is usually the last trail across the Continental Divide to open each summer. The eight-mile climb from Upper Kintla is a stiff one—around three thousand feet. Even as late as this August weekend, snowbanks still lay athwart the trail as we broke from forest into alpine terrain. There was considerable evidence of bear activity, so our little four-person group bunched together for security, which meant the muscles-in-the-eyebrows younger three slowed to my elderly pace. We also kept up a running commentary to warn brer bruin we were on our way.

More bear sign was apparent in the alpine tundra where rocks and dirt had been excavated by *Ursus* in a search for marmots or ground squirrels. With views unfettered amid the open terrain, we all fell silent, struck by the raw high-country beauty. Cameras were unlimbered and our pace slowed to accommodate shutterbug needs.

"Scottish highlands must look like this," I muttered to no one in particular.

Wisps of long hair whipped back and forth across Sherry's face. She was four months pregnant, and that fact softened her features even as the climb and wind and sun and perspiration gave it a ruddy sheen. The lady's eyes were bright and excited. "Do you think we'll see a bear?" she asked above the keening wind.

I shrugged. Her husband Tad carried a can of bear-deterrent capsaicin spray on his belt.

John went no farther than the false summit, where he found a comfortable rock niche out of the wind but with a commanding view back down the valley to Kintla Lakes. There he rested until we three labored on the final mile to the top of the pass in order to gaze into the Waterton Valley beyond.

We met a party of a half-dozen hikers in that last mile. They were headed for a tiny campground near the false summit, where they planned to set up tents and spend the night. I envied them. Such a beautiful place: a tiny, sheltered campsite within a copse of alpine firs, none growing more than ten feet high; a small snow-melt lake just beyond the camping place, waters ruffled by a steady breeze; fabulous mountain vistas in any direction.

There were snowfields to clamber across on our way to the pass. And soon after we reached our destination, the keening wind and a late-afternoon chill sent me scurrying back to join John. I paused halfway down, however, to glass a huge open basin spreading below. Off to one side, the earlier group had erected their tents. I saw a flurry of activity there and turned my glasses upon them. The boys were throwing stones at a family of mountain goats who'd invaded their camp, apparently searching for salt.

Another hiker chanced by. He paused and sat down. He was telling me he was a schoolteacher in a small town in central Montana when something new caught my eye. "Those fellows camped down there are having trouble with goats. There's one coming back now."

I snatched up my binoculars. "No, that's no—my God! It's a grizzly!"

"Where?"

"Across the lake. See? He's . . ."

"I see him!"

I panned the glasses toward the camp to see if those lads were aware that a grizzly approached. They knew, standing clustered, pointing. The bear, for his part, walked as if he owned all the surrounding estate. He strode to the lake and splashed in, swimming directly for the hikers, now not fifty yards away. The cluster broke apart, scurrying like barnyard chicks when a hawk's shadow falls upon them.

The bruin swam so strongly that four inches of his back showed out of the water. "I don't believe what I'm seeing," I murmured. "He's heading right for them."

We were safe enough, perhaps six hundred yards away and upslope, but I chewed a lip over the grizzly's course. Though he appeared to be heading for the hiker's camp, the trail we must take down from this lofty place also lay in the direction the bear headed.

I studied the hikers. Some tested the stunted trees; others backed away from their camp as the paddling grizzly neared. Then the bear did a curious thing—he flipped over and swam back in

Richard Jackson

the other direction. Next he paddled left and paddled right, then paused and appeared to tread water, with only his head poking above the icy lake surface. My memory of the ensuing show might be hazy—it seems crazy now—but I think the bear even did a few backstrokes.

The hikers crept back to cluster in audience as the mighty bruin cavorted porpoise-style before them. He was in the water for a good ten minutes. Then he clambered out on a rock ledge that thrust from the same side where he'd entered the lake. There, he shook himself like a dog, spray flying in every direction, catching the sunlight in thousands of tiny rainbows.

Finally, without an encore—not even so much as a glance at his admirers—the bear ambled off toward the basin below, and disappeared beyond the lip of a distant hill.

For years, I'd heard others talk of observing fearsome adult *Ursus arctos horribilis* at play. But the Boulder Pass grizzly was the first playful bear I'd ever been privileged to view. Others have written of watching grizzlies slide down snowbanks on their bellies, then rise to hike to the top and do it again. The great bears have been filmed cavorting in rivers and streams while fishing. Others have been spotted playfully chasing after deer they had no chance of catching. There've been mothers reported at play like schoolkids, with their cubs, and cubs in ribald sport with their siblings. But it was the Ole Creek family who provided the most evidence of playfulness to me, even surpassing that of the Boulder Pass Bruin. Yet we never saw the Ole Creek bears.

It was during a late-March crosscountry ski tour up Ole Creek—three couples on a day-long thirteen-mile trail circuit, following a remote drainage in Glacier Park—when we ran into their tracks in the snow-covered trail. There were three, a mother and two cubs, padding along the same sidehill path we followed. The tracks were so fresh we caucused, debating whether to proceed or abort our journey. We were nearing the halfway point, with the worst of the sidehill behind. No one really cared to return, but how far ahead were the bears?

"Those tracks can't be more than a couple hours old," Royce pointed out.

"But they're moving steadily," Ruth said. "How much farther before we turn out of the bottom? A couple of miles?"

"Isn't this early for a sow and cubs to be out?"

"If we make enough noise, surely they'll get out of our way."

I muttered, "I've never been through here. I want to go on."

Jane was willing. So were Lyle and Phyllis. Royce gave in.

The narrow canyon broadened, and our trail dropped down to the valley floor. No dummies about outdoors adventure, the bear family chose the same trail we followed onto the bottom. And it was in the bottom where their play began, written plainly in the snow for all to see.

First one cub darted a hundred yards out to the side, only to come galloping back to crash into the other cub, where both went rolling and tumbling in frolic. Then both would dart away in different directions, reverse course, and come careening back in wild abandon to crash into their plodding mother.

She cuffed one, knocking him sprawling into the snow—to little apparent effect. The cubs galloped away together into a wil-

Prints of a family group of grizzlies on top of elk tracks in snow. Note #2 pencil for size comparison.

low thicket where they rolled in play, then came charging back upon their mother. She began to dance and gallop short distances with them. One could see where she leaped into the air just before the cubs collided with her, then charged away through willow brush like a runaway freight as the cubs careened after her.

They walked logs across the creek. They walked logs partway across the creek, then plunged in to emerge fifty yards down, streaming water from their coats. A cub crashed into its mother even as she shook water from her coat, and all galloped away again in wild and erratic abandon.

Then all three would slow and pace sedately, cubs on either side of the mother. Of a sudden, she made a mighty leap and fled across the creek, splashing water onto driftwood and snowbanks, then ambushed the cubs as they galloped belatedly up, looking for her.

Then it was the cubs' turn to gallop ahead and spring their own ambush. Once, while cubs lay in wait, the mother crept around to their rear and ambushed the ambushers.

We had great sport unraveling their tracks. All wanted to see the family at play. But alas, they sped along their own Interstate, heading for God knows where, and we never saw them before we turned off their trail for our parked car and U.S. Highway 2, six miles away. ■

Chapter 29

Changing Rules

It's true there are fewer grizzly bears today than roamed the wilds during the previous century. There are, after all, fewer wilds, fewer places free of survey stakes and cutting-unit boundaries, fewer alpine meadows without prints of vibram soles, fewer lakes without colorful tents pitched along their shores, fewer streambanks without fisherman's trails. Today, basketball hoops hang from the gable ends of garages perched on hillsides where bushes once hung heavy with huckleberry or serviceberry or mountain ash.

There are fewer valleys without Interstates or U.S. highways or state roads or county roads or, at least, forest haul roads full of ten-wheelers in a hurry. There are fewer riverbottom flats without landing fields, or marshes that haven't been drained to raise hay or barley or potatoes or mint.

Yet there are still places amid the ruggedest peaks of the northern Rockies where humans and their toys and lairs are absent. Some of those places are big, very big: Yellowstone and Glacier Parks, the Bob Marshall, Great Bear, Scapegoat, Absaroka-Beartooth, and Lee Metcalf Wildernesses. Grizzly bears dwell therein. And in those places, evidence leads some folks to believe numbers of *Ursus arctos horribilis* are increasing. If, indeed, grizzly numbers are on the rise, it's because a change has occurred in human attitudes toward the bear. That change may be a result of status protection, habitat management, or social transformation. But whatever the cause, it's real. And it bodes well for the future of the great bears wherever their living space is not too confined.

But such is not the case in smaller enclaves where subpopulations of the bears teeter on the brink. Though mountain summits in the Missions are still natural due to Tribal and Congressional mandates, critical spring and fall ranges for the bears have little protection, and their fate in those ranges remains largely dependent upon the benevolence and tolerance of individual valley-bottom landowners. Farther west, bears in the Cabinet Mountains likewise dangle, hanging by a thread frayed by forces traceable to civilization, Manifest Destiny, the industrial revolution, and new technology.

Even were the Confederated Salish and Kootenai Tribes somehow to acquire immediate ownership of all lands within their Flathead Reservation's boundaries, and implement rules to benefit the bears, some scientists question whether the animals could survive without access through the Swan Valley to the larger ursine gene pools found amid the vast Wilderness and Park lands spreading along the Rockies into Canada.

Spirituality, then, is not enough. It wasn't enough to bring back the buffalo and it won't be enough to save the grizzly without being complemented by science and by, above all, a continuing shift in social attitudes.

There's hope, however—a message thread I hope runs throughout this book. When I first arrived in Montana during the 1960s, grizzly bears were considered, at worst, vermin; at best, a nuisance. Hunters came to the Treasure State from all over the world in the hope they would take the ultimate trophy: a huge grizzly pelt to hang on the wall or lay as a rug before the fireplace. I was such a hunter, and accept no shame nor blame that in my youth I was disposed to a pursuit that was both socially acclaimed and perfectly legal.

That I did not take the grizzly rug of my dreams is not at all to my credit, but rather the fault of fate—and the magic the great bears work on people who are speedier at contemplation than pulling a trigger on a high-powered rifle.

Perhaps the most perplexing mystery relevant to shifting attitudes is how *Ursus arctos horribilis* managed to work his medicine-magic on so many of us in such a short period of time. In my lifetime alone (no, scratch that: in but half of my lifetime) the great bears have reversed their image as a symbol of malevolent ferocity to one representing nothing less than the antithesis of pollution and exploitative habitat destruction. From roadblocks to mankind's progress, they've emerged as perhaps the best indicators of nothing less than our own survival. That the animals have attained such an astounding human attitude reversal in the face of sensationalistic journalism portraying them as bloodthirsty killers towering over scantily clad maidens is even more mystifying.

Yet the bears haven't changed; it is we who have changed. And there's poetic justice—as well as some comfort—that the journalistic profession, which contributed to the great beasts' brush with extinction, is also contributing to their recovery through information.

Tabloid journalists, you see, aren't the only reporters covering today's ursine "revolution." No longer are readers content with gruesome attack tales about murderous grizzlies when there are dozens—hundreds—of "Grizzly Daughters" and "Dairy Queen Bears" doing normal bear things on a daily basis.

An excellent example of that transition from pariah to partner can be gleaned from the concern that's evident in a December 6, 1995, account written for Kalispell's *The Daily Inter Lake* by respected outdoors writer Ben Long:

> . . . *Although the final numbers aren't in yet, it's clear that 1995 was tough on bears.*
>
> *At least 12 bears were shot or hauled to zoos in 1995. Biologists say conflicts were high this year, partly because of a spotty huckleberry crop."*

Ben recorded the losses:

- Cubs of the Allentown Sow who nearly starved to death after emerging from the artificial winter den where biologists placed them upon the death of their mother. Re-trapped and sent to a zoo.

- Unnamed sow first trapped after raiding ranches along the Rocky Mountain Front and released amid west-side mountains; finally captured at the Flathead County Airport and shipped to a zoo.

- Boar destroyed after raiding sheep sheds on the Blackfeet Reservation.

- Sow killed near Coram after raiding garbage cans (the Lindbergh Lake Sow); her cubs captured and placed in a zoo.

- Three separate grizzlies killed by mistake by hunters pursuing black bears.

- Two bears killed by trains.

- Boar killed as result of research mishap (tight collar).

Ben goes on to say:

> Of the 12 bears known to be killed or removed, six were females.
>
> . . . Biologists often see high numbers of grizzlies killed and removed during years with poor huckleberry crops. In 1992, 15 bears were removed. In 1993 and '94, years with better berry crops, six were removed.

What struck me about Ben Long's story, however, was not so much what was reported, but what was *not* said. Yes, twelve bears, including six females, were taken out of the Northern Continental Divide ecosystem, either through mortalities or removal. I found it fascinating to note that those numbers were within limits established scientifically by Montana's Department of Fish, Wildlife & Parks while they still had management responsibilities. And we're talking about a year of naturally occurring berry famine.

But the real clincher might lie in the fact that only four of those losses were bears moving into populated Flathead Valley, despite the fact that *fifteen* different grizzlies were known to have worked the valley floor for at least a portion of the spring, summer, or fall. There are snapshots and video footage taken through picture windows of the mighty *Ursus arctos horribilis* grazing cattle-like on lawn grass or eating apples from beneath fruit trees.

Over three decades ago, when I first arrived in Montana, most of those bears would have perished under the guns of frightened humans supposedly defending their turf from ursine invasion. Never mind that the bears were merely re-occupying habitat they'd utilized for millenniums. Make 'em stay in their place: high in the mountains where no people go (and food is scarce). Let 'em eat cake.

The real point is not that four Flathead Valley grizzlies were lost as a result of human activity during a period of huckleberry famine, but that eleven *survived*.

True, three of those survivors were captured and transported to distant release sites. But six visited my valley for a short period and left on their own. And two spent most of their waking year amid the fleshpots of civilization, with at least tacit support from a significant number of people who knew they were there. Furthermore, odds are good there were other, uncollared grizzlies slipping along the valley fringes, moving by night, sleeping by day, raiding orchards or garbage or lawn clover.

Mel Ruder, Pulitzer Prize-winning newspaper editor, wrote an October 14, 1976, story about how a young grizzly bear was separated from his mother and, in an effort to stay alive, tried to exist on fish entrails left along riverbanks by fisherman. He told how the young bear had wandered into town and discovered garbage; how he'd been hounded and finally wounded before being dispatched by a homeowner. Ruder, whose weekly *Hungry Horse News* was famous for its photos, had a picture of the bear. The caption read:

> *End of a young grizzly came Wednesday about 6:30 p.m. at Hungry Horse. He'd been wounded, by persons unknown. Grizzlies and people living next to each other doesn't work.*

By 1995, however, staff writer Michael Jamison could write a feature front-page story for the now editor emeritus' former paper:

The departure of the two cubs whose mother was killed last month in Coram has left residents along the southern border of Glacier National Park missing what had become a familiar family of three in their neighborhood.

"It's too bad she was shot," said Jan Smith, who lives east of Essex with her husband, Don. "She wasn't aggressive at all. She turned tail if you hollered at her. In fact, I wouldn't be here to tell you about it if she had been aggressive. I bumped into her on my way to the garage one day and I yelled and ran and she ran and I don't know who was more startled.

"We saw her on a regular basis for years," said Smith. "On one day she was spotted at four different homes. This fall, hunters saw her near the railroad tracks a lot. I suppose she was feeding on gut piles left by hunters."

But while many residents were sorry to see their neighbors, the trio of bears, removed once and for all from the area, Jan Smith knew it was inevitable.

"They just wouldn't stay away from homes," she said.

. . .

Jan Smith wasn't the only one who regretted the death of the sow and removal of her cubs to a zoo. Recent emigre Paul Grimberg wrote a letter to the editor critical of individuals with slovenly garbage habits. Grimberg was, in turn, attacked by letter writers Ilse Knight and Jim Wright, challenging him as an ignorant newcomer. Those letter writers fell afoul of Judy Shanks, who claimed over two decades' residency and echoed Grimberg's sentiments. Shanks wrote:

. . . We have lived up the North Fork for many years and have not had problems with bears or any other animals in our garbage because we use our heads and care for it properly. . . .

Kirk Giroux, the Coram homeowner who killed the Lindbergh Lake Sow, is not the only person to feel the weight of public opinion after shooting a grizzly bear foraging around his home.

Gordon Pouliot was quoted in an October 5, 1995 news report as saying he "feels lousy" about shooting a grizzly bear that broke into his shed. "I've had several bears in and out of here since August. None have caused any problems." But, according to the report, "late last week, a bear raided his bird feeders. He put the feeders away, but the bear returned."

Despite Pouliot's own spirited letter-writing defense, a storm of criticism arose about his and Giroux's shootings of the foraging grizzlies. The vitriol was civil, however, compared to that breaking around Robert Crump after he pleaded guilty to shooting and wounding the Allentown Sow from a window of his home.

It might be a truly significant watershed that opinion even favors some bears who kill humans. It was unusual when considerable public support manifested itself for the sow who, in the spring of 1987, killed photographer Charles Gibbs as he encroached on her territory in an effort to get the "perfect" photograph. And it may have been a first when Glacier Park Rangers declined to pursue and kill the bear whose attack was proved by Gibbs' own posthumously published photos to have been in defense of her cubs. But the case of John Petranyi had a markedly different outcome.

A Board of Inquiry was convened by Glacier National Park administrators to investigate Petranyi's death and make recommendations. The Board's findings, in part, were:

> *Based upon the available information, investigative reports, and circumstances surrounding this event; it is the opinion of this Board that the action leading to the death of Mr. John Petranyi was a surprise encounter between Mr. Petranyi and a female grizzly bear with two cubs-of-the-year and the bear's subsequent efforts to protect those cubs. This occurred on the Loop Trail approximately one-half mile below Granite Park Chalet.*

Petranyi, a forty-year-old Wisconsinite, was hiking alone on the morning of October 3, 1992. He apparently surprised the bears at close range. The grizzly sow, programmed to defend her cubs, launched a pre-emptive strike.

Later investigation indicated the sow broke off her attack and retreated after immobilizing the man. It was then that Petranyi attempted to flee, provoking a second, this time fatal, attack. The sow dragged Petranyi's body to a nearby wooded promontory and the family began to feed.

The Board of inquiry found no evidence of prior food conditioning of the bears involved; that the subject bears were found to be healthy and taking advantage of available natural food sources; and there was no evidence to suggest that these bears were "food-stressed" and in a predatory mode.

Several days later, following lengthy evaluation, Park Rangers hunted down the "offending" bears—to considerable public criticism. This criticism took two different tacks: (1) that throughout the Petranyi affair, the bears exhibited standard evolutionary bear behavior; and (2) because of the long time lapse between the man's death and the decision to remove the bears, there was some doubt that the actual transgressor bruins were the ones dispatched.

It's remarkable in today's world that even bears physically interacting with humans find plenty of defenders of all stripes rallying to their side. If numbers are any measure, each dead bear lives on through its supporters to win a public relations victory over even a self-publicist like Gordon Pouliot, who has been said to brag of the number of grizzlies he's killed.

Still, it's an uphill battle for men like Management Specialists Madel, Manley, and Frey, and all the game wardens and biologists and wildlife managers. It's difficult to come up with a better example of the educational job ahead than the Coopers Lake landholder who deliberately fed as many as a dozen black bears so he could watch them from his home. Wardens, acting on complaints from neighbors, approached the man, who laughed and told them there was no law on the books to prohibit him from feeding bears!

It's true! The wardens beat a retreat. The resolution came a few days later, however, when one of the bear-feeder's Coopers

Lake neighbors surprised a black bear in his own garage. The bear, accustomed to obtaining food from humans, turned aggressive, and the neighbor killed the bear. He then threatened his neighbor the bear-feeder with civil damages for attracting bears into the area.

Warden Jeff Campbell, working now with a formidable lever, was able to extract a verbal commitment from the homeowner to discontinue his ursine feeding program.

By the grace of God, no grizzly bears were attracted to the Coopers Lake smorgasbord, despite its location just outside the south end of both the Bob Marshall and Scapegoat Wildernesses.

Dan Carney, the quiet, unflappable biologist for the Blackfeet Nation, solved just such a problem by asking the Tribal Council for a rule prohibiting anyone from utilizing food in a manner that attracted grizzly bears.

According to Carney, neighbors complained of grizzlies hanging around the tourist community of East Glacier. As a result, Dan trapped two bears. He traced the problem to one homeowner's yard, where sunflower seeds and dog food was heaped on a roofed-over bird-feeding platform. The proof was grizzly hair, found where the animals had climbed up under the roof to reach the feeder. The homeowner resisted the biologist's suggestion that he discontinue his feeding station. Result? The Tribal Council passed the rule in the winter of 1994-95.

With the enforcement tool in place, it was no longer a mere biologist making suggestions, but Tribal Police. The homeowner discontinued his feeding station, and grizzly bears were no longer a nuisance in the East Glacier neighborhood.

Chuck Jonkel, who studied black bears, grizzly bears, and polar bears for decades, believes we must teach people how to live with bears, "because bears already know how to live with us."

Chuck says we have to teach people to "talk bear." Bears, according to this master researcher, have developed a polished sense of etiquette in their relations with other bears, and readily transfer that etiquette to humans, whom they treat as sort of a "super bear."

Our problem is that most people don't know how to deal in bear terms. "If we only knew how much they take care of us, all summer long; there's hundreds and hundreds of real close encounters, and nothing happens time after time after time. The bear knows what to do, we're the super bear, the bear has better senses than we do, he knows the country better than we do, the bear does the right thing and the people don't even know it."

The man waved his hands for emphasis. A lock of his bushy, salt-shot black hair fell over his eyes and was flicked back with an unconscious gesture. "And that's how we're going to have to manage bears in the future—teach people bear behavior and teach people bear etiquette."

Jonkel says the bears simply can't cope with each human doing things differently. "They can't learn to live with people when one guy feeds them and another tries to shoot them."

Hikers follow trails. But foresters follow a straight line, hanging colored ribbons. Ranchers stock "boneyards" with dead livestock, then become agitated when a bear feeds on carrion outside the boneyard. One homeowner feeds bears, the next sics dogs after them. The list is endless. "We've got to get educated about bear behavior, develop sensible rules and be consistent," says Jonkel.

To illustrate his point, he cited Alaska's McNeil River Sanctuary, where fifty or sixty of the great bears come within a few feet of a group of photographers. "The photographers are under extremely strict rules to stay on 'the pad.' The pad is their 'fishing spot,' as far as the bears are concerned. The bears all have their fishing spot. And they all respect the others' space, the sequence of who can fish when, and they're all very courteous in that they look away, and pretend they don't see the other ones. Well, the bears just automatically transfer all that behavior to people. All they have to do is teach the people how to do it."

Jonkel said photographers come to the McNeil Sanctuary year after year without incident. "Time and again bears will walk by within ten or fifteen feet from four or five people who just 'click,' 'click,' 'click,' 'click.'" The man smiled at the recollection, then said, "They all get the back side of the bears' heads, because the bears will be looking away saying, 'I don't even know you're there.' That's good bear behavior."

Later, as I drafted the results of this two-hour interview with America's foremost bear expert, I was struck by the similarities in tolerance between McNeil River bears fishing for abundant salmon and bears in the northern Rocky Mountains digging in talus slopes for copious quantities of cutworm moths. Is an individual bear's tolerance of other bears—and possibly, people—dependent upon an abundance of food?

Jonkel says food is extremely important to bears. "They den for up to seven months out of the year, which leaves only five to feed. And out of those five months, only two are good months. They can't make up for screwing up in July . . . they can't make up for it in January, like an elk can. They're stuck with their success during that two or two and a half months. They're very exploitive of food. And they are very good at it."

The man's teeth flashed through his graying beard. "I've always said if finding food was a game of chess, grizzly bears would be the Russians of the world. They'd beat the pants off us. They're extremely clever."

Jonkel concedes there's a growing public awareness and interest in *Ursus arctos horribilis*. But he credits that interest to a general public interest in all things natural.

He believes grizzly numbers are on the rise, but thinks today's gain is only a short-term increase because the great bears' habitat continues to decline at an alarming rate.

Chuck Jonkel, arguably the world's foremost bear researcher, believes the only really viable way to increase habitat is to reintroduce grizzly bears into suitable areas where they are presently absent.

And that's an electrifying issue. ∎

Richard Jackson

Chapter 30

Learning To Talk Bear

"We don't need the grizzly bear here," the man said, eyeing one particular listener. "If backcountry users are attacked and mauled by a grizzly," Darby's Gene Honey asked, "who's going to pay the medical bills?"

Montana's Governor Marc Racicot leaned forward attentively. Earlier, he'd told the hostile crowd of three hundred at the Hamilton City Hall that he continues to support a plan which, according to its authors, will put management of the grizzly bear into the hands of the people most affected. "We will not support any plan that does not give the state certain rights."

The plan to which Governor Racicot referred was a proposal to reintroduce grizzly bears into the nation's largest wilderness south of Alaska. Largely located in Idaho, the contiguous Selway-Bitterroot and River of No Return Wilderness complex spreads into extreme southwestern Montana mountain country. Grizzly bears once roamed there, but have been absent for half a century. Governor Racicot spoke at a meeting called by opponents of grizzly reintroduction. At one point, he told the crowd he's "sick and tired of standing back and watching the process take off. We haven't been able to stop the wolf. If it's going to happen, I want Montanans to have a say in how it's done."

The same reasons that impelled Governor Racicot to participate in the process also motivated elements usually opposed to conservation initiatives to join the reintroduction effort. Seth

Diamond, a wildlife biologist for the Intermountain Timber Industry in Missoula, said the proposed citizen-management team would be able to minimize the federal government's role in management of introduced grizzlies.

Still, there's plenty of heat over reintroduction, especially in the rapidly developing Bitterroot Valley. All the heat is not con, however, as a survey for the Idaho Fish and Game discovered. In this survey, conducted by Responsive Management, a Virginia firm, pollsters contacted nine hundred Americans in three different groups: (a) local people in Idaho and Montana counties that might be directly affected by grizzly reintroduction; (b) people scattered regionally throughout Idaho, Montana, Wyoming, Washington, Oregon, Utah, and Nevada; and (c) people across America.

In each group, reintroduction supporters outnumbered opponents: 62 percent of local residents in support, 73 percent regionally, and 77 percent nationally.

Response to the idea of reintroducing grizzly bears to one of their former ranges was different in the Evergreen State, where the Washington State House voted *Ursus arctos horribilis* "ursa non grata."

"First thing you know, a bear will eat a backpacker, and then nobody will want to hike in the mountains anymore," Senator Alan Bluechel of Kirkland said. "Moreover, the federal government might decide the bears are endangered and declare the whole region off-limits to hikers."

The bill, SB6387, bars the state's Department of Wildlife from taking part in any plan to import grizzlies to Washington. This is in response to a proposal to augment a fragile population of remnant bears still holding out in the North Cascades region, along the state's border with British Columbia.

"I recognize that we can't stop the feds," the bill's sponsor, Brad Owen of Shelton, said, "but we hope this will send them a message that we don't want the bears."

Unthinkable as some might believe it to be to reintroduce grizzly bears into vast tracts of wildlands where they once roamed, consider this headline from a July 20, 1995, Associated Press release:

Should Grizzlies Be Returned To California?

The story was about a suggestion to reintroduce the great bears to what is left of the California wilderness.

"I think it would be absolutely lovely if there were a place for grizzly bears in California," Dave Graber, a scientist with the National Biological Service in Sequoia and Kings Canyon National Parks, is quoted as saying. "But I do not think there is a place for grizzly bears in California. We used it up."

But Stephen Herrero, an expert on bears at the University of Calgary in Canada, wrote that the idea is "refreshing and at least worthy of serious consideration. . . . It would be an act of unprecedented conservation significance, but it would also change the basic nature of the wilderness experience in the State of California."

The problem isn't that grizzlies require complete solitude, Graber said, "it's that people require no grizzlies." The King's Canyon biologist added, "Humans will put up with a thousand times more risk from street crime, but not the threat to campers, backyard pets and farm animals that grizzlies might pose."

I find it fascinating that more rhetoric about people not tolerating grizzly bears is heard from people dwelling where there are no grizzly bears than from people where the great beasts occasionally roam. That's what this book is about: how people who live in proximity to the animals are learning to *live*—not just with the mighty creatures but in the kinds of high-quality landscapes the bears, too, can tolerate.

That attitude wasn't always apparent among either ursids or us. It's interesting to note that such change stems from both bears and people learning more about each other—like Chuck Jonkel says, "learning the rules." We who live with the bears have more information—and thus, more understanding. Those who know little about the bears have nothing for counsel but their own fear.

Were grizzlies to be introduced to the Selway and North Cascades and, yes, even California, I should fear most for the animals. Imagine being plopped down amid a frightened bunch of humans *unaware of the rules*! It's not enough they must adjust to different food sources (do cutworm moths migrate to the Bitterroot Range or North Cascades or Sierra Nevada talus slopes?) and security retreats, but they must also adjust to humans who haven't a clue about proper behavior around bears.

And how about the rules of engagement? While it's patently untrue that the presence of grizzly bears in the North Cascades would lead to closing that vast wilderness to travelers, it *is* true that certain limitations might be emplaced to enhance recovery: Like regulations for handling residential garbage near grizzly habitat. Like the Blackfeet Tribal rule prohibiting anyone from utilizing food in a manner that attracts grizzly bears. Like precluding new highways and homes amid the grizzly's best living space.

Those who are motivated chiefly by their own fears need also to understand that much better tools exist today for accommodations between bears and people. Whereas yesterday, advice for living near grizzlies was pretty much limited to shoot, shovel and shut up, today there's a great deal of information on how to live with the bears—much of it in easy, readable, hand-out form.

In addition, there are much more sophisticated trapping and monitoring systems for controlling potential problem bears. And the development of pepper-spray bear-deterrents provides a more easily used defense tool in the hands of ordinary people than yesterday's heavy-caliber firearms.

But better tools and added knowledge for defense might not be enough. The continued presence of nature's greatest indicator of wildness may require deeper thought and a higher level of commitment on the part of us humans. It's not just that we hunted and hounded the mighty bruins to the brink of extinction, but that we still give insufficient thought to their survival. Recall for a moment how we believed the great bears were feeding on McDonald Peak ladybird beetles and how, during the Great Depression, researchers analyzed those beetles to determine whether they would be suitable to collect and sell to orchardists. Though the beetles proved not be of a type suitable for pest control by fruit growers, would it have mattered if we disrupted the huge grizzly's food chain?

In this case, the joke was really on us because it turned out bears weren't feeding on ladybird beetles after all, but on army cutworm moths. . . . Yet one still wonders if it occurs to us more refined, educated, sophisticated, 21st century beings that bears feeding on moths clustered under rocks in isolated Rocky Mountain talus slopes might be affected by insecticides used on army cutworms in Nebraska?

Is public support for retaining grizzly bears enough? After all, the public supports lower taxes and less crime.

It was for a selfish reason that I conceived the idea for this book. I wanted to know more about the grizzly. True, I'd had a great deal of experience with the great beasts as a wilderness out-fitter and guide. But I'd learned just enough to know I knew little. Fortunately, I had lots of contacts within the scientific commu-nity, as well as a journalistic track record to inspire trust. I decided to proceed all ahead, full. That confidence in my assets proved to be a stumbling block when preconceived ideas got in the way of reality, however. Take the bitter wrangling among biologists, for example:

I've always considered field biologists to be arrayed some-where near the right hand of God. They are, without exception, men and women who dedicate their life to their work, sacrificing all to their profession, spending lonely hours in remote places, compensated only by a close communion with nature at its best—and its rawest. I've never known a biologist to have a Swiss bank account. Most are poorly paid, perhaps most poorly of all college-educated professionals.

Believing all the above is why it was so difficult for me to see they have feet of clay.

I expected different government agencies to be at each other's throats—after all, I read the newspapers. However, in my naivete, I never suspected the depths to which those turf battles could descend. And to discover my biologist heroes and heroines likewise engaged in mud wrestling was not only distasteful but dis-tressing.

I thought I could use my experience and draw on the experi-ence of others whom I respected—scientists and management specialists—to find a clear path to the pot of gold at the rainbow's end: recovery of the grizzly. Now I'm not so sure.

Though I consider myself committed to conservation, I'm still unclear about the objectives of environmental activists. I understand what they *say* they want, which is to recover the grizzly bear. I understand they have the high moral ground; that they've refined their own lay professionalism until they may well be America's best at using an overabundance of laws to tie up our system's orderly advance.

No, I cannot argue point for point with one of their polished point men or women. But still, logic whispers in my ear that Chris Servheen cannot possibly be wrong on *everything*. I mean, give me a break! Even if the poor guy deliberately tried to screw up grizzly recovery for fifteen years, simple mathematical odds would guarantee that he would have screwed up to benefit the bears *once*. Thus my only conclusion must be that Servheen is in a role that would have led to crucifixion for even Jesus of Nazareth.

There seems to be no compromise within the community of environmental activists. In all fairness, they believe the bear to be on the brink of extinction. They believe we can afford no more compromises without losing the bear altogether. But am I dense in sensing such a tremendous gulf between the recovery aspirations of the U.S. Fish & Wildlife Service and the huge multi-state grizzly habitat and management proposal of the Alliance For The Wild Rockies that any future bridge between is not only impractical but impossible? And why do I have this gnawing feeling that saving the Grizzly by protecting vast wilderness tracts is not the solution? That he must also have acceptance of his place in the minds of people dwelling in, or passing through, suitable areas for the great bears to roam?

Neither do I understand the activists' fear of state management. I suppose I'm firm in my belief that Montana has both the track record and present interest in beneficial management. The state also has the staff to accomplish comprehensive *Ursus arctos horribilis* management. On the other hand, the activists' concern over whether the state could develop both dollars and authority for proper management seems to have merit.

If Montana (or Wyoming) wants to manage its own grizzlies, let the state satisfy the concerns of environmentalists, as expressed by the Federal Courts:

1. Prove that any future hunting season will (a) eliminate only problem bears and (b) not be detrimental to overall Ursus populations.

2. Prove the state can dedicate necessary funding for future management and research.

3. Guarantee that the state can at least match the present authority of the U.S. Fish & Wildlife Service in preventing other federal and state agencies from taking management actions negatively affecting the bear.

It's entirely possible that no such guarantees can be developed without the umbrella of the Federal Endangered Species Act. I'm not sure if I yet understand why that's a problem for my state's wildlife managers. If it's in America's interest to retain the great bears into futurity, perhaps the nation should pay a portion of the cost and guarantee proper authority to those entrusted with management.

But can anyone ever convince me that the Treasure State's Mike Madels, Tim Manleys, and Kevin Freys, backed up by supervision from the Dan Vincents and Mike Aderholds, backed in turn by the full support of Fish, Wildlife & Parks, the Governor, and best of all, the schoolkids of Montana, cannot do a better job of managing Montana bears? Run it by me again: Who can respond better to problems local people might have with bears? Or turn it around: Who *already has* responded better to problems Montana bears might have with people?

There is nothing so important to ensure survival of the grizzly as continuing public education and understanding. Obviously, such intelligence must stem from continuing research. And here's where the future becomes clouded because of agency turf battles, research competition, and political and judicial manipulation.

Who takes it in the shorts when natural-resource managing agencies do not grant either opportunity or support for ongoing bear research, in-house or independent? The public.

Who is shortchanged when researchers must dot every "i" and cross every "t" before releasing information that could enhance both public interest and understanding? The public.

Or how about media sensationalism? Whose interest is served by presenting a horror image of the great bears, based on a distorted sampling? It's not the guy walking down main street.

Okay, how about this book? I've tried hard not to err just as grievously by presenting an image of a cuddly, huggable, oversized teddy wearing a long fur coat. I hope I've succeeded in presenting an objective, realistic picture of the grizzly.

The truth is, big, bumbling Digger et Number 19 et the Dairy Queen Bear—the one who slummed among humans in downtown Bigfork, who eats apples off foothill trees, who gives up his tasty horse carcass to a human who surprises him—can and will kill schoolkid or preacher, housewife or teacher should they dare cross his invisible and still undefined line. Rick Mace developed a deep affinity for the animal he called the "grizzly daughter I never had." But that grizzly daughter would have killed Rick in a heartbeat if he'd not applied the same careful techniques in handling that he used on the biggest, meanest ursine in the forest.

That more of the creatures aren't less restrained is a wonder. Can you imagine how obnoxious we humans would be if creation had endowed us with a bear's superior musculature, personal weaponry, outdoors savvy, native shrewdness, and ability to absorb punishment?

There's little question the bears are making every adjustment possible within the parameters of their genetic framework to survive in our human-filled world. There's no question the public better understands the great bears today, and that through even more understanding tomorrow we may learn better ways to live with the animals, instead of *against* them.

But there are, oh, so many roadblocks! It's a fallacy to expect that we humans will ever be able to develop effective management and research through a system that has only worked fitfully in the past. There needs to be another better design. Such a design must tie the bears' future to the only positive development with a proven track record: *public education and understanding.* Obviously, such intelligence must stem from continuing research. And that research needs to be applied on the ground—without interference from plans influenced by divisive philosophies or personal agendas.

A giant mountain rises but a mile east of my home. It stands four thousand feet above the valley floor and fills each facing window; I'm looking at it as I type this. I buy hay for my horses from a farmer who lives just a short way south, along the foot of that mountain. Summer before last, Gene discovered a grizzly bear feeding on apples from a tree in his yard. He stepped out his door and shouted at the bruin. It looked up at the man, then began shuffling toward him. My friend stepped back inside his house, and returned with a rifle. He fired into the dirt before the bear's face. It continued toward him. My friend abandoned the field to the bear. The animal hung around long enough to establish a point, then wandered away, back to his mountain and forest and berry patch. My friend told me it was the first grizzly he'd seen during his three decades of farming that land.

Two Little League baseball fields are across the highway from my home, toward Columbia Mountain. During the summer just past, Rick Mace stood on one of those Little League fields with a hand-held receiver, tracking two grizzlies that had been radio collared in the study he leads.

There's an apple tree growing in my front yard. A couple of biologist friends have good-naturedly chided me about not cleaning up my apples, but they don't understand: it's perfectly all right with me if grizzlies find those apples, eat those apples, "impose" upon me.

It's all right that my life has been—and is—tied to the great beasts. It's all right that they've enriched it as has moonlight on a mountaintop, a grouse drumming in the forest, the far-off bugle of a rutting bull elk, the gurgle of a freshwater spring, the soft soughing of wind through the treetops.

I wonder, though. I wonder that I've spent well over half a lifetime amid the great beasts and never seriously been charged or mauled or batted around by a grizzly. I wonder if I'm just lucky.

Or, have I inadvertently *learned to talk bear*? ■

The author.

Afterword

Its writing was complete. Learning To Talk Bear was on its way to the printer and I should have been in fine fettle. But something gnawed about the book. For one thing, Laura had read the manuscript and when I asked if she thought anything was missing, the lady said she wished for information on what she could do to help the bears.

Laura expected too much. The book was never intended to be a call to arms, but a situation analysis. Its focus was how attitudes change as knowledge about the great bears advance. Ignorance is, of course, the villain—a hurdle that must be overcome if the grizzly is to survive through the 21st century. The bears' best hope lies in an informed public. That's how Laura can help grizzlies—by continuing to learn of them.

But can she? Dollars for research are scarce. The information flow about grizzlies slows to a trickle just as public interest surges. It's tragic that our information wellheads are drying at the same time we're rich in wildlife biologists and hungry for information they're eager to ferret out. We've learned so much in such a brief span—a modicum more of the fruits of research passed on to a curious and intrigued public and we might really learn to talk bear.

Then the thought struck: But why should the public fund research when its results have never been designed to provide knowledge for them? In fact, some biologists—and even public resource managers—endeavor to shield the fruits of research from their public patrons, not trusting layfolk to responsibly handle such knowledge.

To be sure, the South Fork Grizzly Study turned out a plethora of information. But its primary focus was to achieve other objectives. Sharing enlightenment with an eager public seemed merely peripheral, largely wrought through efforts of prying journalists rather than a result of original design.

This is the *information age!* People are demanding information and they're being flooded with it from the worldwide web to interactive CDs to a plethora of periodicals to 43,000 books per year to 500 television channels. Yet, they're not so much being flooded by information as demanding access to knowledge. Today's average American is better informed and more eager to learn than ever before. And still, wildlife research lives in the dark ages, suspicious of the motives of layfolk, sometimes sheltering their work from the curious, designing studies to provide information for scientists, not for the folks paying for it.

It's marketing, plain and simple. The solution to this problem won't be found in Biology 101, but in business schools. Why should people be expected to buy a product when there's no clear benefit to them? Even NASA changed focus in the space program to provide information about the wonders of space and make benefits more readily apparent to those who must pay for it. Why should wildlife research be exempt from the same market-driven advertising and promotion principles?

The answer is, it shouldn't.

- Roland Cheek / 1997

Resources

Chapter 3

The Beast That Walks Like a Man, Harold McCracken, University of Oklahoma Press, 1955.

The Journals of Lewis and Clark

Chapter 4

"The Day The Bears Go To Bed" / *Reader's Digest*, 10/10/66

Chapter 8

"Ladybird Beetles and Army Cutworm Adults As Food For Grizzly Bears In Montana" / *Ecology, Vol. 36, No. 1,* 1/1/55; John A. Chapman, John L. Romer, John Stark.

"Grizzly Bears, Insects, And People: Bear Management In The McDonald Peak Region, Montana"—1986; Robert W. Klaver, James J. Claar, David B. Rockwell.

"Grizzly Bear Use of Alpine Insect Aggregation Sites, Absaroka Mountains, Wyoming / Sean L. O'Brien and Dr. Frederick Lindzey, Wyoming Cooperative Fish and Wildlife Research Unit, University of Wyoming (1992).

"Grizzly Bear Use Of Army Cutworm Moths In The Yellowstone Ecosystem;" Stephen P. French, Marilynn G. French, and Richard R. Knight / A compilation of selected papers from the *Ninth International Conference on Bear Research and Management.*

"Two-Year Summary For Grizzly Bear Management Specialist, Western Montana (1993-1994)" / Prepared by Timothy L. Manley, Montana Department of Fish, Wildlife & Parks, March, 1995.

Selected news reports.

Key interviews: MDFWP Grizzly Bear Management Specialists Mike Madel and Tim Manley; MDFWP Region IV Supervisor Mike Aderhold.

Chapter 11

Track of the Grizzly, Frank C. Craighead, Sierra Club Books, 1979.   Key interview: Terry Werner, South Fork Team Leader, Border Grizzly Project.

Chapter 12

National Park Service Board of Inquiry Report / Mary Pat Mahoney Bear-Caused Fatality, October, 1976.

Selected news reports.

Key interview: Robert Frauson, Retired Glacier Park Ranger; Kate Kendall, U.S. Biological Survey; Steve Gniadek, Glacier National Park.

Chapter 13

Brown Bear Resources, Twelfth Report to the Swan Valley School, October 20, 1992.

Key Interviews: Pat O'Herren, Swan Valley Schoolchildren, Bill Collins, orchardist.

Chapter 15

Key interviews: Rick Mace, Team Leader, South Fork Grizzly Study; Shawn Riley, MDFWP Region I Wildlife Manager.

Chapter 16

Selected news reports.

Key interviews: Rick Mace, Shawn Riley, Art Whitney, Jack and Ursula Whitney, Mr. and Mrs. Jim Lafever, Dave Coe, Mr. and Mrs. Royce Satterlee.

Chapter 17

Interagency Nuisance Grizzly Report Form, dated September 27, 1985. U.S. Forest Service advisory letter, Spotted Bear Ranger District, September 24, 1992.

Selected news reports.

Key interviews: Rick Mace, Tim Manley.

Chapter 19

Key interview: Rick Mace.

Chapter 21

Selected news reports.

Key interview: Dr. Charles Jonkel, Director, Border Grizzly Project.

Chapter 22

Informational letter from Charles Jonkel, Director, Border Grizzly Project, dated August 10, 1987.

"Descriptions of Five Promising Deterrent and Repellent Products For Use On Bears" / Final Report, Carrie L. Hunt, U.S. Fish and Wildlife Service, Office of Grizzly Bear Recovery Coordinator, March, 1985.

Fourteen "Case Incident Records" / Glacier National Park files, from June, 1989 to July, 1993.

Abstract: "Field Use of Capsaicin Sprays as a Bear Deterrent / by Stephen Herrero and Andrew Higgins, Environmental Science Program, Faculty of Environmental Design, University of Calgary.

Selected newspaper/magazine reports.

Key interviews: Bill Pounds, manufacturer of Counter Assault capsaicin pepper spray; Dan Carney, Blackfeet Tribal biologist; Steve Gniadek, Glacier National Park biologist; Art Soukkala, Confederated Salish and Kootenai biologist; John Waller and Rick Mace, Montana Department of Fish, Wildlife & Parks biologists.

Chapter 23

Grizzly Bear Capture Form, 6/5/90.

Drugging Information, 6/5/90.

Interagency Nuisance Grizzly Bear Report Form, 8/18/93.

Selected newspaper reports.

Key interviews: Tim Manley, Rick Mace.

Chapter 24

Brochure: "Living With Grizzlies," published by Montana's Department of Fish, Wildlife & Parks.

National Forest camp sanitation rules, Region I, U.S. Forest Service, January 19, 1994.

"Incidence of Human Conflicts By Research Grizzly Bears" / Wildlife Society Bulletin 15:170-173, 1987 / Richard Mace, Keith Aune, Wayne Kasworm, all MDFWP; Robert Klaver and James Claar, Bureau of Indian Affairs, Flathead Agency.

Selected newspaper reports.

Key interviews: Harvey Nyberg, Regional Wildlife Manager, MDFWP; Jim Claar, Region I, U.S. Forest Service; Fred Flint, Resource Forester, Hungry Horse District, U.S. Forest Service; Dr. Stephen McCool, Department Head, University of Montana's Department of Recreation & Tourism.

Chapter 25

"Report of the Montana Fish and Game Commission For Years 1917-18."

"The Role of Hunting in the Recovery and Conservation of Grizzly Bears" / Montana Department of Fish, Wildlife & Parks (date unknown).

"Final Programmatic Environmental Impact Statement: The Grizzly Bear In Northwestern Montana" / MDFWP, March, 1986.

"Comments on USFWS, 1990, Grizzly Bear Recovery Plan, Revised Draft," submitted by Dr. Lee H. Metzgar, Professor of Biology and Wildlife Biology, University of Montana, to Dr. Chris Servheen, Grizzly Bear Recovery Coordinator, U.S. Fish & Wildlife Service, January 7, 1990.

Letter to Lorraine Mintzmyer, Chairperson of the International Grizzly Bear Committee, relative to attempts to delist the Northern Continental Divide Ecosystem grizzly bear, from Keith J. Hammer, January 24, 1990.

"Affidavit of Keith J. Hammer," appearing before the United States District Court in behalf of the Swan View Coalition, plaintiffs in litigation against the U.S. Fish & Wildlife Service and Montana Department of Fish, Wildlife & Parks for their proposed Spring Grizzly Bear hunt, September 16, 1991.

Selected newspaper reports.

Key interviews: Arnold Dood, Endangered Species Coordinator MDFWP; Chris Servheen, Grizzly Bear Recovery Coordinator, U.S. Fish & Wildlife Service; Keith Hammer, Chairman, Swan View Coalition; Mike Bader, Executive Director, Alliance For The Wild Rockies; Mike Aderhold, MDFWP Region IV Supervisor; Glenn Erickson, MDFWP Wildlife Management Bureau Chief; Montana Governor Marc Racicot, in a personal letter to Roland Cheek; long time grizzly bear researcher Chuck Jonkel.

Chapter 26

"Grizzly Bear Recovery Plan" / U.S. Fish & Wildlife Service / prepared by Dr. Christopher Servheen, Grizzly Bear Recovery Coordinator (original approved: January 29, 1982; updated and approved September 10, 1993).

"Interagency Grizzly Bear Committee Biased and Manipulative In Grizzly Bear Delisting and Monitoring Scheme" / Keith J. Hammer paper, November 25, 1991.

"Keeping the Grizzly Bear in the American West—An Alternative Recovery Plan" / The Wilderness Society / Dr. Mark L. Shaffer, October 8, 1992.

"Response to Issues Raised Concerning the Grizzly Bear Recovery Plan" / U.S. Fish & Wildlife Service, January, 1994.

Letter to Bruce Babbitt, Secretary of the Interior and Mollie Beattie, Director U.S. Fish & Wildlife Service from Hal Salwasser, President, The Wildlife Society, January 31, 1994.

"Report on the Application of Trend Monitoring Techniques on the NCDE, Selkirk, and Cabinet-Yaak Ecosystems" / Interagency Grizzly Bear Committee, U.S. Fish & Wildlife Service, December 14, 1994.

Letter to Chris Servheen, U.S Fish & Wildlife Service Grizzly Bear Recovery from Guy Woods, British Columbia Provincial Wildlife Biologist, March 8, 1995.

Letter to Dave Mihalic, Superintendent, Glacier National Park and Harvy Nyberg, Montana Department of Fish, Wildlife & Parks Region I Wildlife Manager from Chris Servheen, March 9, 1995.

"1995 Grizzly Bear Research Proposal for the North Fork of the Flathead River" / prepared by Christopher Servheen and Wayne Kasworm, U.S. Fish & Wildlife Service, March 9, 1995.

Paper prepared on North Fork Grizzly Bear #834 / by Nancy Kehoe, March 25, 1995.

Selected newspaper reports.

Key interviews: Tom Parker, Dr. Christopher Servheen, Keith Hammer, Mike Bader, and Dan Vincent, Region I Supervisor MDFWP.

Chapter 27

The Old North Trail by Walter McClintock, University of Nebraska Press, June, 1910.

"Flathead Indian Reservation Grizzly Bear Management Plan," Review Draft / Confederated Salish & Kootenai Tribal Council and Bureau of Indian Affairs, Flathead Agency, July 9, 1981.

Undated paper, "Flathead Indian Reservation Grizzly Bear Management Zones."

Giving Voice To Bear by David Rockwell, Roberts Rinehart Publishers, 1991.

Press Release, June 1, 1994 / prepared by the Wildlife Management Program, Natural Resources Department of the Confederated Salish and Kootenai Tribes.

"Chronology of Events Involving Female Grizzly and Three Cubs (the Allentown Bear) and One Male Grizzly (the Ninepipe Bear), Summer, 1994" / provided by Dale Becker, biologist, Confederated Salish & Kootenai Tribes.

Plea Agreement, Judgement and Sentence in the United States District Court For The District of Montana Missoula Division; United States of America vs. Robert Crump, filed November 10, 1994 and November 16, 1994.

Selected newspaper reports.

Chapter 28

Key interview: Rick Mace.

Chapter 29

"Board of Inquiry Into the Death of John Petranyi, Date of Death: October 3, 1992." Date of Report: February 5, 1993.

"Additions to the Blackfeet Fish and Wildlife Code," December, 1994.

Selected newspaper reports

Key interviews: Dr. Charles Jonkel, Dan Carney.

Chapter 30

"The Conservation Biology Alternative for Grizzly Bear Population Restoration in the Greater Salmon-Selway Region of Central Idaho and Western Montana" / Alliance for the Wild Rockies, Special Report #8, January, 1996.

Selected newspaper reports.

Index

Other Books by Roland Cheek

Nonfiction

Chocolate Legs 320 pgs. 5½ x 8½ $19.95 (postpaid)
An investigative journey into the controversial life and death of the best-known bad-news bears in the world. by Roland Cheek

My Best Work is Done at the Office 320 pgs. 5½ x 8½ $19.95 (postpaid)
The perfect bathroom book of humorous light reading and inspiration to demonstrate that we should never take ourselves or our lives too seriously. by Roland Cheek

Dance on the Wild Side 352 pgs. 5½ x 8½ $19.95 (postpaid)
A memoir of two people in love who, against all odds, struggle to live the life they wish. A book for others who work and play and dream together.
by Roland and Jane Cheek

The Phantom Ghost of Harriet Lou 352 pgs. 5½ x 8½ $19.95 (postpaid)
Discovery techniques with insight into the habits and habitats of one of North America's most charismatic creatures; a guide to understanding that God made elk to lead humans into some of His finest places. by Roland Cheek

Learning To Talk Bear 320 pgs. 5½ x 8½ $19.95 (postpaid)
An important book for anyone wishing to understand what makes bears tick. Humorous high adventure and spine-tingling suspense, seasoned with understanding through a lifetime of walking where bears walk. by Roland Cheek

Montana's Bob Marshall Wilderness 80 pgs. 9 x 12 (coffee table size) $15.95 hardcover, $10.95 softcover (postpaid)
97 full-color photos, over 10,000 words of where-to, how-to text about America's favorite wilderness. by Roland Cheek

Fiction

Echoes of Vengeance 256 pgs. 5½ x 8½ $14.95 (postpaid)
The first in a series of six historical novels tracing the life of Jethro Spring, a young mixed-blood fugitive fleeing for his life from revenge exacted upon his parents' murderer. by Roland Cheek

Bloody Merchants' War 288 pgs. 5½ x 8½ $14.95 (postpaid)
The second in a series of six historical novels tracing the life of Jethro Spring. This one takes place in Lincoln County, New Mexico Territory. It was no place for a young fugitive to be ambushed by events beyond his control. by Roland Cheek

Lincoln County Crucible 288 pgs. 5½ x 8½ $14.95 (postpaid)
Third in the Valediction For Revenge series chronicling the adventures of mixed-race fugitive Jethro Spring. Also set in Lincoln County, New Mexico Territory. by Roland Cheek

Gunnar's Mine 288 pgs. 5½ x 8½ $14.95 (postpaid)
Fourth in the Valediction For Revenge series chronicling the adventures of mixed-race fugitive Jethro Spring. Set in southwestern Colorado mining country. by Roland Cheek

Crisis on the Stinkingwater 288 pgs. 5½ x 8½ $14.95 (postpaid)
Fifth in the Valediction For Revenge series chronicling the adventures of mixed-race fugitive Jethro Spring. Coming in May, 2004. by Roland Cheek

The Silver Yoke 288 pgs. 5½ x 8½ $14.95 (postpaid)
Sixth in the Valediction For Revenge series chronicling the adventures of mixed-race fugitive Jethro Spring. Coming September 2004. by Roland Cheek

Order form on reverse side

Order form for Roland Cheek's Books

See list of books on page 278

Telephone orders: 1-800-821-6784. *Visa, MasterCard or Discover only.*

Website orders: www.rolandcheek.com

Postal orders: Skyline Publishing
P.O. Box 1118 • Columbia Falls, MT 59912
Telephone: (406) 892-5560   Fax (406) 892-1922

Please send the following books:
(I understand I may return any Skyline Publishing book for a full refund—no questions asked.)

Title	Qty.	Cost Ea.	Total
_____	_____	$ _____	$_____
_____	_____	$ _____	$_____
_____	_____	$ _____	$_____
_____	_____	$ _____	$_____
_____	_____	$ _____	$_____
_____	_____	$ _____	$_____
_____	_____	$ _____	$_____
		Total Order:	$_____

We pay cost of shipping and handling inside U.S.

Ship to: Name _____

Address _____

City _____ State _____ Zip _____

Daytime phone number (_____) _____-_____

Payment: ☐ Check or Money Order

Credit card: ☐ Visa ☐ MasterCard ☐ Discover

Card number _____

Name on card _____ Exp. date ___/___

Signature: _____